*This is the Eskimo World....their native home*

*....the great place called Alaska!*

# Frost Among the ESKIMOS

MEMOIRS OF HELEN FROST, MISSIONARY NURSE
ON THE SEWARD PENINSULA, 1926-1961

"ALASKA IS MY HOME; THE ESKIMOS MY PEOPLE"

Published by
Lutheran Pioneer Press
CONCORD, CALIFORNIA

Cover Design by Lance Hidy

Native Art by George Ahgupuk


Library of Congress Cataloguing in Publication Data

Helen Frost Memoirs

*Frost Among the Eskimos*

Prologue:   Early History:

Library of Congress Catalogue Card Number: 2001094722

ISBN   0-9642228-0-9

First Printing:    2001

EDITOR:  Ross F. Hidy
Advisory Committee:
Mary Miller, Helen Frost Thompson,
John and Louise Maakestad,
Harvey Brandt

Published by
LUTHERAN PIONEER PRESS
5242 Park Highlands Boulevard
Concord, California  94521-3706
(925) 687-2414; E-Mail: rosshidy@astound.net



Printed in the United States of America

# FROST AMONG THE
# ESKIMOS

## CONTENTS

# FOREWORD

The Memoirs of Helen Frost report her experiences as she served for thirty six years with the Native People in Alaska. She went to Alaska to help care for the boys and girls in the Teller Orphanage. Many readers may wonder what had happened to their parents? Who had started this Teller Home to care for these children? We need some history to understand this story.

A noted Eskimo artist, George Ahgupuk, sketched some scenes that tell the history of the Eskimo people in northern Alaska. These portray the events that led up to the tragic epidemic that left so many orphans needing special care.

George depicts the whalers that came to the Arctic Ocean and harvested not only the whales, but also the walrus and seals, making hunting difficult for the Eskimos. That led to the Reindeer chapter of the Eskimo story. Why were the Reindeer brought over from Siberia? Why were Lapp reindeer herders brought from Norway? How did the reindeer experiment work out? Why was a Lutheran pastor invited to come to Alaska? What was the impact of the Gold Rush that brought thousands to Nome, crowding the sandy beaches to search for gold? What started the tragic epidemic that took so many lives and left so many orphans? When we know this history we can understand Helen Frost's report on her life with the Eskimos on the Seward Peninsula of Alaska.

Helen Frost grew to love this Great Land and the Native People. When out on a furlough she was homesick and wanted to go back. She wrote about her love for Alaska to Dr. Aasgaard, the President of the Evangelical Lutheran Church. "As for me, I feel that Alaska is my home, and I do not believe I should be satisfied anywhere else whether in direct mission work or other employment. In spite of many discouragements, these people have grown very dear to me. Many times I have felt like giving up and admitted that someone else should come. Possibly he could do much that I cannot do or haven't done. But then the Lord has sort of put me back on my feet again and made me realize that here is where He wants me and here is where I want to be until He changes it."

Helen explained why she spent thirty six years with the Eskimos when she wrote, **"Alaska is my home; the Eskimos my people."**

*From across the waters came the Eskimo. First only the hunters. What they found in the "Great Land" was good. Better than what they had. So family oomiaks sailed over and people grew in Alaska.*

*The Eskimos hunted in the hills. They followed the game. They learned the land in all seasons. Up and down the shore they went with their dogs and their wives. Where fishes were many, they stopped.*

*Where the rivers joined the ocean, where seals and salmon were thick,
Eskimos pulled their oomiaks high on the shore. With plenty to eat,
and much good fur, they were happy. Babies came like the tide.*

*Eskimo wives are good for babies and fishing. From snow shelters they
jig for tomcod. They seine for sheefish. The Eskimo lives from the sea.
It fills his stomach and puts clothes on his back.*

*Good fishing places grew into villages. Brothers and uncles brought their families. Young men came to see strong daughters. Generations, more than fingers and toes many times over, came and passed.*

*Then came the white men. In great ships with big sails they came to catch the whale. Some liked Eskimo life and stayed. They married. They, too, caught whales. Some white men brought loud guns and bad drink.*

So many whalers came into the Arctic waters that they not only depleted the supply of whales, they took so many walrus and seals that before long the Eskimo hunters had less and less success. The future looked bleak and some warned of the danger of starvation.

Someone suggested, "Import domestic reindeer from Siberia to provide food and clothing. Even in winter the deer can dig into the snow and feed on the lichen or deer moss. And the herds will multiply, making them a renewable source of food and clothing." In 1891 Sheldon Jackson, Presbyterian minister who led this venture, brought over 16 deer and they wintered successfully. In 1892 171 deer were imported and the first Reindeer Station was established at Teller Reindeer Station on Port Clarence. Young natives were to be trained to herd the deer. When the Siberian teachers did not get along with the Eskimo, they tried to bring over skilled Lapp herders from Norway. But they would not come unless a Norwegian speaking Lutheran Pastor will be there. Jackson asked the Norwegian Lutherans to find a pastor and Tollef Brevig accepted. He and his wife, Julia came with the Lapps by train across the US to Seattle. Then after a stop in San Francisco, they came by whaler to Alaska, landing at the Teller Reindeer Station on July 31, 1894.

The Lapps were excellent teachers and got along well with the Eskimo. Pastor Tollef Brevig and his wife, Julia somehow managed to get through the harsh winters. The Reindeer herds multiplied, some young men finished training and became owners of herds. There were also herds at Wales, at Point Rodney near Nome, another at St. James Mission on the Yukon, and at the Swedish Mission at Golovin Bay. The venture was succeeding.

In 1897 eight whaling vessels were icebound in the Arctic Ocean near Point Barrow. They had stayed too long and the crew faced starvation. Congress authorized funds for a rescue attempt that started on December 18, 1897. Hundreds of reindeer, many from Mission herds with skilled Eskimo herders in charge, were driven north over barren tundra and across icy bays toward Point Barrow. When they arrived with the large herd of deer on March 26, 1898, they discovered that the Eskimo hunters had been able to go out and get wild game for themselves and the whalers. The news coverage of the icebound whalers put the reindeer in the national spotlight. The "loaned reindeer" were replaced and now more Eskimos wanted to receive reindeer herds for their villages.

However, difficulties arose. Around Teller, the reindeer moss had been pretty well consumed, so a new main reindeer station was needed. They chose a place about 300 miles to the east on the Unalakleet River. It was named Eaton Station and in 1898 it had a large herd of 446 deer and 177 fawns. But a seed herd was maintained at Teller Reindeer Station. The reindeer program was growing quite well but there were special problems coming in the next years.

But the great tragedy that hit that area came after the Gold Rush brought thousands of miners crowding into the Nome area. A tragic epidemic hit the region and hundreds died.

# BRINGING REINDEER TO THE SEWARD PENINSULA ESKIMOS

Presbyterian Minister Sheldon Jackson led the project to import Siberian Reindeer to help the Eskimos. On July 4, 1892 the first reindeer were landed at Teller, where young Eskimos would be trained to herd the reindeer. Who trained them? Norwegian Lapps, when assured that a Lutheran pastor who spoke Norwegian would be with them. In 1894 Pastor Tollef Brevig and his wife Julia, came with the Lapps to Teller to serve them and the Eskimos. When an epidemic killed many parents, the Brevigs started the **Teller Orpha**nage in their home.

Native drawing of the Teller Reindeer Station in winter. Lower:
Eight ice-bound whalers were caught in the Arctic Ocean by an early freeze. Eskimo herders played a key role in the rescue expedition that drove 400 reindeer north to save them from starvation. Despite storms and freezing weather they arrived at Point Barrow on March 29, 1898.

*Later other white men came with shovels and pans. They scratched in creeks and on the beach for yellow pebbles. When they found them they shouted. Women came running, hugging and kissing. They cried, "More, more."*

### Nome Gold Rush and the Tragic Epidemic that took hundreds of lives

When the Brevigs returned to Nome in July of 1900, they were amazed to find more than two thousand miners were sifting the beach sands for gold. Those miners took over one hundred million of dollars in gold. Two years before Rev. Brevig had written, "Nome is nothing but terrain and tundra and beach." Now there were eight steamships out in the harbor and along the beach miles of tents and shacks. 'Robbery, assault and murder seemed to be the order of the day.' In many places, the Eskimos had been crowded out of their fishing areas. Then an epidemic started in Nome.

### The Tragic Epidemic

A whaler had put in to Nome and left two sailors who were sick with the measles and the disease quickly spread. To avoid the epidemic the Brevigs rushed back to Teller. There they discovered that the miners had vandalized their buildings. So instead of moving into their snug quarters, they now had to clean out the debris and filth left by the miners then try to weatherproof their home for the winter. But they had little time to do this for the epidemic had struck full force at Teller Reindeer Station.

Up and down the coast the sick and dying people lay uncared for, while half-starved children clung to their dead parents. At Wales, almost the entire population of 550 was afflicted and calls for help came for the fifty surviving children. Sick miners crept into the mission and begged for care. While the Brevigs worked to renovate their buildings for occupancy they had to assist those who were sick or dying. Three homeless girls were the first to be taken into their crowded home. They were Bessie Sagan, five year old Alice Alalie who would spend the rest of her life at the mission until another epidemic claimed her, and the infant Emma Willoya, who had been found in a snowbank half frozen. Julia Brevig gave her special care. During the night other refugees arrived, as word spread that the missionaries had returned. Three more children were brought in from a hut where their dead parents lay. This was the beginning of the Lutheran orphanage in the Arctic, the need for which was to continue through the next three score years.

## TELLER MISSION BECOMES A REFUGE

With the Brevigs back the natives began to return to the area around the Mission. The Brevigs soon learned that the tragedy was not limited to Teller. Up on the north coast at Cape Prince of Wales almost everyone was sick and calling for help. Severe weather raged and many patients froze to death. Some who were sick with raging fevers ran out into the cold and were stricken with fatal pneumonia. So many died that 72 were buried in one grave. Some miners brought boilers of steaming water to thaw the frozen earth at the burial grounds. One large trench was made, the bodies were placed side by side, with a wooden cross to mark the spot. In the course of three weeks only five grown-ups remained in the community and forty-six children had lost their parents.

The Brevigs opened their home to care for them then they used tents until a station building was repaired to provide shelter. This was the beginning of the **Teller Orphanage.** Before 1901 passed half the population in the Teller area had died. During these months the Eskimos saw all the Brevigs had done to help their people in this tragic time.

## REV. SHELDON JACKSON'S REPORT ON THE WORK OF THE BREVIGS

What the Brevigs had done to ease the suffering was reported to Washington by Rev. Sheldon Jackson in his official Report to Congress on the Reindeer Project. His report tells of almost unbelievable suffering after the epidemic hit the area:

> "During the measles epidemic in the year 1900 when the Eskimos died by the hundreds and those who were alive fled from their homes, almost dead with fear, leaving the dead bodies of their dear ones to be eaten by dogs, and when the sick and dying were without care, Brevig gave himself completely for weeks and months in the labor of alleviating the distress of the sick, and to bury the dead, and gather and care for the orphan children. When from the beginning neither the Government nor the Synod in the States were prepared to give aid, he placed even his own family on short rations so that he could feed the dying and the children that had been saved. When the old and partly dismantled Government building which had been reconditioned at the expense of his Synod became too small to house all the sick and orphans, he went and acquired tents so that he might give them shelter. Although he was a poor man, he was so concerned about the welfare of the Eskimos, that during the three following years he gave his salary received from the Government which was two thousand dollars, and even six hundred dollars besides, for their help and support."

**A U. S. Senator praised Tollef Brevig's work:**

After U. S. Senator Dietrick inspected the various stations in the area, he praised the work of Tollef Brevig at Teller Station. "This is the cleanest station I have seen in Alaska.... The Brevigs have come down to the native people and become thoroughly acquainted with their manner of thinking. They have convinced the natives by their life that they are their true friends who do not look down upon them or despise them. They do not set themselves above the natives, something which the natives are quick to note and which they will not tolerate."

**Tollef Brevig was "Adopted by the Eskimos" as a sign of their complete Trust**

One night Brevig was visited by twenty Eskimos wearing painted wooden masks. They called him outside and then circled the missionary in an initiation ceremony. Brevig was now adopted, — one of their own. He even had the right to go into their "Kashegi," the public assembly hall which no white man was allowed to enter. The ceremony and the masks frightened Mrs. Brevig, for she feared her husband might be killed. But the Eskimos took off their masks, smiled and explained to her that she, also, was now an Eskimo. The new name the Eskimos gave Brevig was "Apaurak,""Father of all." Julia Brevig was now called, "Amerora", the "Mother of all." The Eskimo people rarely extend this honor to white people.

When Helen Frost completed her nurses training at Ancker Hospital in St. Paul she had no idea she would be going to Alaska. That call was a shock to her, but going to the Teller Orphanage opened a new world to Helen. A world where she never knew what she would be asked to do next.

"Alaska is a place where you go ahead and do things you never expected to do or thought you could do." She discovered that in her three years at the Teller Orphanage. It became even clearer to her during her sixteen years in the isolated village of Igloo. Not only was she the nurse, dentist and doctor, she opened her home to care for the sick or injured, led the worship services, played the organ, directed the choir, and organized the village orchestra. During the war Helen taught school, cared for the village store, was postmistress, sent out weather reports on the radio, and was marriage commissioner. In the village she often was called out at night in the dead of winter when it was fifty below zero. She would put on her parka and mukluks and go out and deliver a baby — by candlelight.

In the summer she traveled with the Eskimos to their Tuxuk River fish camps and held worship services outdoors, using her guitar to lead the singing. In the winter she traveled by dog sled with her Eskimo friends who knew how to dig in if a storm caught them on the trail.

She baked delicious bread, made dozens of cup cakes and doughnuts. The children loved the popcorn balls she made for their parties. Helen loved life and her warm spirit of friendly hospitality made being in Igloo fun, even in winter.

I often thought as I read her Memoirs, "No one could do all that!" But she did. This is the story of a caring nurse who lived with those amazing Native People whose home was on the Seward Peninsula, near the Arctic Circle in Alaska.

# THE ORPHANAGE AT TELLER

The Captain of the Silver Wave pointed up to the white building on the hill. "That's the Orphanage at Teller Mission! That's where you are going. Now we will go on around to Teller Town and drop you off. Then they will bring you back." But seeing how close we were to the Orphanage, I asked, "Do we have to go around to Teller Town? Can't we get off here near the Orphanage?" The Captain said, "We can try. I'll blow the whistle to signal we have someone who wants to get off. If they hear and send out their Mission boat, you can get off here." He blew the whistle, the crew dropped anchor and we all watched to see if they had heard his signal. Yes, they had, for soon we could see people run down to the beach and put the Mission boat in the water. When the Captain saw it coming he said, "They will be here before long. Better get all your gear so you will be ready to get off. You can take their mail sack with you." We quickly gathered our things then watched the boat coming. I was excited for this was the end of a long, long journey. I had been invited to come and help care for the orphaned children.

Before long the Mission boat reached the Silver Wave. The crew handed down our bags and the mail sack to the boat. I thanked the Captain for signaling, then Martha Brennum, Katherine and I climbed down into the small Mission Boat and it headed for the beach. As we neared the shore I was surprised to see so many boys and girls waiting there with the adults to greet us.

## A WARM WELCOME TO THE ORPHANAGE

As we walked up the hill Sister Anna told me more about the Orphanage. "Rev. Tollef Brevig and his wife started an orphanage after a horrible epidemic and they cared for many children. Later it was closed for a while, but after more epidemics, – the measles, small pox, it was reopened again. The last epidemic was the terrific influenza siege of 1918." Then Sister Anna stopped and pointed over to the crosses at the cemetery on a nearby hill. "Up there are the graves of seventy-two people buried in a single grave during that terrible epidemic. Many of them were parents or relatives of these children." Seeing that cemetery helped me understand why the Orphanage had been started. As we came to the door of the large white building I said a prayer of thanks for our safe journey. We had come thousands of miles from Minnesota by train and ship to get here. But now I was ready unpack our things then look around. I wondered what life would be like living with these children up near the Arctic.

## LOOKING AROUND

My first day at the home was interesting. We toured the missionary quarters, then the children's dining room, kitchen, laundry and upstairs in the various bedrooms. It was really not spacious — in fact, considering the number who lived there, it was rather crowded. The first orphanage building had burned down and this had been the missionaries' quarters. I realized I had much to learn.

## LIFE AT THE ORPHANAGE

Since Sister Mabel was soon to leave, I wanted her to tell me all about her work as a matron and what was expected of me. I learned I would be busy! First there was the planning of the children's food. She told me that they tried to use as much Eskimo food as possible, such as dried fish, seal meat, fresh fish and reindeer meat when it was available. The girls baked the bread. There were also cooked beans, soups, cereals, dried fruit and canned milk, which had to be shipped from the States. Then there would be the supervision of clothing, making of mukluks by the big girls, knitting of socks and stockings also done by some of the girls. A schedule was made out at the end of each month showing who was to be the cook, assistant cook, bread baker, who would scrub and clean the various rooms, who would fill the water tank with spring water or snow, and who would carry in coal or wood. There were also turns doing the laundry, running the washing machine by hand, etc. Certain boys were delegated to build the fires every morning. With eleven stoves in that building that was quite a job during the coldest weather. One or two of the boys also made the sourdough hot cakes for breakfast, frying them on top of the stoves while the girls cooked the cereal and set the tables. All of this rather overwhelmed me and I wondered if I would be able to handle it.

Being a nurse I asked how they isolated any children who were ill. Sister Mabel told me, "We just do the best we can with what we have. Tuberculosis is very prevalent. We try to keep those patients isolated, but with so many in our small building, it is very difficult at times."

In the missionaries' quarters we would do our own cooking with a little help from one of the Eskimo girls. Martha Brennum, the teacher, would eat with us. When time would permit, she would also take her turn getting meals. The school was in the old reindeer building and one of the boys built the fires in that building. I could see we all would be very busy. But soon I was reminded that as a nurse I would have some special duties.

## MY FIRST PATIENT

I had been at Teller only a few days when Sister Anna brought in Mikshuak, (Eskimo for a little girl) with a serious skin condition. That reminded me that I had just finished my nurses training and should take over the medical work. I immediately started treating her, first with hot boric acid packs and then other medications. Each day when I came in to get the girl I would hear a remark by one or the other of the children. I told Sister Anna that I wished I could understand what they were saying. Sister Anna listened then smiled as she told me, "You have received your Eskimo name, 'Manakshegut' which means 'the one who takes care of us.' " I was proud to hear this and hoped that I would be worthy of the name, taking care of the children in spirit as well as in body. Mikshuak and I were happy when the skin condition cleared up and she was forever grateful.

Soon after I arrived both Sister Anna and Sister Mabel asked if I should also be called Sister Helen as it would be easier for the children. They thought it was quite appropriate since I had also spent time at the Deaconess Hospital as a sister. We really were a little Lutheran Deaconess community up here in Alaska, I agreed and after that the children called me Sister Helen.

### NURSE — AND DENTIST!

One day a boy came in with a bad toothache. Sister Anna called me over, gave me a tooth forceps and said, "Sister Helen, please pull his tooth!" I hesitated, "I've never pulled one before, — but I'm willing to try." To my surprise the tooth came out quite readily. From then on I was the emergency dentist and pulled many teeth,— not just for the childen. Patients even came over from the village or across the bay, asking me to pull teeth. At first I did not know how to use novocain. But some time later a government doctor came through and showed me how to inject Novocain before an extraction. After that I used it often, for it made it much easier, especially for older people.

It did not take me long to realize I had so many duties that I would need all the skill I could muster. Being a mission pastor's daughter had given me many very valuable experiences. In Alaska every one of them would be used and I thanked God often for those years of preparation. I could cook and knew how to sew. Very soon I was thankful for my special training as a teacher, seamstress and, most of all, my nursing training. Most of all, I appreciated the training and influence of my pastor Father who had encouraged me to come to Alaska.

### MY EARLY YEARS

Spiritually I know that I owe a great deal to my father who was a devout Christian. Born in Denmark, he came to Cleveland, Ohio to join his brother who was a carpenter. For several years he helped his brother build homes. He soon joined a Lutheran Church for he was a devout Christian. As time went by he decided he did not want to be a carpenter. He felt a call to the ministry so he enrolled at Luther Seminary in St. Paul and, after completing his training, he became a mission pastor in the midwest. Being fluent in English, Danish and Norwegian, he did well and started several new missions. The midwest was growing, many little towns were springing up, so pastors were needed to start new missions. Father loved his work and was a sincere Christian. He lived what he taught and believed. He loved to play with us and was much concerned about our welfare and love for Jesus. I remember that during the quiet evening hour he would take me on his knee as he told us stories from the Old and New Testament. I still remember those Bible stories and the little prayers and songs he taught us in the Norwegian language.

There was lots of snow when we were living in Sheyenne, North Dakota. We had a little sled and one morning Father had a surprise for us. In the yard he had built a high snowslide. What fun we had on that slide!

Another day the snow had piled high against the back door but Father knew what to do. He dug a tunnel right through it. How we loved playing in that tunnel. Later he bought each of us a pair of skates and took us down to the Sheyenne River to skate with our school mates.

## THE DEATH OF MY MOTHER

I do not remember much about my mother. She was in poor health and later we found out that she had quick consumption. Shortly after little Reuben was born she became worse and was in bed much of the time. Then one day father called us in to give her a good-bye kiss. Not long afterwards Reuben became very ill with pneumonia. Before he died, he lifted up his arms toward heaven and said, "Mama." We knew then that both Mama and Reuben were in heaven with Jesus.

That first year after Mother died Papa's sister Marie came to stay with us. The next year I stayed with my mother's parents in the country and Herbert went to Esmond, North Dakota with mama's sister, Aunt Marie and Uncle Otto.

Two years after Mother's death Father married again and Herbert and I went back home to Sheyenne. I was then eight years old and Herbert six. Life at the parsonage became a busy one, but happy, too. Two sisters and two brothers were added to our family. First, Esther, Reuben and Gerhard and later Florence. I started taking music lessons and at eleven years of age I played the organ at the church services. Often it seemed a chore to come in from the playgrounds to practice, but Father insisted. I have been thankful many times, for music has been very important in my years in Alaska.

## WE MOVE TO MINNESOTA

When I was almost sixteen, we moved to Minnesota to a country parish near Spring Grove. Father served three congregations, Riceford, Newburg and Blackhammer. I stayed at home part of the year and, since I liked to sew, was able to learn sewing at the shop in Caledonia nearby. Then for two years I went to Sioux Falls Normal School, and received a second grade teacher's certificate. I had intended to teach but, because of the schooling facilities for the younger children, my step-mother asked me to live at home with Father during school days while she stayed with the children in town. During the winter I taught parochial school. All of this was wonderful preparation for my years in Alaska.

### THE CHALLENGE OF MISSIONS

One Sunday there was a big Mission Festival. Dr. Birkelund, who had been in China, was our speaker. I remember vividly his description of the needs in China. That Mission Festival touched me and I prayed that if the Lord wanted me on the mission field I would be shown in some way. I told some people how I felt but they claimed that it was just my fantasy. But to me it was more than that. I began speaking to my father about my concern. He was always interested in mission work and often said that it would make him happy if any of his children felt called into the ministry or to the mission field.

### HOW I BECAME A NURSE

Suddenly the flu epidemic of 1916 reached us and almost all of us were ill almost at the same time. Since I did not get sick I became the nurse. Suddenly the thought of becoming a nurse appealed to me.

One day while cleaning in Father's study I saw an article that touched me. It was from the Lutheran Deaconess Hospital in Chicago about the service openings for nurses. Somehow God seemed to be saying to me, "Why don't you become a nurse?" After retiring that night I became restless thinking that I should go to the Deaconess Hospital in Chicago for training. My father apparently heard me for the next morning he asked me, "Helen, is something bothering you?" I told him and that weekend when my step-mother and the younger children came home we talked about my wishes. They encouraged me so I wrote to the Deaconess Hospital in Chicago and later applied to study there. In the fall of 1919 Father went with me to Chicago when I was admitted for training. I never regretted that decision, received many blessings from my study there, and met many fine people. Several Sisters left for China and Madagascar but somehow my time to enter missions had not come.

The influenza was still raging and during my second year I became very ill. My condition was so serious that one night my Father was called. But God had other plans and my condition improved. After three months of hospitalization I was permitted to go home for a short while before returning to duty. This was a valuable experience, both physically and spiritually.

After graduation I worked at the hospital for two years and gained valuable experience. But as it was not at that time a registered hospital, my friend, Bly, and I decided to leave and go to Ancker Hospital in St. Paul, Minnesota for further study. In one and one-half years I received my R. N. degree. Looking back I realized how important this decision was for we had an excellent training and studied many kinds of diseases. All of this was very helpful to me in Alaska.

# MY CALL TO ALASKA

After graduation while I was doing a little private duty work in Minneapolis I received a letter that changed my life. It was from Sister Anna Huseth who was in charge of the Eskimo Orphanage at Teller, Alaska. This is what she wrote:

**"Sister Mabel Lien is going to the states this year. Will you please come and take her place as matron here? We need you."**

This hit me like a bomb shell. Alaska? — I had never thought of going to Alaska. What should I do? I thought and prayed about it, wondering if this was really God's call to me. Then I wanted to talk to my father for I had always confided in him. When I got home we sat down and I told him. "There is an opening for a nurse at the Orphanage at Teller, Alaska and I have been asked to go up there to help. There are forty five children there in that home. I did not want to decide until I could talk to you. What do you think I should do?"

Suddenly he was very excited. His eyes were shining as he told me something I had never known. "I am so pleased Helen, that you have this invitation, this call to go to Alaska. Years ago, when I was in Seminary, I offered to go to Alaska. The government asked for a Lutheran pastor to go to Alaska to minister to the Lapp reindeer herders and to the natives. I volunteered and so did T. L. Brevig. They chose Brevig for he had been a teacher and was better in English as well as Norwegian. Brevig went to Alaska in 1894. I stayed and have been a home missionary pastor here in the midwest." Then father took my hand and said, "Perhaps, Helen, you are to go and do the work I wanted to do when I was a young man. Perhaps, you are to go in my place. I could wish no greater joy than that one of my children be a missionary."

My reaction was an intense desire to go and give him that joy. Then I was concerned that I might make this decision just to please my father. He had encouraged me but I knew I needed to be sure it was the call of God and not just my desire to please my beloved father.

Sister Anna Huseth in her letter had told me to go over and talk with Ruth Dahle. She had previously spent a summer visiting her brother, Elmer Dahle who had spent three years at Teller. I took my friend, Petra Bly, and we talked with Ruth. She told us she was planning to return as a teacher in the government service at Teller Mission. She told me about the Orphanage and life in Alaska.

Knowing I must decide I went to see Dr. Hoel, the Director of Home Missions, to talk about the work. He immediately turned to me and asked, "Do you want to go?" I hesitated, then asked, "Do you think I can do it?" He briskly responded, "This is not the question. Do you want to go?" I said, "Yes." That settled it! Before I left the office, he had made reservations for my sailing date in August. Unfortunately, Ruth Dahle became ill and could not go, but Miss Martha Brennum from Concordia College volunteered to take her place and she and I would travel north together. But first I had to go home and get ready to move up to Alaska.

## SUMMER OF 1926 — GETTING READY

In July I went home to Spring Grove, Minnesota to begin preparations for my journey to Alaska. Our parsonage was unusually busy that summer. We had a large yard and many shade trees which made it a comfortable place for gatherings. Father decided it would be a nice place for families to gather on the Fourth of July, and the young people could sell ice cream, cake and coffee. It was a beautiful day and many families came.

The next Sunday was the Picnic of the Young People's Society from the three congregations which Father served. It was an enjoyable afternoon and people came from all around. In those days most people used horse and buggy and could not go very far. Afterwards, while washing the dishes, I happened to say to one of the girls, "You have been here two Sundays in succession-- perhaps you will be coming next Sunday, too?" She did not answer, but she looked at me strangely.

## THE SURPRISE

Sure enough, they were back next Sunday. The three congregations had planned a surprise for my Father, and also for me, since I was soon leaving for Alaska. Each of us received a money gift. Although I had a slight suspicion about that farewell, it meant a great deal to me. I will never forget the many friends who wished me well that day and promised to be with me in prayer.

## A SPECIAL COMMUNION SERVICE

The night before I left Father had a special service and gave me communion. His words to me that night were from Matthew 28:20, "Lo, I am with you always, even unto the end of the world." Since that night those sacred words have always reminded me of my Father and that God is with us at all times.

## OFF TO ALASKA!

Neither will I forget seeing my Father, step-mother, sisters and brothers standing on the train platform waving as I left for Minneapolis to take the train to Seattle and then the Steamer Victoria for Alaska. I was glad that I was fulfilling one of his ambitions by serving the Lord as a missionary.

## SAILING NORTH

After traveling by train from Minneapolis we sailed from Seattle on the Victoria. Ocean travel was a new experience to me. When I suddenly became seasick during the night I could not imagine what was the matter with me. I crawled down from the top bunk, scampered across the lounge to the ladies' room and quickly lost my dinner. I soon discovered that Martha Brennun was feeling the same way. However, in a few days we recovered and could enjoy the beautiful ocean, the delicious meals and meet other folks going to Alaska. Some of them had already spent years there and they enjoyed telling their adventures and tall tales, some of which we hardly dared believe.

One evening we were told we had better put clothespins on our noses as we were about to come into Akutan, a whaling station. It was interesting to see the large whales being pulled in, skinned, cut, etc. Many drums of oil were on the dock ready for shipment.

## MY THIRTIETH BIRTHDAY

After eleven days we docked out in the ocean in front of Nome. It was very shallow there so we were lightered on to a barge and pulled in by tug boat. Though it was evening, it was not dark but rather dreary looking. We found a room at the Golden Gate Hotel. It was not very luxurious, but we were just happy to be sleeping in a bed again instead of rocking out in the ocean. As we went to bed I realized that this was my thirtieth birthday. I did not say anything to Martha for we had enough to worry about. But later when I looked back I often said, "I was thirty years in Nome!"

We had to wait in Nome for a few days to get a smaller boat, the Silver Wave, to take us to Teller Mission. The Methodist pastor and his wife, Rev. and Mrs. Baldwin invited us for dinner one evening. In Alaska all churches worked together.

Then one evening we were told that the mail-boat for the north was leaving for Teller. As we got ready a little Eskimo girl who was going to the orphanage was placed in our charge. Of course we could not speak the Eskimo language nor did she speak English. When we asked her name all we could get in response was "Ella." That became her name ever after, — but much later we found out that her name really was Katherine!

In the morning we boarded the Silver Wave and, after another taste of seasickness, we finally came into the quiet waters of Port Clarence Bay. The pilot pointed out Teller Mission up on the hill. Then the Mission boat came to get us. I remembered I had been told that I might have to live in a snow hut. How mistaken they were. In those days people knew very little about Alaska.

# LIFE AT THE ORPHANAGE

Alaska has often been called Uncle Sam's Icebox, Seward's Folly, or the Forgotten Land. To the Eskimos Alaska was "The Great Land" and soon it also became that for me. I loved the waters in front of the orphanage, in its various moods, colorings and weather conditions, winter or summer. The home was located on Port Clarence Bay which connects with the Bering Sea. It is eighty miles S. E. of Cape Prince of Wales, the westernmost point of the North American continent, some 600 miles from Point Barrow, the northernmost point. A two-day ride by dog team (weather permitting) would bring us to Nome, about ninety miles south. There were road houses or shelter cabins on the way for storm-bound travelers.

As I helped to clean around the home, I noticed some of the chairs and the desk in the living room were so unusual that I asked where they had come from. They told me about the large boat, the Fred J. Wood, that had been wrecked in front of our home when its anchor broke loose in a terrific storm. At first it stood almost straight up but through continuous storms and high tides it began tilting and finally it was abandoned. Since no one claimed it, people began salvaging some of the contents. The home got some of the furniture, dishes, utensils, water tanks and other useful articles. Then the Eskimos began tearing the ship to pieces, taking some lumber for building and the rest to burn in their stoves. They had to work hard to get it removed. All that was left of the Fred J. Wood were some large spikes and iron bars.

The Eskimos also liked to tell about what happened on May 13, 1926 when the Dirigible Norge landed on the ice at Teller. I had heard about this before I left for Alaska for it was in all the newspapers. Now I saw where it happened. Capt. Roald Amundson and his men stayed at Teller while the Eskimos had helped pull the Norge down and dismantle it. Then by dog teams they hauled parts of it to the edge of the ice and later it was shipped to Nome. They gave me a piece of the covering removed from the dirigible. Later one of the Eskimos gave me an etched ivory napkin ring with the picture of the Norge. Some say that Capt. Amundson proposed to Sister Anna but she was more interested in the children than this Norwegian explorer. Those must have been exciting days.

## GETTING READY FOR WINTER

Fall was coming and it was getting colder so there was special work to be done. The school house had to be painted. I told Sister Anna that I had never painted before but she handed me a brush and said, "This is a good time to learn." I learned and since then I have put on many gallons of paint. While we did that the Eskimo boys were busy banking earth around the Mission and also the school house. I was impressed to see how they cut the exact square blocks of sod and fit them in to insulate the buildings.

## TIME TO PICK BERRIES

Then one sunny day in September Sister Anna said, "We should go over to Teller to pick blackberries (moss berries) before the freeze up." Two of the Eskimo girls, Martha, Sister Anna and I were to go in one of the row boats pulled along the shore by dogs. Two of the boys handled the dogs. I found this new way of travel very interesting. When we got to the channel of Grantley Harbor we had to row to Teller. The dogs were tied up and left behind until our return. We found good berry patches a little beyond Teller and toward the hills. The ground was covered by the berries so we had a great deal of fun filling our buckets. Then we ate our picnic lunch and it seemed that I was never so hungry. We again continued to pick but before long Sister Anna said, "A wind is coming up so we had better be going back. " But by the time we had reached Teller Town the water was too rough for our little boat. Mr. and Mrs. Tom Peterson and Mrs. Ethel Marx of Teller Commercial Company were very kind and asked us to stay with them overnight. This gave me a chance to get acquainted with these true friends who helped us through many an emergency. The following day one of the Lomen Company's lighterage tugs brought us back. On the way we picked up our little boat and the dogs. Though it was only seven miles across Port Clarence Bay it had been an exciting trip getting berrries for winter use.

## SISTER MABEL LEAVES

When Sister Mabel left to return home I became matron. I could not have managed without Sister Anna as my teacher. As a "cheechako" I wanted to learn all I could about the Eskimos, the Home and how we worked together. Then we had to care for our Christian program of worship and teaching. On Sunday mornings we had services, followed by Sunday School and Bible Class in the afternoon. Each evening after supper we had a Bible study and a devotional hour.

## SAM ALIAK, WHO COULD DO ANYTHING

Sam Ailak was our Eskimo helper and interpreter, together with Leonard Suluguak. When Sister Anna had been at Igloo Sam had been her helper there. He had since married and they now lived in a little house close to the Mission. Leonard also was a fine man and he had studied in the States. But he became tuberculous and was sent back to Alaska. For a time he seemed to be quite well, but later he became ill and died. He had been a dependable man and a helpful witness to his Lord. Sam Ailak was hired by the Mission Board and we never could have managed without him. He was a good worker who could do anything. He directed the work on the beach with the fishing, caring for the boats, sleds and dogs. He could repair equipment, do carpentry work and other things that had to be done.

## LEADING SUNDAY SERVICES

I was surprised when Sister Anna asked Martha and me to take our turn in conducting the Sunday morning services. I really had not expected to be a preacher, too. At first it seemed quite difficult but I did my best, using my Bible and a few other books given me while at the Deaconess Hospital. My father had given me a very good book, "Sermons of the Gospels of the Ecclesiastical Year," by Henry Sieck. These sermons followed the Life of Jesus and it became my constant guide, with my Bible and a few other books given me while at the Deaconess Hospital. The Eskimos seemed very receptive, and treated me kindly, overlooking many of my shortcomings. I learned to love the children at the home very much and also the folks in the nearby village. At first I was very hesitant about giving devotions in their homes or at the sick bed. But the Lord guided me and seemed to put the words in my mouth. I often remembered my Father said, "If you have something to say, you will get it said, though it may not be in the best way."

Father also had told me, "You may be asked to baptize a baby or even give communion to a dying person." I asked him "How could I do that?" "If there is no pastor, you, as a Christian have a right to do this," was his reply. So here I was, supposedly only a nurse by profession, but later finding myself preaching, teaching, baptizing, even giving communion privately, when we had no pastor. The day also came when I was given a license to perform marriages. Many times I felt very inadequate, but when there was no one else to do it, I did what had to be done. With God all things are possible if we are in His will.

## MY FIRST DOG SLED RIDE

The days were getting shorter and it was getting much colder. Soon the ground was frozen hard and the first snow covered the ground. We could hear the barking of the village dogs and see the teams go by. Then one day Sister Anna said, "Today you must have a dog-team ride." She had me put on her parka, mukluks and other warm clothing. Sam hooked up the dogs, I got into the sled, and off we went before one could say, "Jack Robinson." The dogs had hardly been hooked up that fall so they were just raring to go. Did we ever go flying down that hill, under the bridge, along the creek and then on to the tundra. When we went over the tundra's hard tufts of grass I felt one terrific bump after another. There was no cushion, only the bare bottom of the sled to sit on, so it wasn't soft. I wondered what it would do to my bones. Finally I said to Sam, "I don't think I can stand this any longer. You should have a spring-seat in the sled." So he told me to come behind and stand on the runners with him. I did but that was terrible, too, because when we hit those frozen tufts of grass my feet would slip off the runners. Suddenly when we went out on the frozen lake, I slipped off and sat right down on the ice. I was glad when we got back to the Home. I surely felt the effects of that ride for a long time. Sister Anna had a good laugh, saying that the next ride would be much smoother when there was more snow on the ground. Then we could ride on the frozen snow and ocean ice.

## KEEPING WARM IN WINTER

Some time later I had that thrill with the temperature of 30 or 40 degrees below zero. But with a fur parka, fur pants, fur cap and mittens, home-knit stockings, woolen underwear and shirt, together with fur mukluks up to my knees, I was warm and comfortable. If there is a snow storm it is very important to have a good dog leader who knows the way and can find the trail.

## A WINTER RIDE TO IGLOO

I shall always remember the nice dog-team ride I had to Igloo with Sam Ailak in the early spring when the trails were well packed and the days were getting longer. Sr. Magdaline Klippen, a classmate of mine from the Deaconess Hospital, was stationed at New Igloo. I was quite anxious to see how she was located. I fell in love with the beautiful Saw Tooth Mountains with their snowy peaks. The house in which she lived was not very large and a bit cold. She told me how it had been moved the previous spring from Old Igloo because of high water. In fact all of our Lutheran families moved to this new location, about five miles down the river. The Catholic families moved farther up the river, closer to Hot Springs Catholic Mission. It had been quite a feat, pulling these buildings by dog-team, then setting them up again, all done by the teacher and the natives who are able to do amazing things.

We stayed over Sunday so we had a chance to attend services there and meet some of the people, both at Church and in their homes. I did not know that some day I would be stationed there. Sister Magdaline decided to return with us the next day when we went back to Teller Mission. She had her own dog-team and was used to traveling. Though the snow had begun melting the trail was still good. By dog team it is about 45 miles to Teller and, if the weather is good, that can easily be made in one day. Later I did it often.

## BUSY DAYS

With 40 Eskimo children to care for, there really wasn't a dull moment. After school hours at 3:30 P. M., we would lock the door to our rooms for about 30 minutes. We hoped the children would take care of themselves while we relaxed and had a cup of coffee. The children were all supposed to go outdoors for a while after receiving their lunch. Sometimes this worked but often I would hear a rap on the door. Someone had gotten hurt, someone asked to go visiting in the village, or they needed something. Then, when the free time was over, everybody was supposed to get busy. Some did mending and sewing, some made mukluks, others did their outdoor chores, cooking or other duties assigned to them. We did not want to wean them away from their Eskimo foods for they were used to them and preferred them. The girls knew best how to prepare their own foods but were also taught how to cook other foods.

### DOGS MUST EAT TOO!

Cooking the dog food was the daily chore of one or two of the boys. Usually they cooked it out of doors or in the dog barn, but sometimes they cooked it indoors. The odor from cooking cereal, seal meat, dried meat, blubber or leavings of different kinds wasn't pleasant, but the dog-team was a very important item so you just had to forget about the unpleasantness.

### MITKU SOLVES A PROBLEM

One day Mitku had left the cooked dog-food standing in the laundry to cool off. Then one of the dogs got in and tipped it over. What a mess! But Mitku was equal to the occasion. He merely brought some puppies in and before long there was only a grease spot left.

### CHRISTMAS

Christmas is a busy season everywhere, but at the orphanage it was really exciting. Martha Brennun prepared and planned the Christmas program. Wherever you went in the building you might hear someone singing or reciting their part. The cook for the children was busy baking the bread and cookies. We had invited a few people over from Teller so, of course, there was extra planning and cooking to do besides special cleaning. But everyone helped, looking forward to this event. The larger boys made the Christmas tree for the school, made from a two by four plank into which willow branches were stuck. When trimmed with popcorn strings and various other homemade decorations, the tree looked very nice. The candles had to be put on very carefully and, when lit, watched closely for fear of fire. Sr. Mabel had left a small artificial one for our living room. Then we had to wrap the gifts, something for each one that friends had sent in the Mission boxes.

### OUR ALASKAN CHRISTMAS DINNER

We tried to make the Christmas dinner as festive as possible, with a special serving of reindeer meat, potatoes, vegetables and fruit pudding, cake and cookies. All gathered in the school house for the program and also for the gifts. The white folks were also there. It was a happy time for all, celebrating the birth of our Savior. On Christmas Day we again gathered in the school house for services, with some extra singing by the children. The room was crowded and mothers, with babies on their backs, often sat on the floor. They didn't mind. They said it was cooler. One day I saw a man even sitting on the coal bucket. Every minute I expected the bucket would tip over and spill the contents on the floor.

## SPRINGTIME

We looked forward to spring when the sun was higher and the days longer. It was often overcast in the long night of winter and for weeks I had watched the ice on the Sound. When there was more sunlight each day, the snow really melted fast. Later we would have twenty-four hours of daylight. Now it was time to clean out the food cache which was up on poles. That was where we kept the seal pokes. All of these had to be washed and ready for the next year. We tried to keep as much of the Eskimo food on hand as possible and this was one way of storing it. We also used a great deal of macaroni, dried fruit, and canned or powdered milk.

### BUSY SPRING DAYS

Spring housekeeping also had to be done, as well as painting. Some of the boys were very handy with the brush but there were times when Sr. Anna and I would also paint because we wanted to get through before camping time. The native families always went camping in the spring and this was a great time for the children for it was in their blood. I made a cloth bag for each one into which they could put a few of their clothes. A list was made of all the things needed,— tents, bedding, sleeping bags, food, medical supplies, dishes, cooking utensils and a number of other things. Then, just before break-up, Sam Ailak took us all over to a creek and lagoon about six miles up the coast and helped set up the tents there. The girls were in one place and the boys in another.

Sam Aliak's brother, Kodshok, was blind but big and strong. It was interesting to see him make little boxes for the girls, working very carefully with his tools. His main job was carrying in water. A yoke had been made to fit over his neck; then, with a hook at each end reaching down to the bucket, he would carry the water. One of the smaller boys was always with him to guide him and see that he emptied the water in the right place. Sometimes it would be a little slippery but he was very careful.

### ICE FISHING IS FUN

Going camping that spring was my first experience sleeping on the frozen ground. Sam showed us how to put willow brush under our sleeping bags so it felt almost like a spring. It was a bit cold the first days but it soon warmed up. The boys and girls went out on the ice, cut a hole and had great luck fishing. I also tried my hand at it and got about forty tomcod in less than an hour! Right then it must have been a very good run.

### DUCK FOR DINNER

Spring was also game season with flocks of geese and ducks flying over us every day. Sam usually supervised the larger boys who were given a gun and a certain number of shells for their game hunting. Sometimes the boys came home with quite a number of birds, — brants, emperor geese, ptarmigan or whoever came their way. During these days we ate very well.

### FRESH EGGS

Sometimes the girls would go out and hunt bird's eggs. They usually found quite a few and these fresh eggs were a real treat. Although we had ordered chicken eggs with our summer supplies, they were usually gone by spring — or by that time had a strong taste.

I was quite surprised at what I saw one day when I came into the children's tent. Some of the girls had found a nest of ptarmigan eggs, immediately boiled them, and were now eating them. As they opened one egg I noticed a little bird in it. "That does not matter," they said. "It is fresh meat."

### A HUNTING ACCIDENT – ONE BOY'S ADVENTURES

One morning in camp as I was getting up I heard a loud shot, followed by a cry. I knew two of the boys had gone hunting. They usually did during the night or early morning hours, as it was light all the time. Before long someone was being brought back to camp on a sled. It was William Nullekin, one of our orphanage boys who had been shot accidentally. Several of the shots grazed the side of his chest, with a few lodged in his flesh. I wondered what I should do. Sr. Anna had gone up the coast a ways where Sam Aliak was camped for a few days with his family. For convenience and better care I decided it would be best to take William home, asking Martha if she would hold the fort. To reduce infection and promote healing I started treating William with hot packs. Suddenly Johnny Read drove in, asking if he should get Sr. Anna. Johnny had married Sister Agnes Nestdahl but she had died about two years afterwards. Johnny did many fine things for us, helping us with various needs. He had a fox farm not far from the Mission at this time.

Sister Anna came home and in a few days the ice broke up so Sam could bring all the children home by boat. William's sores healed and he was soon bouncing around again. The next year at camp he was again accidentally shot. This time it was in the foot, almost causing him the loss of one toe. This time we sent him to the doctor at Nome. Then one day, when out in our Mission boat, together with Sam and some of the other boys, William fell overboard. The quick action of Sam and his helpers soon had him back on the boat. I think he was one of those that had more than one life.

I often said that if God hadn't been with us in His protecting way, many tragic things could have happened.

### CATCHING SALMON

The big salmon run started the fishing season and everyone was busy. Nets were placed out in the bay and they caught many salmon that way. Soon they were cleaned and hung up to dry. We also sent two boys up the Tuxut River where the Igloo natives always camped. They would stay there fishing for salmon for possibly a month, drying some fish for the home. The boys were given a certain percent for their catch and they appreciated that very much.

I shall never forget my first delicious Alaska salmon, — the whole baked salmon Sr. Anna prepared. She seemed to know just how to do it. She taught me how to prepare Alaska foods and also how to can salmon. We would fill the glasses with nicely cut pieces, add a little oil and salt, seal the jars tightly, then place them in a boiler with a rack on the bottom to be cooked for at least six hours. The result — delicious salmon to enjoy in the winter.

## BARRELS OF BERRIES

Later came the berry picking time on the Tuxuk River. Some of the larger girls and I were taken up to a cabin located in the berry patches. We must have picked two or three small barrels full of delicious blueberries which we froze when the cold weather came. We also picked salmon berries and blackberries, but these were stored in seal pokes and frozen, —the Eskimo method of canning. I discovered that the blackberries made good jelly if I ran them through the meat grinder to extract the seeds. This seemed to soften the seed and gave the jelly a delicious flavor. Later we got a pressure cooker and would put the berries in jars, pressure cook them, preserving them and then we could have delicious pies in the winter.

Late in August or September would be the herring season run. There was a little smokehouse on the beach where Sister Anna would smoke some herring. Much of the herring was stored away for dog feed. Then there was the run on smelt when as many as possible had to help string them for drying, — all for winter food for the children.

## REINDEER IN ALASKA- A FASCINATING BIT OF HISTORY

Reindeer meat was another food necessity for our home. But how did we get it? I learned that Teller was Alaska's first Reindeer Station. For years the whalers had depleted the supply of seal and walrus and finally the situation was critical. Searching for an answer to the problem, someone suggested importing reindeer from Siberia. This suggestion had many critics but a few bold people explored this solution to help the Native people. Could reindeer be imported from Siberia to Alaska?

Dr. Sheldon Jackson from the Presbyterian Mission and Captain Healy, of the US Government boat, first checked the possible supply of reindeer in Siberia. Then they brought over a small herd to see if they would survive in Alaska. They did, for the reindeer could dig under the snow and find moss to eat. If allowed to graze, the herds would double every three years. After lengthy negotiations with the government and friends, the Bear carried a total of 1,289 deer across to Alaska at various times. Then the government brought Siberians over to teach the Eskimos how to herd and care for the deer. But the Eskimos did not like to work with the Siberian herders. In 1898, the Eskimos said they would rather have Christians teach them how to herd. Jackson's research revealed that there were Christian Lapps in northern Norway,

Sweden and Finland. They happened to be Lutheran. But these Lapps said, "We will only come if a Lutheran pastor is there." Dr. Jackson asked the Norwegian Lutheran Church,"Could you find a pastor who speaks Norwegian and would be willing to come to work with the Eskimos on the Seward Peninsula in Alaska?" Rev. T. L. Brevig volunteered for this mission. A special task force went to Scandinavia and persuaded some Laplanders to come to Alaska to teach the Eskimo how to herd reindeer. They also brought some reindeer from Scandinavia. J. W. Johnshoy's book, "Apaurak of Alaska" tells the story of the early days of our Eskimo Mission and the reindeer business. A new book, "Where Did the Reindeer Come From?" by Alice Postell is a delightful volume. The project succeeded, young men were trained to be herders, A certain number of deer were given to each Eskimo who finished the training. The herds grew and became a valuable source of food and clothing.

Some of our boys owned some deer, inherited from their fathers. Others worked as herders and were given a certain number of the deer as pay. Every fall or spring when the deer were rounded up and marked, a few of these were killed and the meat given to the home. I learned to like reindeer meat just as well as beef. We tried to dry some pieces by hanging them under the eaves, but we soon stopped that. The temptation was too strong for some of the older boys. The meat was usually frozen and kept for winter use. We had a cache built upon four posts, with tent material over the frame. This is where the dried salmon, smelt, tomcod, meat, seal pokes with seal oil or berries were kept for winter use.

### The Mail Boat Brings Sad News

During the last part of June or first part of July the ice pack was gone and we began looking for the mail boat and the freighter with our food supplies. It was a real holiday when our first mail boat came into Teller for we knew there was mail for us. During the winter mail came once a month by dog-team, but in the break-up season the dogs could not travel. Sam Aliak, together with some of the boys, would then go over and get the mail. What a thrill that first time when I was handed a package of forty letters, some about three months old. The last dog-team had brought the sad news that my Father had passed away. Now came the detailed news. I remembered my last night together with Father, receiving Communion and his parting words. It seemed as though I could see him waving good-bye, with God's blessing in my new venture. Now his working days were over. He had been a faithful pastor, a good father and husband. How happy he would be today in 1979 if he could see his children in their various positions of service in the Lord, and see his many fine grandchildren.

Long after father died I received a book of devotions witten by my brother, Gerhard. One was about father's final illness. Since I had been far off in Alaska, I had no way of knowing what had happened in those days. Gerhard had a rare gift for writing devotions and I was comforted to read it. Apparently he had remained at home so Mother could be there with father in his last days. Here is what he wrote:

"I wasn't there;
he wouldn't have known me;
 he knew no human face,
 not even hers, my mother said.
 He couldn't find words
 to speak his crying needs;
 yet two remained:
*"Praeke evangeliset! Praeke evangeiset!*
 Hour after hour, day after day
in that his final week:
"Preach the Gospel! Preach the Gospel!"
Blessed residue,
 two words,  one thought
 expressive of the habit
of one spent life—
 to us the last, the best,
the greatest gift."   ...

*from "Blessed Is the Ordinary"*

A beautiful tribute to a faithful Pastor and loving Father.

### THE CHILDEN SAW IT FIRST

Suddenly we heard a shout, "Oomiak, oomiak — the big boat is coming!" Before the boat became visible the children could see the smoke above the horizon,. Suddenly it appeared and now came a very exciting time. Sam and a few of the big boys quickly pulled the boat out and went over to Teller to help with the lightering.

### SUPPLIES FOR A WHOLE YEAR

As soon as the weather was right, our second-class mail and supplies were brought over to the Mission by the Lighterage Company. Sometimes the wind would be too strong and they would have to wait a few days. This annual shipment included many sacks of flour, cereal, beans, sugar, macaroni, coffee, canned milk, dried fruit, Christmas candies, some fresh eggs and fruit. For ourselves, we also ordered considerable canned food, some bacon, ham, etc. Many mission boxes also arrived with some fine things for the children, both clothing and in gifts. How were all these supplies carried up to the Mission?

### SISTER ANNA'S LITTLE RAILROAD

For a long time they had been carried or brought up by wheelbarrow. Shortly before I came, Sr. Anna had asked Sam and some of the boys to build a track across the creek below the Mission. The government helped supply some rails and posts. An old rail-car was resurrected from somewhere. Then using a pulley from the top, the supplies were pulled up quite easily. Sister Anna had many inspired ideas to improve life at the Orphanage.

How good that first orange or apple tasted. The first fresh eggs and a piece of bacon were a real treat! Later on we used dried eggs or dried milk, especially for cooking. The children were real excited about opening the Mission boxes, hoping there would be something to fit them. Some of the big girls and boys helped us sort all of these things and put them away for the Christmas season.

### A NEW FURNACE!

There was another surprise aboard the freighter. Before Sr. Mabel left she said she would see that we got a furnace, radiators, pipes and all the necessary fittings for steam heat. An old boatsman, who was also a carpenter and engineer, offered to put it in for us. As soon as the supplies came he and Sam started right in to install them. How thankful and happy we were when they finished their work. Then the old heating stoves were taken out and the furnace turned on. This new furnace made life much easier. Sr. Mabel had also sent a new set of dishes for she knew we really needed them.

### ANOTHER SURPRISE — ELECTRIC LIGHTS!

The following year when Rev. Dahle came back to Alaska to be stationed at Igloo, he put in a Koehler plant and electric light system for us. This, too, was a wonderful new convenience. We really felt we were on top of the world then. No more kerosene or gas lights to worry about.

### MARTHA BRENNUN LEAVES FOR HOME

Martha Brennum was not in good health and suddenly she decided she would have to go back home. Who would we get in her place? It was a late hour for the government to get a teacher to replace her. Then Sr. Anna suggested that I take the school and one of our big girls, who had been at White Mountain School, would teach the little folks in the afternoon. At first I hesitated, knowing that I had plenty of work as it was, but I was willing to try. The government immediately agreed and arrangements were made. The village children did not usually get back from their camping until the latter part of September. Although I had my teacher's certificate from the Lutheran Normal School in Sioux Falls, I had not taught regular school before. This would be a new experience. If I had not had the matron's job, too, it might have been fine. However, before the year was over I decided that I could not attempt it another year. I did not feel that I could do justice to either job and that it was not fair to the other workers.

### SISTER ANNA BECOMES ILL

Then, to add to our difficulties, Sr. Anna became quite ill. I felt it was quinsy, infected tonsils,— for she had such a high temperature that she was almost delirious at times. There was no way of getting a doctor nor could we get her to the hospital at Nome. I felt quite helpless — as I did whenever something serious happened. Everyone was praying for her recovery — the village Eskimos and the children at the home. I tried to treat and care for her as best I could. I often said, "I should have been a doctor and a dentist, too," but God was watching over us. Finally, the abcess broke and she was able to get rid of that choking feeling. She soon felt some better but I could see she was not well. This was her year for a furlough so she asked the Mission Board if she might go home early and rest that summer. We learned that a plane was now beginning flights into Teller and it could pick her up right at the Mission. The Board agreed so Sister Anna did not have to wait for the boat. We helped her pack for her journey and many of us watched her plane take off as she left for a much needed rest. A wonderful Christian and marvelous leader had left us for a rest.

## ALL ALONE AT TELLER

Now I was alone with the work. However, Sam was a great help and the larger boys and girls also did what they could. The days were getting longer, school would soon be closed and the work would not be quite so heavy. But longer days meant it was time for spring cleaning and painting.

One evening I went up to the boy's room as they were going to bed. I reminded them to open the windows a little, saying, "You don't want to get T. B., do you?" One boy responded, "Everyone dies from that." To him it almost seemed that way, because of the recent deaths in his family and among friends.

There was a little Lars hobbling around, whose father had died from tuberculosis. He had a sore leg for some time, but we did not know why. One day, one of the girls happened to drop an iron on his leg. The swelling broke open and continued to drain for some time. When the government boat came in that summer, Lars was brought aboard. There the doctor recommended an amputation. Lars went home to his Heavenly Father some time later.

One of the older girls continued to have a drainage from her shoulder for some time. It finally healed but she never had the full use of her arm. This must have been another tuberculous infection.

Although the government boat came in every summer and treated these cases in the best manner they could, — leaving medicines and instructions, — this was not enough. We knew many people needed better care. Today there are hospitals for them and the tuberculous situation, checked regularly is more under control.

### MARY ELLEN DOYLE

Mary Ellen Doyle, who had recently come to the home, was a very bright little girl. Her grandfather was a Laplander. When her Eskimo mother became ill she had been sent to a sanitarium. Her father, a bookkeeper at the Nome Mining Company, could not care for her, so he asked if she might be brought to our home. This eight years old girl became quite a favorite at the home. Later, when I went to Igloo, I took Mary Ellen with me.

A little baby suddenly became very sick, no doubt of pneumonia. We tried every treatment we could think of, — putting a woolen cloth over the chest, camphor rubs, and even tincture of benzoin inhalations, but nothing helped and the baby died. The men immediately began making the coffin, covering it with white cloth. Some of the girls made artificial flowers to decorate the coffin. The grave had been dug in the nearby cemetery. After the funeral Mary Ellen came running up to me, took hold of my hand and asked, "Was that baby baptized?" "Yes," I assured her, "and she is now up in heaven with Jesus." After a few moments Mary Ellen asked, "Am I baptized?" I told her, "I do not know but we will write to your father or your grandfather and find out."

### EARLIER BURIAL CUSTOMS

In the above I described a Christian funeral. But in former years they had different customs and up on the cemetery hill were the remains of earlier burials. In those days a little platform had been built on four posts, just large to hold a coffin. In those days when a man died, his hunting gear was buried with him, —perhaps his rifle, knife, furs or even his kayak. If it was a woman, her needle and skin sewing tools were placed near her body. These things were supposed to be needed by the spirit in the next world. With the passing years the cover might have blown off but the skeleton was still there, together with some of the belongings. Everything had a spirit. Therefore, it did not matter if the things rusted or decayed or were carried away by dogs. They believed the spirit made use of the spirit of a gun for hunting, or the spirit of the boat to make a water voyage, etc. Edward L. Kiethahn has written a very interesting book, about the early folklore of the Eskimos. It had illustrations by George Aden Ahgupuk, one of our Eskimo boys from Shishmaref who became a nationally known artist.

### WEDDING BELLS

Soon after Sister Anna left one of the older girls wanted to get married to a village boy. I decided that although she was young —only 16— it was perhaps the best thing. Then it wasn't very long before a second girl wanted to get married. Each couple had to go over to Teller town for the marriage license and be married by the commissioner. For those weddings, we always had an extra little ceremony here at the home, followed by refreshments such as cake and tea or cocoa, which they all liked. (Later I was authorized to conduct marriage services.)

Many years later when Eva Swenson visited me in California, she reminded me of those wedding parties at the Mission. As she put it, "I was quite amused at your speed. First finding a wedding dress in the Mission box, stirring up a big cake with decorations on it, getting the school room ready for the audience from the village and home, then you rang the bell, conducted the service, which was followed by the refreshments at the home. Then came the happy ending (we hope) where the couple strode off to the village. There, no doubt, an Eskimo feast had been prepared." Looking back I think she was right!

## MORE CHILDREN LEAVE

Then there was a third girl who wanted to go to Nome and stay with her brother. He felt that he was old enough to take care of her. She went and we later learned that before long she, too, was married.

One of our little two-year old boys had been staying with us since his mother died. The father had remarried and one day he came and asked to take Ernest home for he wanted his little boy with him at home. So we packed his things and home he went.

Of course, some of my friends in Teller began teasing me, "Are you trying to marry off all the girls?" No, I was not, but I did find that when they got to be fourteen or fifteen years of age it was a little harder to manage them and keep them at home. The Eskimos in the villages usually married quite early, especially the girls. Some of our boys also left that year. They, too, were growing up and wanted to work. Some of them went north to Wales to be reindeer herders. Others wanted to be with relatives and make a living. As a result, the number at our home decreased considerably, but I felt that it was the best for all. Our home had been very crowded and I'm sure that if a health inspector had come around our building would have been questioned as an orphanage. Many times I felt that we did not have adequate staff help to carry on the program that was necessary. Also we might have provided better education, handicraft or social activities for these growing children. Instead, we cared for their basic necessities as best we could. We had very little time for the nearby village, except to conduct Sunday services, Sunday School and women's meetings once a month. These meetings were held in our own small quarters. However, in spite of difficulties, we believe many childred were helped. We tried to do the best we could under the circumstances. Later we met many of the girls who had married, had a family and were doing well.

## A SAD VISIT

One day I was suddenly called to the village. Dora, who was expecting a baby, was seen outside her door calling for help. She had suddenly gone into labor and when I got there she was having convulsions. I told the woman with her to stay while I rushed home for the ether and mask, thinking of what we used to do at the hospital. Each time a convulsion started I would give her a whiff of ether to calm her down.

Suddenly an Eskimo medicine man, a shaman, from Teller Town walked in, just as she was going into a convulsion. I stopped my procedure to see what he would do. He just looked, became frightened and walked out. I then proceeded as usual. Her husband, Jerry Kaloki, was sent for and we both sat by her through the night, as she lay on the floor with her reindeer skin for mattress. This was the Eskimo custom. Finally, I gave her a good dose of castor oil and, before morning, this was effective. The baby was born, but, sad to say, it was dead. For some time we were afraid that Dora, too, would leave us. She became delirious and spoke very strangely. Then she would begin singing some of our church songs. But I was glad to hear that and as we prayed for her recovery I knew that she was in God's hands. Yes, she became well again and today Dora and Jerry are living in Nome and have two adopted children. Once later, while visiting Nome, Dora and Jerry invited me to their home and gave me a beautiful piece of ivory. They said that I was like their mother and they wanted me to have it as a special gift. Another time, they gave me a lovely pair of Eskimo slippers.

### A HAPPIER ENDING

Some time later, I was again called to the village. A mother was in labor. The baby came rapidly but the placenta was delayed. The husband and friends sitting there were very worried. I know the husband was praying and there certainly was a prayer on my lips. The abdomen was becoming quite distended and I feared internal hemorrhage. Then one of the women said, "Can't you do something?" I knew now I would have to go in manually, so turned to the husband and said, "Please continue praying." With much care and caution, I soon had the placenta removed. How I thanked God for my nurse's training and His help. I knew the mother would be quite sick and need watching. With the home to care for and Sister Anna gone, I was quite alone. So I asked if they would bring her over to the Home, for there I could watch her better. They did not answer right away, for I had said we would put her in the sick room. A little later Sam Ailak said to me, "They did not want to put her in the sick room because of the deaths there." Recently one of our big boys had passed away there. So I said we would put her on the couch in the living room. That was fine, and before long they had her carried over. She improved quickly and we were thankful when everything went well with both mother and baby.

### MY PRAYER IS ANSWERED

One day I was called over to Teller. The Lomen Company storekeeper had a terrific swollen check, could not open his mouth and was in great pain. Again, I used the simple medications I had, consisting of sedatives and heat, but it did not help. "Cut it open," he said. "No, I can't do that," I replied. "Yes, you can. I must have relief," were his words. I thought of all the things that might happen if I didn't do the right thing. They had tried to contact Nome for a plane, but the weather was not good. When I started preparing the instruments, that seemed to calm him down. But I was taking time just stalling and praying hard that the Lord would tell me what to do.

Just then we heard a shout, "A plane! A plane is coming!" What a relief that was, for I knew I could not have used a scalpel in this case. He was taken to Nome where he got the help he needed. One more instance of God's guiding hand.

### EVA SWENSON JOINS US AT THE ORPHANAGE

Before summer was over we had the good news that Miss Eva Swenson was coming to teach the school. That was welcome news. Without the help of Sam Aliak and his wife, Viola we could not have kept going. It was too much for one person to handle. And now the berries were ripening. When we needed someone to go up the river with the girls for berry picking, Eva offered to go.

We knew that Sister Anna would not be back until early fall. Then came the sad news. Sister Anna was very ill at the Deaconess Hospital. First it was an ear infection and later appendicitis. Now she had developed endocarditis. The Board assured us that if she couldn't come back, someone else would be sent. This troubled us a great deal. How would we ever manage without Sister Anna? She was such an enthusiastic person to work with, a good manager and capable, a real Christian and always concerned about each person. Then I received a letter from Sister Anna saying that another nurse, Anna Matheson was coming to be the matron. That left me as manager. We believed Anna Matheson was God's choice and asked for His direction and help. We wondered, of course, what she would be like.

### WE WELCOME SISTER ANNA MATHESON

The day came when a plane landed in front of our home. When Leonard Sooluguk brought Miss Matheson in I knew as I met her that she was God's choice. We became warm friends and co-workers. Now there were three of us again — Anna, Eva and Helen. Anna Matheson had also worked at the Deaconess Hospital. Sister Anna Huseth had met her there and told her about the immediate need at the Mission. Since she also had been at the Deaconess Hospital as a nurse, everyone called her Sister Anna.

### LETTERS FROM SISTER ANNA HUSETH

We kept receiving unfavorable news regarding Sister Anna. I cannot help but quote a little from her last letter to me, dated October 29, 1928: "Dearest Helen: How I wish I could write a real long letter. There are so many things to write about. But it is not so easy where one is flat on one's back. I have not been sitting up for some time. As for writing letters, the bunch I wrote to Alaska and other business letters that had to be taken care of at that time, just about finished my further attempts at writing. I was very sick a little later. When I got over that siege and was feeling pretty good again, Dr. Solum told me what the score was. It did not surprise me for it was about the conclusion I had come to, because both he and the Mayo doctors had evaded my questions. Perhaps you have already heard just what is the matter with me. But, in case you have not, I know you are anxious to know. It is streptococci infection of the endocardium with some other complications. There is no known cure for this disease but the Lord can cure anything. I believe that this disease of mine is meant to be a particular blessing to me and perhaps to others. I have asked that if it can glorify the Lord, that He make me well. But if it can glorify Him more, for me to keep this illness, then I am satisfied. I know that no matter how he arranged it, all will be for the good of us all. Yes, I even see now that a greater interest has been created for the Alaska Mission just because folks are sympathetic and think it is too bad I could not go back. I wonder if you heard that the Daughters of the Reformation of our Church have organized into a National D. O. R. (later L. D. R.) They adopted as their first project **to build the new station at Shishmaref.** Isn't that wonderful?"

November 2 — in same letter. "Dear Helen: I wonder if you are getting tired and worn with much responsibility. It really was asking too much for you to carry on alone for so long. How I have prayed for you. 'Cast your burdens on Him.' He can carry them all for you. In fact it is when we are so tired and helpless that we feel we simply cannot carry them and go to Him in our despair, then is when the Lord really can make use of us to His Glory...."

"Is Sam staying by you and still doing well? I hope Miss Matheson and Miss Swenson are both going to like Alaska. I should write to them but I guess that will not happen for a while. I pray for you three. 'They that grow under His shadow shall return; they shall revive as the corn and grow as the vine.' Hosea 14:7. May the Lord watch between thee and me while we are absent one from the other. Lovingly, Sister Anna"

## A SAINT IS CALLED HOME

Sister Anna passed away in the spring of 1929. I know that everyone here missed her, — the Eskimo folks among whom she had worked, here and at Igloo, and the children at the home. She had been a friend to all, a sincere Christian worker for her Lord. We, as missionaries, were saddened when the news of her death came to us, but the Lord has rewarded her, in His own great and wonderful way. We appreciated what she had done for our Alaska Mission. She was a blessing to me for she had invited me to come to Alaska and taught me the power of prayer.

## "WANTED: A MISSIONARY FOR SHISHMAREF"

Sister Anna had often spoken of the need for a missionary at Shishmaref. On the north coast of Seward Peninsula is a little island about two and one half miles long and a half-mile wide. About two hundred Eskimo people were living there. Our early missionaries had made trips there every year. Sister Anna had also been there, together with Sam Ailak as driver and interpreter. Each time one of our missionaries went up there, some Eskimo would ask, "When is a missionary coming to stay with us?....Can we be saved if we do not read the Bible and go to Church?" These were vital questions. What were they to believe if no one was there to tell them? Though many of the older people could neither read nor write, they had a good memory, repeating over and over the things they heard. When they gathered in the school house or in their homes they talked about the things our missionaries told them during their visits. Yes, they had pleaded many times that someone would come and tell them more about that wonderful Savior, the "white man's God" as they called Him. It was this prayer that was being answered through Sister Anna Huseth. In one more year, the Lutheran Daughters of Reformation had the funds to assume that responsibility. The young girls in our Church had accepted this challenge and, in 1930 with the gifts of many other friends in our Church and with God's help, the funds had been raised.

### OUR 500 MILE TRIP BY DOG SLED

Sister Magdaline Klippen had left Igloo but Rev. and Mrs. Dahle were there. We enjoyed having them come down and visit us at Teller. One spring day during my third year at Teller Mission, Rev. Dahle stopped by on his way to Shishmaref. He said, "I would like you to come along to see the village and meet some of the people. We want to bring them the good news from the L.D.R. That a missionary will be coming very soon!" I was happy to go along and it was quite an experience. For our trip we used a low sled, perhaps two or three feet wide and seven or eight feet long. It as loaded with our sleeping bags, a minimum amount of food for man and dogs, extra clothing in case we should break through the ice and get a bath in the "Arctic" or its tributaries, a bag of dog "mukluks" made from old coats or denim, a few protectors in case of severe weather and several other indispensable articles for a trip of this kind. All of these things were packed quite tightly inside of a canvas and strapped just as tightly as possible to the sled for fear of a "tip over." That happened quite often.

With thirteen dogs ahead, Rev. Dahle on the runners behind, manipulating the brake at the same time, and me sitting astride the load, we sped along at quite a pace, perhaps six or seven miles an hour. We had gone about 25 miles when we ran into a severe Alaska storm of wind, snow and sleet. All that was visible at times was the last three pair of dogs. Many times our eyes were so blinded that we could scarcely see them. Once we found ourselves almost going down a rather steep incline. Another time the sled turned turtle on an ice hummock, and I was on the snow behind in a snowdrift. Finally we saw something black looming up in front of us. We were in York, forty-two miles beyond our starting point. This used to be a mining village and now the building was only used by travelers for shelter. The shelter cabin was full of Eskimo travelers. Close by there was a miner's cabin, but it was locked up. But Rev. Dahle knew the man who owned the cabin so he carefully opened the lock and we went in and first the dogs were put under shelter. We then had something to eat for we were very hungry. Finally we crawled into our sleeping bags and had a delightful sleep and rest.

### A STOP AT WALES, THE FARTHEST WEST VILLAGE

The following day we arrived at Wales which is the western-most point of the North American continent. We were in the vicinity of the Arctic region. Wales was a village of over one hundred people. The Presbyterians had formerly taken care of this village but they had left. For a while the Swedish Covenant Church had served there but they left, too. Rev. Dahle had stopped there before, conducted services and been asked to baptize children. So the people welcomed him.

### A NATIVE HOUSE

It was interesting to visit the native homes, providing you could find them. Some of the houses were completely covered with snow. On close observation a stove pipe would be visible through the snow. Then you would also detect a window made from walrus skin. Walking bent low I made my way through a small entrance dug down into the snowdrift. Then through another rather long tunnel and a two foot square door, I found myself sprawling on the floor. In one corner sat the grandmother tanning reindeer skins for a parka. The mother was busy biting bottoms from oogruk (sea lion) skins and sewing mukluks (shoes) for her many children. Where was the father? He had gone some twenty miles down the coast to gather wood. They had no chairs to offer us but instead invited us to sit on the floor. A native home, especially at that time, was very simple. A stove and perhaps a bunk bed made from logs or lumber was often the only furniture. At mealtime all sat around a board table laid flat on the floor. Dishes were few. Spoons and an Eskimo "oolu" knife was many times the extent of their silverware, thus the fingers were a handy implement. They used to make wooden bowls but one seldom sees that anymore. Enamel dishes became a popular necessity in their homes. Many times the little ones ran about with only a dress on. It always surprised me how fairly orderly the homes were with such small quarters and so many living within. At Wales we stayed with the teachers who welcomed us.

The next night was spent in an Eskimo home at Sinrock. These folks were from Shishmaref and were glad to see us. There we placed our sleeping bags on their floor while the whole family slept in various nooks.

### BRINGING THE GOOD NEWS TO SHISHMAREF

The second day after leaving Wales (about 120 miles), we drove into Shishmaref. As we drove up to the school there was quite a procession of young and old following us along the street. Since we hoped to have a Mission station there in the near future, this visit was very important to us. How happy they were to hear a pastor would be with them soon. We reported that the Lutheran Daughters of the Reformation had taken up the project and that many people were praying and giving that the needed funds so a missionary could come soon. They were pleased.

Here I stayed with the government teachers. Rev. Dahle stayed with Mr. George Goshaw, who had a fox farm and ran the store. When Rev. Dahle conducted Sunday services, morning and evening, in the schoolhouse I believe most of the village population was there. They asked that I speak in the evening. I was the organist and, together with Rev. Dahle, we tried to sing a song. It is strange what one will try to do in Alaska, and get by with it. Things that you would not do in the lower states. At that time that was called 'outside',

### THE STORMY NIGHT WE LOST THE TRAIL

We planned to start out again rather early Monday morning but the weather didn't look too good. However, Mrs. Dickson, the teacher, packed our lunch and by 11:00 A. M. the weather seemed to clear so, after a memorable and pleasant stay, we started off, Mr. Schmitt, the reindeer superintendent of the district, was also there and leaving at the same time. He had a young boy along who was to show us the way to Serpentine Springs. We planned to spend the night there then go on to Igloo. For some reason our guide became a little mixed up in directions and we never got there. Later, we lost track of them. Every little while Rev. Dahle would point to something dark in the distance and say, "That must be it." However, it never was "it." Instead some rush or a knoll was sticking out of the snow. We were riding out in the open spaces. The country seemed very flat with few landmarks. Then it began to snow and get dark. We drove on for there seemed to be a trail ahead of us which the dogs were following. However, every little while Rev. Dahle would take out his flashlight and examine the trail to be sure the dogs stayed on it. We did not dare to stop for fear a terrific storm might blow up and, not knowing exactly where we were, this might be dangerous. It was getting past midnight. The dogs were tired but still we pushed on. Suddenly Rev. Dahle said, "There! I see some shovels and traces of a mining camp. I know where we are now!" It was about 4:00 A.M. when we reached Taylor. It was dark at the roadhouse but Rev. Dahle rapped at the door. Finally an old grey-haired man appeared. Rev. Dahle asked if he had a place for us to sleep. "I think so." he said. He took me upstairs to his own bedroom. I placed my sleeping bag but I was so tired I didn't go to sleep for some time. But it was good just to be on a bed. Rev. Dahle must have slept downstairs somewhere. In the morning I was awakened by sounds in the kitchen and the smell of sourdough hotcakes frying. I was so hungry it did not take me long to crawl out of my sleeping bag and join them.

After having some breakfast we started on our way to Igloo, where we stayed one night, then on back to Teller Mission the next day. We had made quite a circle, about 500 miles in all by dog team, but were no worse for the wear. It had been a real experience and I was happy to have had this privilege of meeting the fine Eskimo people at Shishmaref and other folks along the way. Anna Matheson and Eva Swenson had had their experiences, too, at home, but all was fine. Sam Aliak was an old hand there and a great help to them.

## MY FIRST FURLOUGH

My three year term at Teller Mission was finished in 1929 — two years as matron and in charge the third year. They had been strenuous years but very instructive as I learned about life in Alaska. Sister Anna Huseth had been a great help to me. I had learned many things about the Eskimos — their habits and customs, how to approach them and their needs. Most of all, in everything I did, I learned I needed God to teach me patience. I had grown to love these Eskimo people, both in our home and in the village. But now it was time to visit my family and enjoy a furlough. I could not believe I had been in Alaska for three years.

My year in the States went very rapidly. After seeing my family and some friends, I decided that I needed more Bible studies so I enrolled at Lutheran Bible Institute in Minneapolis. Those wonderful weeks of study, worship in Chapel and fellowship gave me just what I would need.

# IGLOO

While I was studying at Lutheran Bible Institute in 1930 I received a letter asking me to go to Igloo. Since a pastor would be needed for Shishmaref, Rev. Dahle was leaving Igloo to begin permanent work at Shishmaref. Mabel Lien would be the village nurse, hired by the government. Mr. and Mrs. Jesse Olson were going to be in charge at Teller, working with Anna Matheson. I had met the Olsons at Bible School. I was excited to be asked to go to Igloo.

## OUR VOYAGE NORTH

On July 5th I sailed north from Seattle on the S. S. Victoria, with the Olsons. Rev. Stub, Mrs. Rynning and Miss Enestvedt, ardent workers for our Mission, were there to see us off. Not long after coming aboard I was handed a package of letters from various friends and relatives who had remembered me on this sailing date. This was so encouraging for, although I was going back to Alaska, this would really be a new venture. I was to be the only missionary at Igloo. Before this I always had other workers with me, but this time I would be all alone. But I was glad to be going back to Alaska to be with the people I had grown to love.

A stiff wind had come up during the night and the next morning we found ourselves rocking to and fro. It was so rough I was glad to stay in bed and I had no desire for food. On the second day we felt better and the seasickness did not bother us anymore.

We made several stops on our way. Our first one was at False Pass, a place very well known for salmon fisheries and canneries. We saw what happens to a salmon before it lands on the grocery shelf. I found that very interesting.

## A WHALING STATION

The next stop was Akutan, a whaling center way up in the Aleutian Islands. Here many a whale has been pulled up and disposed of. One was just being hauled in the day we landed. We saw men sawing through the whale as if it were a huge log of wood. They told us it was 65 feet long and weighed 65 tons. The blood was continually running down the platform and at the same time it was being washed with a stream of water from above. Some distance away were several large pots where the bones were prepared for fertilizing materials. Akutan has often been called the place of a thousand smells. It was very fittingly named.

### A Visit to Dutch Harbor

A seven hour ride brought us to Dutch Harbor and Unalaska. We dropped anchor about 3:30 in the afternoon. We were told that we would be stopping there until about nine that night and that there were various interesting things to be seen here. We were glad to get off and stretch our legs, so some of us immediately started off on a hike.

At Dutch Harbor there was a remnant of a beautiful summer home owned and formerly inhabited by Molly Garfield and her husband. For a short time they had the rich contract for seal hunting off the Pribiloff Islands. At one time there been about 40,000 people in and around Dutch Harbor. Now in contrast it was quite deserted and forlorn. The seal hunting had been taken over by the government and a company from St. Louis had the contract. When the Alaska gold rush came on in the 1800's, many went north and others south. Nevertheless, it was interesting to see this home, though forlorn, forsaken and misused as it now was. Some batchelors had been using it for the last winter and they surely did not know much about housekeeping or how to live in a respectable home. I wonder how things are there now.

Close by was quite a high mountain. Mr. Olson and three others climbed it that day and signed their names in the book in a chest at the top. The rest of us wanted to see Unalaska. We climbed over a small hill and crossed a stream in a boat rowed by a little Indian boy. He grinned when each of us gave him 25 cents for transporting us.

On the other side of that stream lay beautiful Unalaska, very picturesque in among the mountains with a small harbor as outlet. There was a Methodist and a Catholic Mission there. We visited both places and found them very interesting.

We arrived at Nome on July 14th at 2:00 A. M. Due to shallow water we anchored about five miles out from Nome, to be taken in about 7:30 A. M. When going ashore, we entered a large basket-like affair and were hoisted by chains and lightered on to the platform. Miss Green, the Methodist worker for the natives at Nome, was at the dock to meet us. She invited us to stay with her until our boat came to take us on to Teller. No one seemed to know when this boat might leave. We were told that the boat was up north, storm-bound and perhaps ice-bound. This might mean a two week's stay in Nome. I now knew I was back in Alaska, where traffic and travel must depend on weather conditions. There was no set time for anything — just "be ready all the time." One had to learn patience when traveling, whether by boat, dog-team or airplane. This was a new experience for the Olsons who were going to Teller Mission.

We picked up our baggage and wended our way to the Methodist quarters. The Methodists had always been kind to our missionaries coming through. On Friday word came that a little trading vessel was northward bound and perhaps they would consent to take us to our destination. We immediately went to investigate. Yes, they were going Saturday at 8:00 A.M. and we could go along. Even though this boat was not equipped for passengers, we were glad to board it as we were anxious to get to our destination. At 8:00 A.M. we were ready, but the water was too low and no boat could move. A large scow was standing on a sand bar with supplies for the Steamer Victoria, but they had to wait for the tide to come in and raise the level. Up to this point the waters had been very calm but suddenly there was a change, filled with power and motion as the water began rising and moving in. By about 10:00 A.M. we were on our way. Little did we know what was ahead of us.

### ON A SMALL BOAT IN A HEAVY STORM

We were not out of sight of Nome when suddenly quite a blow came up. Then the engine stopped and we were being tossed to and fro by wind and water. There is nothing worse than losing power on a stormy sea. Soon they got the engine going and the boat was moving again. We were on our way, but my head was swimming and my stomach turning. I quickly disposed of my breakfast and wished I were home again. Mrs. Olson fared no better and followed suit. We finally found our way to the cabin below, but there it was stuffy and close. Soon we were sprawling on some rather filthy and unkempt bunks that no doubt belonged to the crew. But in our misery we were glad to have even this. Had I been seasick before? If I had, I certainly didn't remember anything like this. Soon we heard the rattling of the dishes, smelled the odor of the coffee and fried eggs. Mr. Olson seemed to survive it all and joined in a hearty meal with the crew. To Mrs. Olson and me it was very distasteful. It is a good things there are a few real sailors in the world.

It was nearing midnight and it seemed we were being tossed about unmercifully. The cabin was dark and gloomy. We were suddenly coming to a very critical point in our trip. Buckets and boxes seemed to be tossed around while water was washing up on the deck. Teakettles and coffee pots came flying off the stove. Clothes on the wall swayed terrifically. Records in the cupboard behind my head came sliding down. It sounded almost as if the boat were going to crack open and its contents swallowed by the sea. In the midst of it all, I saw Mr. Olson kneeling in prayer. Yes, there was power on high and One who could still the tempest. Suddenly, we felt ourselves coming into calmer water. We had passed Point Clarence and made it into the Bay on whose waterfront Teller Mission Orphanage is located. At 1:00 A.M. we saw the Mission in the distance, but due to the storm we had to go on to Grantley Harbor, in front of Teller Town, where there was perfect calm. "Oh, how beautiful" was all I could say. "Praise the Lord we are safe." It had been a troubled night.

I think I must have felt something like the disciple out on the stormy sea, with Jesus sleeping in the stern. Suddenly Jesus arose and with his commanding voice and power bade the water "Be still" and there was calm. I am sure that my prayer must have been that I would always trust in the Lord, knowing that He can carry us through whatever may come, all kinds of storms, whether on land or sea, physically or spiritually.

About noon as we landed at the Mission, we could see our boat was again plying its way out of the harbor and bay, going farther north. Our thanks was directed to God, but also to the Captain of "The Good Hope" and his crew for a safe landing. But tragically, some time later, in a freezing storm, this boat was wrecked and all passengers lost.

It was wonderful to be back at Teller, step on solid ground and see the smiling faces of the children and the village folk. They gave a warm welcome to the new Missionaries, the Olsons. It was Sunday and we had come just in time for their afternoon services. As we worshipped that day I was convinced more than ever that Alaska was to be my home, — until the Lord told me otherwise.

After a few days at Teller Mission and showing Mr. Olson around, I was anxious to get to Igloo. I knew I would need a helper so I took with me a rather promising young boy by the name of Samuel. He was about fourteen years old and I felt he might help with chores and other work.

With Sam Aliak as pilot of our Mission boat, the Julia B., we enjoyed a lovely trip up the Tuxuk River. We stopped at various camps along the river where the Eskimo people of Igloo were fishing and picking berries.

## MARY'S IGLOO

Igloo was a very nice little village, forty-five miles inland by dog-team and seventy-five miles by boat from Teller Town. To the south about seven miles we had the foothills of the beautiful Saw Tooth Mountains. On one side of the village was the Pilgrim River and on the other, close to the Mission was the Kuzitrin River. These two rivers met just below the village and also about two miles above the village. We used to say that Igloo was a floating island. Then a few miles further down we had Little Salt Lake, which led into Big Salt Lake. About fifteen miles across Big Salt Lake we would come to the Tuxuk River, leading into Grantley Harbor and Teller Town. All of these places are familiar spots, especially to the Eskimos who camp on the Tuxuk River every summer to do their salmon fishing and their marketing at Teller. There were about 150-200 Eskimo people at Igloo when I arrived. I understand the village had been much larger before the flu epidemic.

When we got to Igloo we found our supplies for the winter were in the warehouse, so that was the first chore to be cared for. I loved the little four-room house with its front entry — it looked cozy and inviting. In fact, the Dahles had left a coffee pot and cup right on the stove, bidding me welcome.

## PICKING BERRIES FOR WINTER

It was berry season at Igloo and what fun we had picking those delicious blueberries close to the Mission, almost at our back door, along the river bank. The salmon berries (called multebar in Norway) were just beginning to ripen. Then came the cranberries and blackberries (moss berries.) But the mosquitoes were a pest and something to contend with. There were few folk back in the village, but we were kept busy with our berries and getting settled.

## GETTING STARTED

Soon it was September. We heard boats coming and going as families came back to the village from their campgrounds. Others were going past to the Old Village or Pilgrim Springs beyond. It was a happy day when I could conduct my first service at Igloo, but also a strange feeling for I was not a preacher.

## THE NEW TEACHERS

The new teachers came, a young couple, Mr. and Mrs. H. Burkher. They seemed so interesting and filled with vim, vigor and vitality. I invited them over for dinner, together with the Petersons, who owned the store. They were bringing another couple later, —Mr. and Mrs. Overbough, to run the store. They were all busy unloading their supplies so they appreciated my invitation.

When Mr. Burkher found out that I was a nurse he asked if I would take care of the medical work in the village. He would let me have access to the medical supplies sent by the government. In turn they might be able to do something for me. Later on they did a lot to help. Both Mr. and Mrs. Burkher seemed quite musical and he had a good voice, so I asked if they would help with the choir. They agreed and we had a good time at choir practice. The Eskimos like to sing.

## SAMUEL GOES BACK HOME

At first Samuel seemed to be quite happy at Igloo, but by and by he showed signs of loneliness. He missed his Teller friends and just did not feel at home. When Mr. Olson came some time later via dog team, the boy was quite determined to return to the orphanage, so he left.

## MARTHA COMES TO HELP

Realizing I did need someone to help I asked Martha, one of our older girls from the orphanage, who was now staying with some of her relatives in the village. Martha had studied at White Mountain Industrial School for a year. The last year she had worked for the former teachers, but they had been transferred to Nome. The new teachers did not need her so I asked if she would like to come and stay with me. She accepted and Martha was a good helper, clean and neat, and I liked her. All went well for quite a while. At first she seemed quite happy, but somehow I did not seem to be able to get very close to her. Perhaps it was my fault. I let her visit the village when she felt like it and there was no trouble there. She went along with me when I was occasionally invited to the neighbors or teachers for dinner. She took part in the choir and Christmas activities, but there was something strange about her. She seemed to draw away from us and was very quiet, busy sewing or knitting on her own. Then later came the crucial day which was a great shock to me.

Sister Anna Matheson, together with Johnny Reed, came for a visit and stayed over a Sunday. Saturday night I was awakened with a rap on the door. A very frightened father told me that his baby had swallowed some kerosene. We told him to bring the baby over and we washed out its stomach with enemas and tried to make the child drink some milk. Pretty soon the baby seemed all right so he took it home, and we went to bed again.

In the morning while we were eating breakfast a man from the Old Village five miles away arrived. His wife had delivered her first baby and he asked if I would see her. She was one of our former girls from the orphanage so I asked Sister Anna if she would take care of the service while I went up to the village. She agreed and all went fine. We had lunch together, then I visited some of the homes in the afternoon.

### A CRY FOR HELP

The next morning Anna Matheson and Johnny Reed planned to get an early start to return to Teller. So I got up early and was making breakfast while they were packing. Suddenly I heard a cry from Martha's room and a call, "Sister Helen, come!" I rushed in and there was Martha — delivering a baby! I was never so surprised or shocked in all my life. How trusting, how ignorant I had been in not realizing that she was pregnant. I had noticed that she seemed rather fleshy and that she wore a parka the greater part of the time, but I had never suspected this. I called Anna to finish taking care of her as it just seemed that I was unable to do so. Of course, all of this delayed their departure, but they finally left. Then I was alone, — with Martha and her new baby.

Martha later told me how it had happened and who was responsible. It was a married man from the village. Of course, I had a serious talk with him and Martha, too. Martha and this man seemed repentant. His wife also came over and they talked together. Martha stayed with me for a while, then decided to return to her relatives in the village. Later she and her baby left for Nome to work for the teachers whom she had been with the previous year at Igloo. She stayed with them for a time then rented a little cabin. Later the baby became sick and died. I'm sorry to say, Martha became a victim of tuberculosis and was found dead one morning. I have always felt badly about this incident and wondered if I had failed her in some way. God only knows.

### GETTING ACQUAINTED....MEETING MARY OQUILLOK

I had met some of the Igloo folks from time to time at Teller but now I had a chance to really learn to know them. Perhaps one of the first ones was Mary Oquillok who had a most interesting background. She often came to visit and then would tell me about herself. Sometimes it was a little hard to understand her, although she spoke English fairly fluently. She told me she had lost her parents when she was a little girl. An uncle cared for her for a time. When she was very young she learned to cook, sew mukluks and parkas. Three of her cousins, Keelick, Jim and Fred, also became a part of the family when their parents died. She cared for them as if they were her own.

Mary's home soon became a hospitality house. When strangers —white men miners and other travelers – came through the village inquiring about shelter, people would direct them to Mary's Igloo and she would welcome them. Therefore, when the village sprang up around her house, this place was called Mary's Igloo.

During the gold rush white families also moved in. One white woman took a special interest in Mary, asking her over to her home and taught her many things. Mary even told how this white lady took her and her three cousins outside — to the states — as it was called. What a wonderful time they had. To them it all seemed like a fairyland. But when spring came and the boats were again going up to Nome, they were all anxious to return to their reindeer meat, fish, ptarmigan and seal. Mary said, "We went back home and I was glad to throw off my white men's shoes and clothing and put on my parka and mukluks again." It had been an adventure long remembered and something to talk about for many years to come.

Some time later Mary married and had two children, who later became ill and died. Her husband became a victim to the white man's vice in the mining camp and was drinking and gambling with the rest. As a result he lost his life in one of the brawls. His death left a terrific mark on Mary. But, as time went on, she met a widower by the name of Oquillok who had a little boy called Apollok. Oquillok was a very industrious man, a fine reindeer herder, and a good man. Soon his reindeer herd was the largest in the community. He was greatly respected by all of his relatives and friends. Mary later married Oquillok and cared for his son, Apollok.

## HOW THE IGLOO CHURCH WAS STARTED

Oquillok had traveled a lot when he was young. During his wanderings up north, working on the whaling vessels, he had met some Christian men. When they taught him about God he was greatly impressed. Later he had the opportunity of hearing and talking with Rev. T. L. Brevig, the missionary at Teller. He became a real convert and began to share his faith with the people at Igloo. Among those who became Christians was his crippled brother, Octuck. They wanted a place to meet and pray so they put up the first church at Mary's Igloo, building it from logs. When this small congregation came to worship, their services were led by Octuck with Mary helping with the singing. As often as he could, Rev. Brevig came from Teller to help and encourage them, teaching them about the Bible and some new songs. Someone gave Mary pictures of scenes taken from the book, "Pilgrim's Progress," which she often used in teaching. Mary showed these to me one day and told me how helpful they had been in her life and teaching.

Unfortunately, Octuck's service as pastor did not last long. One day while traveling with his wife and baby on the river by dog-team, they had a tragic accident. Their boat struck an overflow, went under the ice and all were drowned. Now the three Octuck children, Tommy, Peter and Lucy were orphans. Mary welcomed them to her home, and now she had a bigger family. By the time I came to Igloo, Apollok and the three Octucks had married and were living in their own homes. Oquillok had passed away just before I arrived, but his name was often mentioned for he had been a great leader, both in the village and in the Church. He also had been a pioneer with the reindeer business. David, son of Apollok, came to live with Mary and later Albert also came. Mary was a mother to many.

When in doubt about various matters pertaining to the village folks, I would go to Mary. When I wanted some skin sewing done, Mary was always willing to help me. Although she could not read, I often used her as my interpreter, especially for women's meetings. Perhaps she did not always say it just as I did, but she knew what I meant.

Keelick was another fine man and a good interpreter for our services. His wife was a fine woman and they had several fine-looking children. Jim Eyuk had spent some time near White Mountain working in a mine, then he married and they moved to Igloo. He was a good leader in the village, always dependable, jolly and outspoken. The younger brother, Fred (Mosquito), married Mary Ann, a girl from the orphanage. When Sister Magdaline was at Igloo from 1923-1927, Mary had been her companion and helper. So I felt quite at home with her and her family. Several years I went down the river to the Tuxuk camping grounds with Fred and his family.

**OUR WEEKLY MEETINGS AT IGLOO**

I enjoyed the work at Igloo and the many fine people there. As I visited them in their homes from time to time I became better acquainted with their family life. The first year our women's meetings, young people's Bible class, choir practice and girls' sewing class all met in my quarters. Sometimes it would be crowded and it did mean much more cleaning. Later, when Rev. Dahle and family spent some time in Igloo again, he enlarged the kitchen and also added a small class room. That made it much more convenient for the smaller gatherings could be held there.

At 2:00 P.M. I would ring the bell for our women's meeting. Often even before the bell rang I might see Mary Ann and little Howard, all dressed in fur, come trudging along the path. Then Mary Oquillok, with one of her adopted grandchildren; Wasak with her two little ones; Gussie, with one child on her back and two more tagging along. They, too, wanted to see what was going on and get some of those cookies or doughnuts I might be serving! Sometimes there would be as many as twelve women and almost as many pre-school children. Usually this didn't make for a very quiet evening. But they all liked to get away from their huts, see the bright light of a "white man's home" and what treats there were. First we would have a Bible study class with an interpreter, possibly on "Women of the Bible." Then there would be prayer or testimony followed by singing. Perhaps someone had learned a new song in Eskimo. I remember once when Mary Ann had been in the Kotzebue Hospital for a time she learned a new song and taught it to us. In the meantime, I would cook the coffee and get the lunch ready. Then there would be considerable visiting, some in the Eskimo language and some in English. Sometimes it was hard for them to break up and leave, but shortly after the lunch was over, most of them would be on their way home, looking forward to the next month's meeting.

On Monday evenings we had our Bible Class for the young folks between confirmation age and possibly twenty-five years old. Tuesday was choir practice night. This consisted mostly of unmarried folks or those who did not have children to care for. On Wednesday night mid-week services were held. At this time I often followed the Old Testament stories, perhaps using Hurlbut's Story of the Bible. On Thursday afternoons, after school, the girls' sewing group came. Friday night was play night at the school house and the Burkhers usually planned some interesting games. I often went, just to see what was going on.

Saturday was always a busy day,  first getting the house cleaned up, then preparing for Sunday. Usually on Monday I started to prepare my sermon for the next Sunday. The school children were also divided into groups and came over once a week after school for catechism and Bible studies, to prepare for confirmation.

## SHORT DAYS AND LONG NIGHTS

Some referred to our days in December as "very short," due to the short daylight period. But I often felt they were "very long" because there were so many things to do getting ready for Christmas. During the first years we did not receive as many Mission boxes as we did later on. The native people fished and hunted for food, trapped and sold pelts or made things to sell, but most of them had little money. Therefore, I spent much time preparing a suitable Christmas gift for each one.  Many hours were spent making flannel shirts for the older boys, coveralls for younger ones, and dresses, aprons, mittens or something else that might fit a real need.

A close examination of the supply of matches, soap or other articles on hand for personal use was made, to see what might be sacrificed as a suitable gift. Yes, at times I went to the village store for some gloves and socks to make the list complete. But in later years we received many more mission boxes with very fine things to use as Christmas gifts. Some years there were coats to be made into parka jackets for the boys. I would use the fur on them for ruffs instead of the wolf or wolverine ruffs which the Eskimos put around their hoods. Some of the women liked to make under-parkas from "white women's coats," and then gingham parka covers over them. Very often these were very colorful, with a ruffle at the bottom and rick-rack braid for decoration above the ruffle and around the pocket and hood.

## THE FIRST CHRISTMAS

The Burkhers were very fine teachers and interested in the progress of their students. Mrs. Burkher liked to prepare programs and I was glad to work with her. So we planned Christmas Eve together in the schoolhouse. I brought all the gifts over for the natives, also practiced some songs with the girls. Mr. Burkher and the boys made a

Christmas tree from willow branches stuck into a pole. We all enjoyed a very pleasant and happy Christmas Eve.

That night at midnight I was pleasantly awakened with singing outside my bedroom window. A group of the young folks had decided to go out caroling. The next day our Christmas services were held and the choir sang fine songs with the help of Mr. and Mrs. Burkher. We again gathered in the evening for a Christmas Vesper Service. The children recited some Bible verses and sang. Then we all sang Christmas songs.

On New Year's Day the natives, together with the teachers, arranged for some dog-team and foot races on the frozen river. I made pop-corn balls to serve in the evening in the schoolhouse, where they would gather for more games. Then the prizes were given to those who had won the races. I had previously made some doughnuts which I quickly warmed and dipped in sugar. These were served with coffee and cocoa about midnight, before going home. Oh, how everyone loved that!

### SPRING ON THE TUXUK RIVER

It seemed that Easter and the break-up season were upon us before we knew it. What a marvelous sight to suddenly see the river ice break up and go floating down the river. Everybody had been busy getting ready to go down the Tuxuk river for their salmon fishing. Mr. and Mrs. Overbough and daughter, who had taken care of the village trading post that year, were waiting for the "Pippen" to come up and get them. This good-sized tugboat belonged to Mr. and Mrs. Peterson at Teller. The Petersons and Mrs. Marx owned the Teller Commercial Company and had a store at Teller. They also owned the Igloo Trading Post. This year I went along with them for I was going to stay in a tent on the Tuxuk River for a while. Except for the mosquitoes, that would have been fine, but I did not enjoy them. However, they did not seem to bother the Eskimos very much, for they kept right on with their fishing activities.

On Sunday many of the Eskimos would come to my tent for morning services, all sitting on the ground, of course. If the weather was nice we just sat outside in the open. After spending a short time on the Tuxuk I went down to Teller to visit at the Missions. When the berry season came, Sam Aliak took some of the girls up the river to pick berries. This gave me a chance to get back to Igloo.

### BRING MARY ELLEN TO IGLOO

This time I took Mary Ellen Doyle with me as a companion. She was a fairly good student and musically inclined. I felt that I could help her by givng her music lessons for there was more time at Igloo than at the Orphanage. I enjoyed teaching her and she was a fine companion. Mary often spoke of her stormy arrival at Nome and then Teller Mission. Her mother while at Unalakleet was unable to take care of her. Mary Ellen was first sent to the Industrial School at White Mountain but she was too young to stay there. Then she was put on a boat for Nome, landing on the beach, with no one to meet her. Finally, someone asked her who she was and where she was going. A search was made for her father and he found her temporary lodging.

Letters had come to our Mission asking if we would take Mary Ellen. She was then put on the mail-boat going to Teller. When our Mission boat went over to get the mail, there she was. It was a stormy day but, in the distance across the Bay towards Teller, we could see a boat coming. It was loaded quite heavily, for Sam was also bringing back the fresh supplies that had come in from Seattle. Sometimes it looked as if the boat was about to be swamped, but God watched over them and they made it.

It was a strange place for Mary Ellen with so many children around, all eager to speak to her. She was a sweet little girl. She spoke English very well and also knew the Eskimo language. Her light hair was quite a contrast for all the other girls had dark hair. She liked to visit the Mission quarters and it was hard for us not to show partiality. Now you can see why I wanted Mary Ellen with me at Igloo. I still wonder why I didn't take her the first year. We became good friends. In fact, she often called me "mother" and later, while off to school and in training, she sent me many Mother's Day cards. I always appreciated this. She became a great help to me.

I started piano lessons for her and Josie Keeling, another Eskimo girl in the village. Josie's father had bought her an organ so she could practice at home. Mary Ellen and Josie became good friends and both got along very well with their music. As soon as they were able to play the hymns they took turns playing for church in the evenings. A few years later, while living in Teller, Josie was organist there so I felt that my time spent teaching these girls was well spent. Mary Ellen also made use of her musical ability in various ways later on.

## THE ORCHESTRA

I was surprised to find what a good ear for music many of the Eskimos had. One day I happened to say to Mr. Burkher, "I wish I could play the guitar." So he told me that if I would get a guitar he would show me the chords and help me get started. He played the ukulele, and his wife the musical saw. One of the Eskimo boys had a guitar, so when I did get a guitar, it wasn't long before we had a little orchestra going. I showed him what I knew and he would go home and play for hours. Before long, playing by ear, he was much farther along than I was. I had to have the music to follow.

One day another boy came in and showed me his violin and what he could do with it. He also played by ear. I became so interested in the violin that I asked to borrow it for a little while to see what I could do with it. I then ordered a violin from Sears and Roebuck and began to practice in earnest. I received some help from Della Vollmers, the music teacher at Teller. But holding the violin bothered my neck and I became too tense, so I had to give that up. I soon decided that a mandolin would be easier for me because I could then lead with the melody and sing at the same time. I ordered a ukulele for Mary Ellen. More of the boys and girls became interested and soon we had quite an orchestra to play for our Sunday evening services and other gatherings. When I visited the village I often found several of them playing together.

Mary Ellen started school with the other children in the village and was a good student. The Burkhers were glad to have her there and I wanted her to get to know the other children. Each Friday I had her invite one of the girls for dinner, taking turns so that each of the girls of her age would visit. The girls that were invited seemed to enjoy coming. Then after dinner we would go over to the play-night program at the schoolhouse.

We had five dogs and Mary Ellen was responsible for their feeding and care. She enjoying taking some of the girls with her for rides. I felt that this was a good sport for her and it gave her an outlet. Mrs. Marx and her daughter Ethel were taking care of the store that year. Ethel had a dog team, and she and Mary Ellen shared a common interest. Of course, Ethel was a grown girl and had handled dogs for years. She taught Mary Ellen a great deal about how to handle and care for the dogs.

Whenever Mosquito Lake at the end of the village would freeze up nice and smooth, then there would be skating. I also had skates but had never become much of a skater. However, it was fun to get out for a little while, watch the others and get some good fresh air.

### WHEN THE SUN DISAPPEARS

Once more on November 26th we watched the sun go down below the beautiful Sawtooth mountains. Then we said "We have seen the sun for the last time this year." But we were not discouraged for we accepted that. We knew that after Christmas, on January 17th we would again see the sun coming up above the mountains. In the meantime, there was much to do getting ready for Christmas

### THE SECOND CHRISTMAS

This Christmas at Igloo there seemed to be so many more things to do. This year we had more Mission packages so two weeks before Christmas I began wrapping the presents for the natives of the village. There were so many to be accounted for. Care had to be taken so that those of the same ages and classes received about the same gifts or as nearly as possible alike. Therefore, I divided out for each group separately, then wrapped them. By making use of the late hours and a bit of the wee morning hours, I managed to get most of the wrapping done the first three days. Of course, Mary Ellen did not find an elaborate lunch ready for her when she came home from school, nor did the house look very orderly. Then there was the baking, washing clothes and special cleaning for Christmas and other preparations.

Just a week before Christmas I was called to the delivery of a baby girl in the Keelick home. The arrival of a newborn is usually a happy moment but I felt very sad about this one, knowing that both father and mother were tuberculous. Keelick had hardly been out of his house all winter and Mrs. Keelick had been trying to keep the house going with the assistance of the older children. The making of mukluks for six children was quite a task and she had to call on them for help in scraping the skins for sewing.

This year I knew the people better and felt that I could plan for activities that I had not been able to do earlier. On Christmas Eve we gathered in the schoolhouse for the splendid program of Mr. and Mrs. Burgher. The gifts were distributed and, of course, all were interested to see what they got so immediately left for home. A few could not wait that long and they beamed as they displayed a colorful new shirt or dress, mittens, stockings, piece of material, yarn, school supplies, or whatever it might be. I, too, had gifts from far and near, piled up at my house, waiting to be opened when we got home. It seemed nice to be remembered this way.

At about midnight I heard carolers at our windows, singing "Silent Night," "Joy to the World" and other Christmas songs. It brought me back to the days at the Deaconess Hospital when the nurses went caroling early in the morning, over to the Old Folk's Home nearby and on the hospital floors.

At noon on Christmas Day we again gathered in the Chapel for our services, to hear the "Glad Tidings" spoken long ago but still the good old story. In anthem and song, devotion and prayer, we, too, rejoiced. I felt very humble at the thought that I was the spokesman, and often prayed for God's guidance that I would say the right thing, bringing faith to someone.

In the evening we gathered at the Chapel around our Christmas tree that had been decorated by the boys. The children circled around the tree and sang songs and quoted Bible verses and told the story of Jesus born in the manger. The adult choir sang and our new Igloo orchestra also played. Then Mrs. Burkher told the interesting Christmas story of "Gretchen's Surprise." It was a delightful evening and much enjoyed by all.

During the week between Christmas and New Year I had various groups over to my house for a social hour and refreshments. On Wednesday night the Junior Bible Class and Catechism class came. For Thursday I invited the mothers for supper (twelve of them), asking them to leave their little children at home except for the babies on their backs. I put an oil lamp on the floor. The Christmas tree was in the center, and in the candlelight they enjoyed the spread of mashed potatoes, reindeer meatloaf, lima beans, catsup, bread, apricot sauce, cake and coffee. It seemed to be a real treat and it was interesting to see how quiet they all were, sitting on the floor during the meal, just enjoying the food. Then we had devotions and sang some Eskimo songs. All was cleared away and everybody sat down in a circle playing games, such as hitting the peanuts with beans, blowing out the candle in the center, bouncing and hitting the rubber ball, putting puzzles together and playing jacks. They all laughed and carried on as children. I could not help but laugh myself, just to see them laugh. All pretended to be very anxious for the awarded prize, trying to snatch from one another. Before they left, Mary Ellen played a few pieces on the piano which they enjoyed. It was amusing to hear their "thank you's" in English and Eskimo. I am sure one mother repeated it at least four times.

On Friday night the adult Bible class came for a good time and twenty-four of them squeezed into my small living room. To make more space we had removed all chairs and movable furniture so all that was left was the piano and the stove. As they came in I asked if they would sit on the floor. One boy spoke up, "Well, I guess we all know how to do that." We all knew that many native homes then had very few chairs. We had various games and contests, and everyone took part. That night everyone enjoyed jello, cake, cookies and peanuts.

One morning during the week I was called to Mary's Mountain, where a group of Catholic people lived, to see a sick boy. The child had a very large swelling on his left groin which had been getting worse. I soon had the swelling lanced and an abnormal amount of pus began streaming out. No wonder he had been so uncomfortable. What a relief to him when it was all over. I will never forget the expression on his face when he looked at me, as if to say, "The pain is all gone. Is it true?" It was and I was glad I could help.

## NEW YEAR'S FESTIVITIES

Saturday morning, before New Year's festivities, I was not feeling at all well but I managed to bake two double batches of dough-nuts for the New Year's Eve party in the schoolhouse. I did, however, have to crawl into bed for the rest of the day. It no doubt was "LaGrippe" as it was called before the word "flu" became popular. By Monday (New Year's Eve) I was out watching the sights. In spite of it being 20 degrees below zero almost the whole village was there to see the races and games. There were men's, boys' and girls' and women's dog races, sock and foot races for various groups and relay races.

Mary Ellen also entered the races and came in second place in the girls' and boys' dog race. Using her five dogs, Ethel Marx won second place in the women's races.

In the evening everybody once more gathered in the schoolhouse where more games were played and prizes awarded. The orchestra played and there was Eskimo dancing. Coffee, doughnuts, apples and peanuts were served. The apples were a gift of Harry Gavin, a miner and old-timer living down the river some distance. He always enjoyed coming to Igloo from time to time when there was dog-teaming.

## STARTING THE NEW YEAR

At twelve midnight we rang in the New Year. Both the school and Chapel bells were heard, besides the shots from guns. Then all was quiet and everybody wended their way home. At twelve noon on New Year's Day we met in the Chapel for services and to thank God for His many blessings to us the past year, expressing it in word, prayer, song and music.

I'll admit I did look forward to January 17th. On that day we would again see the sun coming up above the mountains. I loved that gorgeous sight with many colorings upon the snow white mountain peaks. Every one in the village was looking to see the sun which had been gone so long. It was as if an old friend had come to visit and give light for another year.

Before we knew it, Easter, with its usual activities, was upon us; then spring and break-up season. The snow would be melting fast and many streams coming down from the mountain sides. Soon the days would be longer, and before you knew it, it would be light all the time. The men and boys would be out hunting muskrats or squirrels for in those years they got very good prices for the furs.

One day I saw a near tragedy. I was watching an Eskimo coming across the river through some overflow on to the slush ice. I watched him hurry and just make it to the bank near where I was standing. Just as he got there safely the ice broke. Very quickly the strong current began breaking the ice as it started moving down the river. I always enjoyed watching the break-up but some years it was at night while I was sleeping. How different the river looked in the morning with the ice gone and only the blue water remaining. Soon we would go down on the Tuxuk to Teller again.

## VISITING SHISHMAREF TO SEE THE NEW BUILDING

Rev. Dahle invited Miss Matheson and me to come up to Shishmaref to see the new station and building there. They had been working for the last two years on that building. After ten busy months at the inland station of Igloo I looked forward to this little excursion. We went up on the mailboat and it was so nice to again see the Dahles and Mabel Lien, who lived in the Post Office building close to the Mission.

Rev. Dahle and the natives had certainly put in some hard work. All as volunteers; no one was paid. Rev. Dahle had planned and guided it to completion. The new two-story building had living quarters downstairs and the chapel above. The natives of the village had helped raise the framework into place and do many other things. What a magnificent job against so many obstacles. I was so happy to see it. I know that it had not been easy for Mrs. Dahle, living in a tent through those cold fall days until they could finally move into the first completed room.

## DEDICATION OF THE NEW CHAPEL

As we got ready for the Service of Dedication I thought how the prayers of Sister Anna Huseth had been fulfilled. Today the Shishmaref Church and Station stands as a memorial to her memory through the efforts of the L.D.R., Rev. and Mrs. E. Dahle, and many friends. The Girls' Club of Central Lutheran Church, Minneapolis, Minnesota had sent a beautiful gold cross for the altar. It was given in memory of Mrs. H. Stub, the pastor's wife. This matched the gold candlesticks previously given by the Lutheran Daughters of the Reformation. An appropriate service on "The Cross." was conducted that Sunday when this cross was first placed on the altar. On this beautiful day the Eskimos were able to come from the near islands where they were camping for the summer. Mabel Lien was also doing outstanding work there. Besides being the station nurse, she also helped with the religious work.

It was a joy to see the natives flocking into the chapel on Sunday morning or lingering about the door, waiting to speak to the missionary about something. They knew they could confide in him.

### My Prayer for a Cabin — and an Outboard Motor

That visit strengthened me spiritually and physically for I received helpful information and encouragement. For a long time I had wanted to spend more time with the natives on the Tuxuk during the summer. Four or five months out of the year, rain or shine, cold or warm weather, they lived in tents. It didn't seem to bother them but, somehow, I found it difficult to live like that for such a long time. I especially needed advice on how I might be there to visit and lead worship services. I had been praying about this for some time. I wondered if a small cabin could be put up on the Tuxut near their camping places. Rowing my little "Ark" was not easy. If I had a small outboard motor I could travel much easier to the various camps. But for this we needed money.

### A Pleasant Surprise

Just as I was wondering about this I got a letter from Rev. Foerde of Starbuck, Minnesota. In it was a check for $200. given by one of the members in the congregation. Mabel Lien knew of this dream and she gave me $50. for the "cabin fund." I knew that my prayers had been answered. This had been a worth-while trip.

Coming back to Teller we discovered that two new workers, Miss Mabel Gunderson and Golelo Hansen had arrived for the Teller Mission. Anna Matheson was leaving for the states. I had known Mabel Gunderson at the Deaconess Hospital so we had a little reunion.

### Back to Igloo

On returning to Teller from Shishmaref we heard that the berries were ripening at Igloo. We needed to gather berries for the children at the Mission so we hurriedly prepared to go up the very next day. We got together sandwiches to eat on the way and seal pokes for the berries. Mabel Gunderson and two of the girls from the home were going to help with the berry picking. Mr. Olson took us up in our Mission boat, the "Julia B".

It was a beautiful and warm day as we traveled up the Tuxuk River, bringing us first to the Igloo native fishing camps. They knew just where to camp for the best salmon fishing. When we stopped at one of the camps, Mr. Olson conducted services out in the open. It was an interesting picture, with the mountains on one side covered with a deep green vegetation. On the flatland below there were seven or eight tents erected and on the fish racks long rows of beautiful red salmon were drying in the sun. On the calm and peaceful riverbank sat the natives, young and old, singing hymns as they took part in the service.

Following the service I told about the new plan of building a cabin on the Tuxuk so that I could stay there longer during the summer, visiting and having services. They were pleased and the men offered to help put up the cabin when the lumber arrived. Their offer pleased me very much.

The lumber came with the fall supplies. The Eskimos chose a site in the largest camp and erected a 16 x 10 single wall cabin, covered with malthoid paper. Now I knew where I would be living the next summer. I was anxious to try it but that would have to wait until later.

We then went on up the Tuxuk where Mr. Olson left us to pick berries. We picked three good-sized barrels of blueberries, blackberries, cranberries and salmon berries. Berries were very valuable in Alaska as there was so little other fresh fruit or vegetables to be gotten.

## My Poor Little Garden

Before going down to Teller I had tried to plant some carrots, turnips and lettuce in a little patch of ground which had been dug up for me. I wondered how it looked now. I discovered that the turnips were about as large as peanuts, the lettuce leaves were one or two inches square, and I needed a magnifying glass to see the carrots. It seemed that ground was just too cold or not fertile. My winter supplies had not arrived but Mr. Olson had put out a white-fish net for us. We landed so many white-fish we had some to dry for winter use. So, with fish and berries, our menu was almost complete. Of course we made some sourdough hot-cakes and bread. After three weeks Miss Gunderson and the girls returned to Teller with one of the natives from Mary's Igloo.

About the middle of September the natives began coming back to the village. The tugboat from Teller arrived with our supplies, so Mary Ellen and I got busy putting them away. When one of the boys returned to the village he stored the coal and oil away.

## Getting Ready for Winter

When we saw snow begin to appear on the mountains we knew that before long the river would begin to freeze. As soon as the village folk got back, we had our regular fall wood-hauling day. This meant that as many boats as possible went up the river to gather wood for the Chapel. It would be placed on the bank and then when the river began freezing and they could not go anywhere, several of the men and boys hauled it to the Chapel, chopped it and put it into the hall or the Chapel. While they worked I would cook a big kettle of beans, make some fruit pudding and tea. I served this at noon or when they were finished. We were always glad when this was done. Everyone helped and we all had a jolly time.

### MISSION BOXES

When I first came to Igloo we had very few Mission boxes. But when we let our friends know of our needs, that changed and help came from various places. I remember Jane Thorpe organized a group called the Igloo Club that made quilts, mittens and other articles we needed. The Women's Missionary Federation began sending boxes and later the L. D. R. or congregational groups started sending donations every summer. They enjoyed doing that and their gifts meant a lot up in Alaska.

One evening while in camp on the Tuxuk River I stopped at one of the tents. There I found a mother very busy trying to patch and fix a worn and ragged coat as a protection for her baby when she carried it on her back. I had just received a bag of clothing from the Riceford Congregation where father had served. In this bag was a nice plush coat. I thought how happy this mother would be to get this coat so I gave it to her. She was very pleased, for the next evening she came to me with a letter asking me to send it to the lady who had sent the coat. This is what she wrote:

*Dear Unseen Friend:*          *Tuxuk River, July 13*

*I am an Eskimo mother in Alaska so you know I cannot write very well. I want to thank you for the coat you sent far away from the states. Sister Helen Frost has given it to me this evening. I was very appreciate to get it, for I was used to wear it before.*

*I was raised down at Teller Mission for few years. I am living up at Igloo now for seven years after I got married. My old home was at Cape Prince of Wales. But after the flu sickness I was taken down to Teller Mission after my parents died.*

*We should be very appreciate for the Mission workers sent Alaska to help Eskimo who are really very need of help by white people. We are fishing in the Tuxuk River for salmon now, dry them and sell them for our own use in winter time. Sister Helen is with us so you see we can have our Sunday services any time when she is with us. There are some other Eskimo fishing in different places, one family here and one family there.*

*We will not stay here very long. When the salmon quit running it will be time for us to move up the river to fish some tomcod for our own use in winter, and herring for dog feed. We have dogs in winter, to take us around in different places, and boats in summer time. We do not have trains, cars or airplanes to take us around, so you know it is handy to have sled dogs and boats up here.*

*I thought I would write promptly to thank you and Sister Helen.*

*from Mrs. Fred Mosquito*

## NEAR TRAGEDY ON THE TRAP LINE

One day Fred Mosquito came over and told me about one of his recent experiences. He and two others had gone out trapping, which took him some distance from Igloo for several days. At that time the price for fox, wolf or wolverine skins was very high. They had no heated cabin waiting for them, so they prepared a snow igloo by digging into the snow bank. It had begun to snow and blow quite furiously and before morning they were completely snowed in. Fred, who seemed to be their leader, awoke earlier than the rest. He lit the primus stove and started to make coffee. The stove had not been going very long before he noticed the flames were quickly going down, then it popped and went out. He now knew that their supply of oxygen was low and, if they were to save themselves, they would have to dig their way out as quickly as possible. But their shovels had been left outside in the sled. They grabbed a tin plate and began digging, but soon Fred fell back, exhausted. Snow was applied to his face and he soon revived. They took turns digging and after about twenty-five minutes, they saw light. A stick was put through and a little air came in. Then they broke a larger opening, but they did not dare stop. They carried out all of their supplies and would not go back. When they began looking for their dogs they found that three of them were dead. The others lay buried under the snow, alive and seemingly quite comfortable. Fred said he never perspired so much before, even though the thermometer registered several degrees below zero. It had been a narrow escape and they were thankful to be alive.

## A VERY COLD WINTER AT IGLOO

That winter the temperature stayed between 30-40 degrees below zero for a month. One early morning I happened to look at the thermometer and it read fifty-two below. I knew that I had been shoveling a lot of coal into my stoves but did not realize it was quite that cold. It was a real job carrying in the coal and carrying out the ashes each day. A boy would frequently come over and help me with this job. The water-carrying was always done by one of the boys. When visiting in the states, people would often ask, "Do you have running water in Alaska?" I would reply, "Yes, we have running water — in the nearby river, but we must go out and get it." The boy would put on the shoulder yoke with straps hanging down in either side and fasten the hooks to the buckets. The buckets were made from gasoline cans. Then with dipper and long ice-pick, he went down to the water-hole in the river. Sometimes it would be frozen over quite hard and needed considerable chopping to get at the water. I had a barrel in the kitchen for drinking water and a tank close to the stove, connected with pipes running in and out of the stove. That gave me hot water when I needed it, and also helped heat the room.

When it was very cold I always checked the thermometer in the cellar, I had a lantern or two in the cellar and they kept my potatoes, eggs and canned goods from freezing. Sometimes we might also have some oranges and apples. We would get our supplies cheaper by ordering them through the Mission Board and a buyer in Seattle. So each year we sent our order to the states for groceries, for the coal, oil, or whatever we would need. There was a small village store but it carried mostly staples which the Eskimos could use.

### Rev. Dahle Visits Igloo

At that time Rev. Dahle was in charge of the Mission. When he would come from Shishmaref to visit us, he would conduct communion services, baptisms or special services. This time he had first stopped at Teller and visited with the Olsons and other workers there. Miss Golelo Hansen wanted to visit Igloo so he brought her along with him. When a pastor came to lead the services all I had to do was to play the organ. This time we had confirmation services in the morning with baptism and communion services in the afternoon at 4:30 P.M. Rev. Dahle, Mr. Burkher, Miss Hansen and I sang quartets together which everyone seemed to enjoy. Our local choir also sang, so we had a fine service.

Their visit seemed to be over all too soon, for on Monday about 10:00 A.M. the guests left for Teller via dog-team. A little later in the morning one of the native women from the village brought over one of her little girls who was three years old. She told me the girl had gotten a bean in her nose and they could not get it out. I got my forceps but when I tried to remove it, the child struggled, kicking, fighting and screaming. I just could not get hold of it. Each time I got the forceps on, it slipped off. I could not understand it. Finally to get her to relax I had to resort to a few drops of chloroform. This worked and out came the "animal." It was not a bean but a "bead,"— and a fairly good-sized one, too. No wonder the forceps slipped. The relieved mother said "Oh, thank you, thank you". That same evening her father came over with their little boy to have a tooth pulled and that came out easily. As they left the father remarked, "How could we get along without you?" I'll admit they often kept me busy!

### Dynamite is Dangerous!

That same afternoon two men, Kopok and his son Alexander, came to my door. "Alexander has hurt his hand," the father said, and pulled off his mitten. What a sight! Handling some dynamite in a careless way he had shot off three of his fingers! I immediately started trying to stop the bleeding and to disinfect the wound. The fingers were so splintered and lacerated that nothing I could do would take care of it properly. Seeing he was about to faint I asked him to lie down on the floor. I knew immediately that he must see a doctor. I called Mr. Burgher (the teacher) and he contacted the Nome government office, telling them what had happened and asked for a plane for him as soon as the weather permitted. I fixed up the cot for the patient in my little bedroom and he stayed there until the plane could come. In the meantime, I stopped the bleeding, tried to keep it from becoming infected and gave him something for the pain which must have been quite severe. However, he was very courageous about it and did not complain. Four days later the plane came and took him to Nome where he was cared for. He returned a few days later with finger amputations. I had to check it for a few days and when no infections occurred I was very thankful.

Later in the spring a boy from the Old Village walked in and sat down on the floor. "I got cut on my leg," he said. It was quite a long cut on the thigh and bleeding very badly. I quickly got out my catgut suture material, tied up the bleeding blood vessel, put in about three sutures and applied a bandage. Soon he was off again with a big grin on his face. At Igloo there were few dull days.

One night Ralph came over and asked if I would come to his house. Tommy had sat on a crochet hook and they could not get it out. It had gone into the flesh about a half inch or more. With careful maneuvering I soon had it out, and that was the end of that! Beans, dynamite, cut leg, crochet hooks! I never knew what a day would bring.

## AN UNUSUAL CHALLENGE

Perhaps the most serious case was that of an old man, Otoyak. He had been out hunting during the day but was back in his home that evening. He complained of a pain in the back of his leg. I looked at it and found a hard swelling on his buttocks. I told him to apply heat and that I would see him in the morning. The next day I brought some boric acid crystals, making hot packs from it, and showed his wife how to do it. It kept getting worse until the whole buttocks seemed to be involved and a red line appeared down the back of his leg. I told him that we had better try to contact Nome and send him to the doctor. I talked with Mr. Burkher and he went over to see him. The next morning we went over again to see if he would go in case a plane could get there. I was positive that something had to be done. I told him that I knew an incision would have to be made. He thought a little while, then he turned to me and said, "You cut, you cut." That meant that, regardless of consequences, he did not want to go and that I should take care of it.

So I went home, prepared the instruments, Ethelchloride for freezing the area, and so on, then went over to make the incision. It had to be a deep-seated one and I was fearful of the results. It took much courage and God had to hold my hand. I did a crosswise incision and soon the pus was oozing out. I came back often and changed the bandage two or three times a day. On one visit I noticed how black the flesh was down below the incision. Gangrene seemed to be setting in. Now, I again pleaded with him to go to Nome, but he said, "You take care of it." The flesh had begun to slough off an area of about six or eight inches square. No doubt during the swelling the circulation had somehow been impaired. By and by I was able to cut all of the gangrenous flesh off, carefully keeping a moist and prophylactic dressing on the open wound. It took a long time for the new tissue to form, but it finally began healing. After three months he was again able to use his leg with little difficulty. How happy he was. Later his wife came over with a lovely pair of mukluks that she had made for me to show her appreciation.

There were countless abscesses, skin and eye conditions and various kinds of infections. Some times a child would get a fish bone stuck in his throat. Yes, even fractures such as the little boy who broke his leg when he fell on the ice. I put on a plaster paris cast and later he had an opportunity to go to Nome for an X-ray. He was told, "It was a perfect break and a perfect setting and healing." Once more I was thankful.

### MIRACLE DRUGS

Many babies died who I am sure could have been saved if we had sulpha drugs and penicillin, the medicines of today. They reacted so quickly we called them miracle drugs. I will never forget the time I gave some sulphadiazine to a little child who had whooping cough. The grandmother was just desperate because the child was coughing so much. At times she feared he might choke to death. I administered the first dose, then told her to give the child more every four hours. The next day when I again saw the child he seemed so much better. The grandmother asked, "What kind of miracle drug was that you gave my baby? He is so much better!" This was not the only case when such quick and marked changes occurred. Then, when the penicillin came out we really thought we had something unique.

How often I wished there might have been a miracle drug for the T. B. cases. We had whole families, with perhaps one or two who had died from T. B. Since at that time there was no sanitarium to which to send them, as a result the whole family was exposed. Living in such small quarters, with improper diet and at times not properly clad, — all may have instigated the disease. But today that picture has changed and tuberculosis is under control. Doctors are accessible through radio, airplane or hospitals. Regular X ray surveys were made. Clinics were conducted in the villages and a general check-up was made regularly. Those with active T. B. were taken in first, then the lighter cases. At first it was difficult to get some of the sick to go to the hospitals, but when they saw many coming back, apparently cured or arrested, the problem was solved.

The medical work was a real challenge. Many times I felt very helpless and wondered what I should do, but, with God's help, somehow the problems were solved. How thankful I was for the training I had received at the Deaconess and Ancker Hospitals. I also realized that, by being able to help the Eskimo physically, I was better able to reach them spiritually.

## CLOSING THE TELLER ORPHANAGE

In the spring of 1933 the Mission Board decided to close the orphanage at Teller Mission. Some of the first children had grown up and some had passed away. Many of those remaining had relatives who were willing to take them in. This seemed to be the solution for, after all, these children will always be Alaskans, and in an Eskimo home they would learn what they needed to know. The out-dated building had not been designed as an orphanage. It was expensive to run and each year it was harder to raise funds. Soon after the decision was made, Mabel Gunderson and Golelo Hansen left. Mr. and Mrs. Olson remained for another year to take care of the village folk and dispose of some equipment in the building.

This was also a furlough year for Rev. and Mrs. Dahle at Shishmaref. We were wondering who would come when I heard from Rev. Dahle that Rev. and Mrs. E. Hartje were coming. He asked, "Would I come up and stay with them for a while until they got acquainted with the place. The freighter was bringing supplies the first part of July and the Dahles would like to take the same boat out." So I began making plans for this, but we would have to wait until the river ice went out.

## THE SPRING BREAK-UP

Finally the break-up season was upon us. The Kuzitrin River had cleared very rapidly. The Eskimos had moved down to Salt Lake or were camped on the sloughs, waiting for the ice there to disappear. Then they would go on to the Tuxuk River for their usual salmon fishing season. I was anxious to get down to Teller in order to catch the boat going to Shishmaref. So I said to Ethel Marx, "How about going down to Teller with me in the "Ark," my little motor boat? Perhaps Mary Ellen could stay with your mother and go down with her when the tugboat comes to get her." Ethel was game, so we talked it over with Mrs. Marx and she agreed.

Such rushing around I never saw in my life. I had to have all my things ready that were going down to my cabin on the Tuxuk so that they could be picked up and put on the tug when it came. Mary Ellen had to get her things together she needed for her stay with Mrs. Marx and then for our summer camping. The house had to be closed up, chimney covered and the place locked up. For my little boat, I needed plenty of gasoline and oil, my primus stove, tent, a few cooking utensils — and food in case we got storm-bound or the motor broke down.

## OUR JOURNEY TO TELLER

Since it was light all the time, we left about 9:00 P.M., for the night hours made for pleasant traveling. In fact, the waters were very calm. We went down the Kuzitrin River until we entered Little Salt Lake. There was still too much ice on Big Salt Lake so we tried to find the little inland rivers which would eventually bring us down to the end of Big Salt Lake, about twenty miles down from Igloo. We tried one stream but soon found ourselves at a dead end so we had to go back again. We traveled most of the night but were suddenly stopped by a heavy fog. This was a good time to have something to eat. Just as we finished the fog lifted. To our surprise, we saw large floes of ice and knew this was Big Salt Lake.— not the lower end of it. We were not quite sure where we were nor where to go for everything looked alike. Suddenly I spied something that looked like it might be smoke, shooting right into the air. I was sure this was God's leading hand, but we never did find out what we had seen.

We again started out, traveling quite a distance in the direction of this smoke. When we approached one point of the Lake we could see some tents across the tundra. We pulled up our boat and walked across but, just as we got there, the tents went down. It was Fred Topkuk and his family from Igloo. They saw an opening between the ice flows and wanted to hurry through before it closed. They told us that we should do the same. It was quite shallow where we were so Ethel pushed up her boots and waded in front of the boat, pulling us into deeper waters so we could use the motor. Very soon we were on the Tuxuk River on our way down to Grantley Harbor and Teller. But once more we ran into trouble. The ice from Grantley Harbor was coming back our way instead of going down into Port Clarence Bay and the Bering Sea. The other boats had stopped at their camping ground farther back. We quickly made it to shore and pulled up our boat at one of the Eskimo camping places. There we made some coffee and had something to eat. We then decided to rest a few hours until the wind changed and took the ice out again. We must have waited there close to twenty-four hours.

Then suddenly the ice disappeared almost as fast as it came. We started the motor and soon were on our way to Teller. When the Ark made it to the beach we were welcomed with cheers and applause. They had expected us earlier and been afraid something might have happened. Mr. Burkher had communicated with Teller and told them we were on our way. We were tired but glad to be there after a real outing.

The Steamer Victoria came a few days later. When I got on I met the Hartjes and we had a good visit on our way to Shishmaref. The freighter had also arrived, and was unloading the Mission supplies. The Dahles were all packed and Rev. Dahle had only a brief time to explain a little about the duties and work there to the Hartjes. Then the Dahles boarded the Victoria and were soon headed south again. Those had been fleeting moments of "Hello" and "Good-bye." Now I was supposed to finish briefing the Hartjes.

The first task was to get the supplies in and the Eskimos always helped with this. On Sunday we had services. I gave the message, then introduced Rev. and Mrs. Hartje to the congregation. It was a nice day and we were all happy to welcome the Hartjes. I spent ten days with them, then went back on the mailboat to Teller, then up to my Tuxuk cabin. I just loved camping there on the River and Mary Ellen and I spent many pleasant days there that summer.

## THE SKAVLANS

In the spring of 1934, Rev. and Mrs. Skavlan were called to live and work at Teller Town and also serve at Brevig Station, formerly Teller Mission. During the summer most of the village natives would go to various places for salmon fishing, berry picking and other activities. The Missionary at Brevig Station could then spend more time in Teller Town. Sometimes there would be quite a few Eskimos there just for the summer, either from Wales or the Diamede Islands,. Once again we were anxious to meet our new workers.

That spring it seemed the break-up came upon us very quickly. This time I was going to travel to Teller with the Eskimos. On the 20th of June Mary Ellen and I left Igloo together with the Fred Mosquito family. Most of our things were placed in their boat, their second boat contained the dogs and all their camping equipment and my little "Ark" was towed behind. It rained very hard the day we left but Fred put a canopy over us which kept us from getting wet.

## ROUNDING UP THE REINDEER

Round-up was one of the most exciting events of the year. Our first stop was at the reindeer corrals, ten miles down from Igloo. Most all the other natives were already there, just waiting for the deer to come in. Some of the herders were rounding them up. Our little tent was put up. Some of the boys chopped wood for us, for it was still a little cold with snow on the mountains and ice on the lake. The handy little primus stove which I used for cooking also gave some heat.

What a sight that was two nights later when the deer came in! Everybody, big and small, was at the marking. Big tubs of reindeer meat had been cooked. Some may not have had any reindeer meat for some time. Oodles of Eskimo bread, tea and coffee were prepared by two of the Eskimo girls. Of course everybody feasted before and after the marking. When the deer were run through corrals and counted, those not marked had to be caught and marked. Each herd had a special ear marking. This marking often took place during the middle of the night,— but that was no problem. At that time of year it was broad daylight, and thrilling to watch.

After about four days of camping at the corral, we started off down the sloughs and streams for the Tuxuk. The snow was melting on the Saw Tooth Mountains and the lake ice was going fast so the water was high. Of course, the Tuxuk cabin needed a good cleaning after the winter's storm and break-up. Many flies had found this a good resting place and I swept up many dustpans full. Soon everything was spick-and-span again and we could relax. That cabin was much more comfortable than a tent.

Then on the 28th of July we received word from Mr. Olson that Rev. and Mrs. O. E. Skavlan had arrived. Would I come down to meet them? Right after the Sunday morning services, Mary and I went down in my "Ark." It was great fun meeting them and hearing their reaction to the new land of Alaska. They showed us pictures of their four children, thus trying to satisfy themselves that they were fine. But I knew there was an ache in their hearts. It must have been hard to leave their children behind and come into the Arctic, not knowing whether they would see them again. But God is good and fills every need of those who trust Him and follow His footsteps. Much later I met their married daughter when I visited them at their home in Garden Grove, California.

After a few days with the Skavlans we went back to the Tuxuk for Sunday services. It was a beautiful day. Before eleven o'clock several boats had arrived with natives from the different camps. Our 12x14 tent was set up beside the cabin and before long everybody was there. I played the guitar as we sang. Everybody was so quiet and listened so intently that it was a real joy. After service there was a good time as people visited and shared the news. Then I took my boat and three of the big girls with me to visit a couple of the upper camps. No one had come from there that morning and at both places we found illness. I visited each one.

An old lady who had lost her husband a year ago was quite sick with tuberculosis and would no doubt soon follow him. To her, death was nothing to dread. She knew that she would then meet her Savior, be clothed in a new garment and would again meet the loved ones who had gone before.

There was another man in the same camp who was quite sick, but he reacted differently. He was not interested in God's word. I had tried to help him, but he resented it very much. Quietly I prayed that I might some day help him. I conducted a short service at both camps, then on our way back we stopped where two Catholic families were camping. They kindly offered us some tea and sourdough hot-cakes. By that time we were very hungry so they tasted good. It had been a good Sunday.

I always felt renewed and invigorated after the summer of camping and visiting the natives as they fished and gathered berries. I loved being out in the open, —in spite of the mosquitoes. I felt prepared for another year's work in the village, whatever it might be.

I hoped that before too long our new missionaries at the Brevig Station would come up and conduct services. I wanted our people to meet Rev. Skavlan and hear him speak. I was sure they would receive much blessing from his sermons.

This year, however, I had to wait in Teller for a few days. Last spring there had been a break-in at our Igloo store and I was called as a witness together with three others. Mary Ellen stayed at Teller and would come when the supplies arrived on the tugboat. I had no idea what would soon happen in Nome.

## MY FIRST AIRPLANE RIDE

On September 10, 1934, an airplane came to Teller and we were off to Nome. I shall never forget that first plane ride. What a thrill this was! I had lived close to the Saw Tooth Mountains, had looked over and watched the changing colors. I had gone over them by dog-team, but now I was seeing them by air. It was a beautiful sunny day and the thousands of peaks were clearly visible from all angles. Below I could see the many streams, rivers, lakes, tundra and villages which looked so different from this point of view. We spied several mining camps where the gold diggers were busy shoveling for the shining ore. Nome looked like a little toy town. Soon we were descending and I had a feeling of relief when I again stepped on the ground. It had all seemed like a vision. What greater inventions did God have in store for His children?

Even though I roomed at the Pioneer Igloo Hotel, most of the time was spent with friends or at the courthouse. The boy who was on trial was from Old Igloo. I had spied him as he was trying to unlock the back door to the village store. One of the native girls had also seen him. Some things had been found gone from the store but we did not know until this happened who had been in there. The storekeepers had left for Teller and I had the only key.

## THE TRAGIC FIRE AT NOME

We had thought that our stay in Nome would be short but we were wrong. We appeared in court as witnesses on the specified date. Shortly after our arrival and some questioning a recess was declared. Ethel Marx was also with me as a witness for the store. We decided to take a little walk downtown and possibly do some shopping. Suddenly the fire alarm sounded and we rushed out to see what it was all about. The report came that the Golden Gate Hotel was on fire. Everybody knew what a firetrap that was. It was old and ready to come down anyway, but no one knew what the outcome would be. This hotel was located right across from the Post Office, which was next to the Court House, near Front Street or Main Street. Many stores and business offices and many residences were in that area. When the fire alarm sounded many people were afraid for the safety of the town. The strong wind blowing from the northeast could carry the flames from the hotel to the Post Office and then on down the street. People rushed in from all parts of town and started carrying things from nearby houses. Trucks were honking their way through, trying to save personal things as well as supplies from stores for the fire was spreading.

## THE FIRE SPREAD QUICKLKY

The fire department worked hard to confine the fire to one building but from the very first it was a hopeless fight. When the walls of the building collapsed the strong wind spread the flames in all directions. Everyone worked desperately to rescue things from houses and stores in the path of the fire but it was impossible to keep ahead of it. Between 10:00 A.M. and 3:30 P.M. the fire had destroyed forty-six

business houses, including a grocery store, dry goods stores, the bank, the theater, five lodge halls, six hotels, two bath houses, U. S. Jail, Post Office, Court House, U. S. Customs, Coast Guard, Alaska Road commission, City Hall, Fire Department, Central Heating plant, U. S. Reindeer Office, Northern Transport Coast Airways, doctors' offices with books and equipment, two dental offices and the Chamber of Commerce building. Nome had suffered a major catastrophe. Most people who lost their places of business also lost their homes. It was a a major tragedy and a sight never to be forgotten.

It was strange to see which buildings were untouched by the fire. Two churches, the hospital and nurses' quarters, two warehouses, Indian Affairs building and about half of the residences were not damaged. The wind did not blow the fire to the area where the natives lived, but about four hundred people were burned out of their homes. Some said, "The fire took the rich people's homes and left the poor people's homes," But that was not true in all cases. Soon after that tragic Nome fire many people left for the States and never returned.

Where was I all this time? At first I helped some friends move out of their house. Then I helped guard some goods from the jewelry store, while the owners went back for more valuables and tried to find a place to store them. Then I realized the hotel where I had been staying was in line of the fire, so I rushed up to get my suitcase and belongings. But in my haste I left a few things in the dresser drawers. I went to the hospital where they were also getting ready to evacuate. Fortunately, the fire stopped just before reaching there. They invited me to stay there, so this became my future lodging place while in Nome. It also became so busy that I was asked to help while waiting to go back to Igloo.

Because of the fire, Court proceedings were suspended. After two weeks I was again able to leave Nome. The Teller folk had left but I was waiting for a plane to take me either to Hot Springs or Igloo. However the rain and fog over the mountains made flying impossible. Finally one morning Father Menanger from Hot Springs said he had a pilot who could get us to Hot Springs, then he would see that I got to Igloo. It was a small two-passenger plane with the pilot in front alone. Father Menanger was quite stout so when we squeezed into the back seats we were so firmly fixed we surely didn't need seat belts.

It was raining a little when we started and more as we went on. As we approached the mountains it looked so thick and hazy I wondered if we could get through. Father Menanger probably saw I was a bit frightened and asked if I was afraid. I do not remember if I answered him but I know I was praying. Then there was a sudden break in the clouds. Our plane headed in over the top of the mountains and landed safely at Pilgrim Springs. I stayed there overnight and the next day they took me home to Igloo by boat. I was never as relieved and thankful to be home again as I was this time.

## To Nome via Dog-Team

One day right after Easter, Ethel Marx wanted to take her dog-team across the Saw Tooth Mountains to Nome. She asked me to go with her on this  seventy or eighty mile trip. Ethel was a good dog musher and had her own team. Two other teams from the village were also going. When we started out about six o'clock in the morning it looked like we were going to have a beautiful day. We reached the foothills about six miles from Igloo and had just begun climbing when the dogs suddenly turned a square corner and over went our sled! Ethel and I were sprawled behind and hanging on to the sled for dear life for fear the dogs would get away. I soon let go in order to let Ethel get control. But the dogs dragged her into a deep snow-drift before she could stop them. When I reached her she stood there much amazed and disgusted with her dogs. She could see no reason for such behavior. Then I told her to look a little farther, for there was small reindeer herd not far away. The dogs had gotten a whiff of them and had decided they would like a  bite. She gave each one of the dogs a beating (not too hard, for she loved her dogs,) then exchanged leaders and we started out once more. As we started, we saw another team coming, waving a package. We had forgotten our lunch at Igloo. But Ethel's mother knew this other team was also going and sent it with them. The lunch tasted good.

As we reached the summit of the mountain we were climbing, a snowstorm started and it was very windy. As we were crossing a little frozen lake the dogs slipped and became tangled. To hold them still Ethel stood on the brake  while I crawled on my hands and knees and tried to untangle their harness.  I couldn't stand up for it was too slippery and windy. We wondered how long this storm would last,  but before long it let up. On a part of our climb I walked behind the sled or even in front of the dogs, to encourage them to keep going. This also eased the load. Going down was fine.

During the afternoon we were calmly traveling along when we suddenly saw an arm reaching out above the snowdrift. Someone was waving and  inviting us to stop and come in to have some coffee. That sounded good and of course the dogs were glad to have a rest. We climbed down into something that resembled a  snow house, although it was just a little cabin covered with snow. The man  living there was a prospector working out his daily bread in gold diggings. He had not seen anyone for a long time and wanted the news of the day. He did not even have a radio. He served us coffee and bread of his own baking — just a little heavy, I'll admit, but it tasted good to us hungry travelers. It was dark when we reached Nome later that evening, and we were very tired. Our visit in Nome was a pleasant change.  Our return trip went very nicely. The colder  weather had frozen the trail real hard and that made for good sledding.

It was nice to have Mrs. Marx. and her daughter Ethel  living next door. They were Catholics but they always attended our morning services,  They were very cooperative and generous in time of need. The Eskimo people liked them. Some

afternoons, especially on stormy days, we would get together and have coffee as we did our sewing or mending, quilt-making or even rug-making (hooked). Sometimes we would eat lunch or dinner together —and then we usually included the teachers. At Igloo we became close friends.

### A FURLOUGH AFTER FIVE YEARS AT IGLOO

The usual term in Alaska was three years, but I had been asked to stay at Igloo for five years. I did not mind and the time went by quickly. Now it was 1935 and time for another furlough. I had hoped that I might take Mary Ellen along with me to Minnesota and send her to school there, but the Mission Board felt it was better for her in Alaska. Her father was bookkeeper out at the mining camp but still lived in Nome. I hoped to talk with him about making other arrangements for her.

Right then there was a shortage of nurses at the Nome Hospital. The supervisor wrote and asked if I could come in by plane and help them out until the boat came and Miss Morgen, the regular supervisor, would be back. This meant that we would have to go before the river ice broke up. Then the Catholic priest from Pilgrim Springs came down and told me that Mother Rose was also going to the hospital as a patient, until the boat came. "Would you see that she is taken care of, and also room with her on the boat to Seattle?" I did and enjoyed traveling with her.

Mary Ellen was permitted to stay with me at the hospital. She did little jobs there and also baby-sitting for a lady in town. In the meantime, I had been scouting around for a good place for her to stay. Then the Methodist pastor's wife asked if she might like to go to the Jesse Lee Home at Seward, — provided there was room. I disliked very much leaving her behind but this seemed to be a good opportunity. I knew that there she would have a good home and there was a high school there. When the Victoria came in and Miss Morgen arrived, she offered to let Mary Ellen stay with her until she left for the Jesse Lee Home. That worked out well.

### TRAVELING WITH MOTHER ROSE

On our voyage south Mother Rose and I had a fine time and wonderful accommodations. We were given the Bridal Suite! We had a very nice trip out and her friends were there to meet her when we arrived in Seattle. I stayed with Peter Myrhres ( my step-mother's sister's family) about two days and had so much fun shopping. After being away five years I definitely needed a new wardrobe. After a few days I left for St. Charles, Minnesota where my folks were living. Then I suddenly decided to go to Cleveland, Ohio and visit my brother Herbert and family. I had earned a little extra money while working at the Nome hospital so I asked my sister Esther to go along. This was a real treat for both of us. Besides some other visiting and a few speaking engagements, the time went very fast.

### ASSIGNED TO WISCONSIN

For two years I was at our Indian School, but I really missed being in Alaska.

# CALLED BACK TO IGLOO

I had been at Wittenberg about two and one-half years when word came to me that there was again a vacancy at Igloo. Would I be interested in going back? After I had left Igloo Rev. and Mrs. Dahle had been there one year then Rev. and Mrs. Klyve were there for two years. Now the Dahles were going back to Shishmaref and the Klyves were going to Brevig Station and Teller. So someone was needed for Igloo.

Somehow, my desire to go back became very strong. Immediately I told Rev. Sihler, explaining that, while I loved working there, my first love was for Alaska. He understood and agreed that, as soon as the  summer parochial school was over, I would be free to leave. So in 1938,  I again packed up to return to Alaska. Knowing that I was going back to Igloo, I was as happy as I had ever been for I felt like I was going back home.

The trip back was interesting because of the various modes of travel I used to get there. First I took the train to Seattle. Then in Seattle I enjoyed the comforts of automobiles, street cars and walking on sidewalks and roads that were smooth with no snow or ice! This is travel in the states as compared to Alaska. Then we took the large steamer up to Alaska, were on the scow as it was towed into the Pribiloff Islands and rode on the truck that brought us to where the beautiful fur seal were roaming. That was a sight I shall never forget.

Ten days later we landed at Nome, were lightered in baskets down to the barge and again towed in by small tug-boats, and then by boat over to Teller. Then another girl and I took the little outboard motor boat that afternoon over the rather stormy harbor. I wanted to see Ethel Marx out in the hills not far away. She was now married and living with her husband who was doing some mining. From the beach we walked about five miles, over hills and big tufts of grass, through the rain, fog, mud and swamp. When we got there,  tired and hungry, Ethel welcomed us with warm coffee and goodies. The next morning her husband gave us a ride back to the beach in a covered wagon pulled by his tractor. That was one more mode of travel. Then we had to hurry back to Teller before the Lomen tug left for Igloo. Quite a trip!

However, the tugboat was delayed for a couple of days so I had a chance to visit with Rev. and Mrs. Klyve. Then the tugboat left to take us  and the new teachers for

Igloo across Salt Lake up to Igloo. The boat also carried the school supplies for Igloo and Pilgrim Springs. The weather was perfect and I really felt like I was going back home!

## BACK HOME AT IGLOO

It was wonderful to be back in the Mission quarters at Igloo. I surely liked the new reading or class room which Rev. Dahle had added to the building. This would be so nice for all our women's and girls' meetings, orchestra, Bible classes, and so forth. No longer would I have to have those meetings crowded into my kitchen or living room. They had also added a very small bedroom which would make it easier to welcome guests.

With my supplies came a nice new rug for the living room, a comfortable little rocker and a few other necessities that would make it more comfortable. Many Mission boxes came, and these were all placed in the new attic above the class room until I could sort them later.

## HAPPY REUNION WITH OLD FRIENDS

The natives had not come back from their summer camps. A few days later I woke up to find the ground covered with snow. What a delightful sight. During the night I had been hearing dogs and motors, so I knew that some of the residents had come back. I was anxious to see who had come, so shortly after breakfast, with my shoe-packs on, I started for the village. Sure enough, there was my piano pupil, Josie Keelick, who was now married to Peter Octuck. Mary Oquillok came running and what a fond embrace she gave me. It was so nice to meet the others who had also returned. When I felt their welcome I knew that I had not made a mistake in returning. I knew that God wanted me here and I prayed that the Lord would guide my every step to His honor and glory.

While I missed my little Mary Ellen, I had been getting mail from her and knew she was doing well at Seward. One of the nurses there had taken a special interest in her, taking her into her home at various times. She also did some little jobs for different people while going to high school. I knew that this had been the best for her.

## THE NEW TEACHERS

Mr. and Mrs. Opland, the new teachers at Igloo, had a son about twelve years old who had a new accordion. He wondered if I could help him with it. I had never played an accordion before but could teach him something about the notes and chords together with the piano. But I know he would have done better with a real accordion teacher. He was an energetic little fellow and said that some day he hoped to study law. This is what he did, and he is now living and working in Anchorage.

## TELLER TOWN WAS GROWING

During my absence things had been happening in Teller Town. During the summer more Eskimo families had moved there so both Rev. Klyve and Rev. Skavlan had been conducting classes and regular services. We surely needed a Church building. When the Loman Company donated an unused store everyone helped remodel it, building a Chapel in the front and two small rooms for living quarters in the back. Though small, this let them start the program.

The Chapel was dedicated on August 13th, 1939. Rev. Dahle came down from Shishmaref and I came down from the Tuxuk camp. Many of the Igloo folks who had planned to come down for the Dedication were held up by a severe storm coming up the river, but some got there for the afternoon services. Rev. Klyve was then in charge at Teller and at Brevig Station (still Teller Mission then). Dedication services were conducted in the morning and at noon Mrs. Klyve served sandwiches, doughnuts and coffee. A song service was conducted in the afternoon, then a social hour for the white folks present in the evening. In spite of bad weather, all went very nicely but it was not quiet there. Since we were on the waterfront we could hear the boats and planes coming and going. A very important person came that same time.

The government doctor and dentist came ashore to set up a clinic. The government doctor comes only once a year, so anyone who needed help had to see him whenever he came. Serious cases were often sent to Nome or Kotzebue. Now those who needed medical attention needed to go over to the clinic. Since I was a nurse and knew the people, they asked me to help. Although the clinic interrupted our celebration we were thankful for this help for the Eskimos and for Rev. Klyve. He had a tooth that was bothering him so he went over and the dentist pulled it.

## "AN EPIDEMIC IS COMING!"

I stayed in Teller only a short time before returning to Igloo. We had been hearing about a measles epidemic at various villages. Many had died and others had severe after effects from it. Teller and Igloo had not had it yet so we wondered when it would reach us. It did come — like a storm.

There were no natives back in the village when I returned. Then Mr. Opland came in and announced that "it" had arrived. One family had rushed back to the village because the mother had measles. Another family was on their way because their children were ill. Some of the older folks who remembered the early epidemics of measles and the flu were quite concerned. We all knew that living in a tent was dangerous at this time of the year. The temperature was dropping, freeze up was near and snow was not far away. Soon all the natives were rushing to get back into their homes.

I had plenty to do then, visiting the homes and trying to help them. I warned them not to get cold or expose themselves unnecessarily. Most of the deaths that occurred in our village or other places were among the babies or tuberculous patients.

The death of an eighteen-year-old girl caused quite an impression on me. A year ago she had had pneumonia and since that time she had not been very well. Her heart and lungs were effected, perhaps even before she was sick. Now she got the measles and with her tuberculosis, she died about three months later. But her death was beautiful for she was a sincere Christian and a witness to those about her. She seemed so glad when I went over to sing and pray with her. A few days before she died she sent me a note, asking if she might have communion. I had never given communion before as this had always been done by the visiting pastor. But I felt that it would be wrong to refuse her this privilege so I gave it to her. I came over to see her a few hours before she passed away. She was struggling for breath but her last words were, "I want to be with Jesus." I replied, "You know that you are going to be with him soon." Then she said, "Yes. Thank you," — and was gone. One of her favorite songs was "There's a Land that is Fairer than Day" so the natives sang that hymn at her funeral service. That fall there were six funerals. It was hard in many ways, but I believe this made many people think more seriously and possibly show more kindness and love toward one another.

The coffins the men made often looked crude but when covered with muslin or outing flannel, — whatever I happened to have or they could get at the store, — they looked fairly nice. Then we usually placed some paper flowers on top. The cemetery was about a mile from the village, up a little hill. We walked there, except for the family who might use a dog team. The grave was always dug by the big boys or men. This was most difficult as they had to dig and chop into solid ice mixed with gravel. Even during the summer time only the top soil, not more than two feet down, would be thawed. At first it seemed strange to me to be conducting funeral services, but I soon got used to it. At the close of the graveside services we always sang the verse I had learned while attending Lutheran Bible School: "Turn your eyes upon Jesus, look full in His wonderful face, and the things of earth will grow strangely dim, in the light of His glory and grace." I wanted all to go home with this thought in mind.

Sometimes I wondered what the early Eskimos really believed regarding death, before the missionaries came. Then I was told that in their religion they believed that everything was controlled by spirits which are in turn controlled by the Shaman or medicine man. Because of this, there was no need of prayer. However, as each village often had their own Shaman, there was considerable variation in opinions on religious matters.

The spirit of the deceased was thought to remain in the house for several days after the death of some person and then to retire to the grave and wait for the birth of the next child in the village. The child was then named after the deceased. It was believed that the Shaman participated in their various activities such as hunting, fishing, etc. So it behooved each one to please the spirits. When the powerful Shaman became too old to hunt, he would sell his power to younger men. They also used a lot of taboos and charms to make people believe in their power. Many Eskimos have turned from these beliefs and now find power and new life in Jesus, our Savior.

## SUNDAY MORNING

Just as I was building my kitchen fire, Ralph Kugruk came to ask if I would please come over. Alice, his sister, was going to have a baby. I quickly picked up my baby-kit and medicine box and followed him across the river ice. Here was a young mother lying in one corner of the floor with a curtain around her. Near by on a wooden bunk lay her sister, ill with measles. She had a baby about a year old trying to get some nourishment but the mother was so sick she hardly knew what was happening. On the floor, in the opposite corner, lay an old man about sixty-five years old. He was a wonderful Christian. He had been ill for a long time, suffering from a lung condition and rheumatism. Yes, it was a sad situation but in the midst of it the old man began to pray. He could not hear us but he saw us and knew what was going on. The mother was a sweet old lady who took everything patiently. She and I took care of the new-born which arrived about two hours later. It was a sweet little baby and I could not help but wonder how long God would permit it to live, since her mother was so ill with tuberculosis. She also had a little boy about two years old. The father was away, working in one of the mining camps.

It was almost eleven o'clock and time for services when I got home. I did not have time for breakfast but needed a few minutes of meditation before ringing the bell for services. After the services I was invited over to Oplands for lunch. I had a good meal and enjoyed it very much. Then I hurried off on my rounds in the village, as there were other sick folk I should visit.

At one home that afternoon, I learned that one of the big boys had just escaped the cold water for his grave. He had been out with his dog sled when they came to thin ice on the river. He tried to stop the dogs but could not and the sled and dogs broke through. He jumped off the sled and managed to get around, cut loose two of the wheel dogs and get hold of the sled. But the other dogs went under and drowned. So I visited a rather sad household. Before I left we had devotions and I tried to point out God's way of dealing with us, which is often hard to understand and unexpected. But we were thankful the boy's life had been saved.

## WINTER CAME EARLY THAT YEAR

This year the river froze up very quickly. Several of the natives were still down the river trying to do some fishing when the river began freezing. One boat went ahead trying to break the ice while others followed. Suddenly, the ice jammed against the side of the boat, making a big hole in it. The other men had to come to his rescue and hurriedly got everything out of his boat so they could tow it alongside their own. They realized they could get no further so they set up camp by the river. In a few days some of the men walked home, but the others had to stay until it froze solid so they could bring their dogs home.

### GETTING READY FOR WINTER COLD

During the freeze-up period some of the men and boys decided to bank up earth around the Chapel to make it warmer. They also chopped the wood on hand and made two more benches for the Church. They put some colored paper on the front windows to reduce the glare of the sun and snow which at certain times was hard on the eyes. They also did some painting and all of this made a wonderful improvement. Before winter set in the natives also had much work to do around their own homes, — especially those who were still living in sod houses. These sod houses almost needed to be rebuilt each year because the snow, wind and rain played havoc with them. However, they surely knew how to cut those blocks and pack them in, so nice and even that I always marveled at their skill. Those sod houses really kept out the cold. The homesteaders in the midwest in the States knew that.

### CHRISTMAS - 1939

The preparations for Christmas this year kept us very busy. Early in November I had checked our mission boxes so I could get an early start wrapping gifts. Some were not very useful. Realizing we needed more I started sewing and burning some midnight oil. Before long I had made two dozen shirts for the school boys and some dresses for the girls. Then I purchased some gloves, socks, stockings and a few other little things at the village store. Two lovely quilts had been sent which would be fine gifts for the two interpreters. The mothers received some yarn or a piece of print together with a hand towel or a dish towel or other article. So we had gifts for each one.

Mr. and Mrs. Opland prepared a program for this year and I helped with the music. There was one little accident which put a slight damper on our festivities. Eleven year old Bobby Opland was helping his mother shake out some gunny sacks that were to be used for the Shepherds in the Christmas play. Suddenly a piece of steel that was in the sack flew up and hit his eyeball, cutting the tissue close to the pupil. A few days later he went to the doctor at Nome and found out that he would have a permanent scar on that eye. We felt very badly about this.

We had our usual Christmas festivities, New Year's party with races, etc. in which the whole village took part wholeheartedly. I even had help with the making of the popcorn balls and doughnuts for our parties. The boys and girls were always anxious to see them come out of the kettle and enjoy a little sample.

Soon after Christmas we began making plans for the confirmation services. Rev. Klyve would come to conduct this service in March and also have a communion services in the afternoon. Our Senior and Junior Choirs were to sing and the orchestra would also play, so there was much practicing and preparing for that Sunday. Then Easter was coming and we had services and programs to plan for. The Annual Church Convention and Reindeer Convention would be at Shishmaref this year. As I was to be at the Convention, we decided to have our Easter activities on Palm Sunday.

I decided to have a little musical play called "The Easter Lily." It took considerable practicing but the children enjoyed it as it was something different. With the singing by various groups, this became an enjoyable program.

### THE BIG STORM IN REINDEER CONVENTION WEEK

Many were getting ready for the convention. The mail plane offered to pick me up so I decided to go by plane. But a storm came up so the plane could not come. I waited for five days and was about to give up when I received a message from Rev. Dahle that even if it were late, I should come,. Evidently the big storm had held up everyone.

This was really the worst snowstorm of the year and one day was especially bad. Starting about seven in the morning it kept snowing and blowing for hours. The snow seemed to be packing in on all sides. The windows were covered to the top on one side and we had a high drift on the other, only a few inches away from the wall. I could not see my neighbors and for eight hours the storm did not let up. But oddly enough, in the midst of this I got some very good radio reception and enjoyed some wonderful music. A major storm kept everyone home and this was a very good time to do some reading, meditating and writing.

At 3:00 P. M. the storm seemed to let up and outside things looked very different. The schoolhouse was almost buried in snow. To get out the Oplands had to climb through a window so they could start shoveling. The strong wind had broken the propeller to my windcharger and my attic was full of snow. Fortunately, a couple of boys came along and helped me to shovel it into tubs and pans before it could melt and leak through the ceiling.

When the storm was finally over, Mr. Opland hired a dog-team and driver to take him to Shishmaref for the Reindeer Convention. I decided to do the same thing and go with Jim Eyuk. We started off about 8:00 A.M. Monday loaded with sleeping bags, lunch, dog feed, primus stove, tent and some extra luggage,. We had not gone far before it began snowing quite hard and at 12:00 noon we were in another blizzard. We stopped at a herder's cabin, made some coffee and devoured some sandwiches. About 4:00 P.M. it began clearing so we were again on our way. We traveled until almost 9:00 P.M., when we stopped and set up camp in a willow patch.

It was interesting to see how quickly the natives had the tent put up on top of the snow, fastening it to sleds and willow trees. Willow branches were placed on the snow for a floor and they served as a very good spring for our sleeping bags. Two primus stoves were lit, coffee was made, some beans and corned beef were mixed together and heated. Being the only woman in the party of four, I was pronounced the cook. You should have seen me on my knees, stirring the stew and pouring the coffee. Of course, we were so hungry we could eat almost anything. About midnight we were all inside our sleeping bags. I was warm and comfortable but, somehow the night seemed rather long and the sleeping hours short. In one corner someone was sawing wood, another chopping kindling and the third talking in his sleep!

Towards morning it began to blow and snow some more. Soon one side of our tent had pulled loose and was wide open. One of the men found his head outside the tent, instead of inside. At 7:00 A.M. we were back on the trail, climbing hills and plowing through soft snow. We reached Shishmaref that night about 8:00 P.M. and figured that we had traveled at least one hundred miles in two days in difficult weather.

The most interesting part of the trip was, of course, the stay at Shishmaref, visiting with the Dahles. Everything was quiet when we drove in but soon we heard singing in the Chapel. There were people from six different villages and three different Protestant denominations, all singing praises to the same God. Each took part in song or music. When we arrived they had already been there for three days, morning and evening. People were still arriving and when the total count was made there were 167 visitors, 56 dog teams and 575 visiting dogs in the village. Some of the Shishmaref folks had as many as fourteen guests. It took a great deal to feed so many but the people of Shishmaref had open houses and open hearts. It was hard on their seal meat, blubber, reindeer meat, berries, etc., but these things were also a treat to those coming from the inland villages.

The Reindeer Convention had started on Thursday, meeting at the schoolhouse and continuing for five days. One evening there was Eskimo dancing. Another day there was dog racing for men and women. Having visitors in the village was always exciting.

I spent eight enjoyable days at Shishmaref. Rev. Dahle had been planning a trip to Igloo and Teller, so I was able to ride with him on my way home. We made it in two days, arriving at Igloo at 10:00 P.M. The others had left before we did so were at home when we got there. The next Reindeer Convention was to be at Igloo.

### WAS IT COLD AT IGLOO?

Many times people have asked me, "How cold does it get in Alaska?" I know one morning at 7:00 o'clock my thermometer read fifty-six degrees below zero and it may have been much lower during the night. Someone at the Old Village reported that their kerosene froze one night and I am told for that to happen it must be seventy below. How thankful I was now to have an oil-burning stove in my kitchen and would soon have one in the living room. Instead of shoveling in coal and taking out ashes, I had one of the boys pump in some oil for me once a week. I could also do it myself but sometimes the drums were hard to open. Then, when I later was able to buy a second-hand gasoline wash machine, I felt like a queen. It almost seemed incredible that all I had to do was heat some water in the boiler, pour it into the wash machine, put in the clothes and soap, then step on the lever, and away it went. Of course, in the winter-time there was a drying problem, but I had lines strung across the kitchen and clothes dried very nicely, especially now that I had oil heat. As I mentioned before we did not have running water in the house, but did, — out in the river. However, one of the boys was always faithful about carrying in water, filling the barrel and hot water tank connected to the stove.

## THE JOY OF SPRINGTIME

Before I knew it, spring was again upon us. How I loved that nice warm thawing weather. Our teachers, the Oplands had left early. The storekeepers had also gone to Teller before breakup. Then the river ice went and all the Eskimos, except one family called the "Mosquitoes," had left for their spring camping ground along Salt Lake and the Tuxuk. Fred Mosquito's wife was not well, and Fred liked to stay for the smelt run which came shortly after breakup. I came over to their place just after they had pulled in a big haul. Fred and the children were busy stringing the smelts on wires, then hanging them for drying. Fred had caught some muskrats during the night and his wife was skinning them. It was a busy place.

On Sunday I went over to the Mosquitos again, to have Sunday morning devotion and singing with them, as there were no other folks in the village. Afterwards, Fred asked if I wanted to go with them to lunch. At first I hesitated, not knowing just what he was thinking about, but then I realized what he meant. I asked,"Are you going out for a boat ride?" "Yes, we were figuring on going out some place, make tea and have some lunch. Would you like to go along?" Of course, I did. It was a beautiful day, so I rushed home for a loaf of bread, some butter, jelly and cookies. A little later they picked me up and we went up the river and found a lovely spot for a campfire. Fred began roasting smelts on a stick placed around the fire. I had never seen this done before so it was very interesting. They had three girls and two boys with them. The girls and mother picked some fresh green willow leaves which they mixed with seal oil to eat together with the fish. Those roasted smelt were really delicious and it seemed nice to be out on a picnic again. I took some pictures of our outing.

I had been giving music lessons to Annie, their oldest girl, so a couple of days later they came over to hear her play on the piano. Later I helped her get started on the guitar and mandolin. She loved music and seemed to pick it up quite easily.

When they were ready to go I went down to the Tuxuk with the Mosquito family again. Before we left Fred overhauled my motor. I would need that down on the Tuxuk River.

### WEDDING BELLS

The spring of 1941 was quite eventful in more ways than one. Mr. and Mrs. E. Ellingson, both Lutheran Bible Institute students, together with Mr. Ray Erickson, decided to take a trip across the Saw Tooth Mountains from Nome, going through Mosquito Pass. This was their first trip this way. As a result, they spent about four and one-half days instead of one or two. They lost the trail, running into storms and then, on top of this, Mr. Ellingson got dreadfully snow-blinded and had to stay in the dark for three days. That same week Rev. Klyve came up from Teller, to conduct communion and baptismal services. He also performed a marriage ceremony.

When I discovered that one of our girls was pregnant I asked if she wasn't getting married. Since they would have to go to Teller or Nome for the ceremony, they kept postponing the trip. Now was their chance. Just at this time I saw the boy passing the Mission so I called him in. It seemed that he was not then sure but said that, if the girl was willing, it was all right. But, when they later came over to be married, there were no witnesses. So I went to the village and brought back a sister and a cousin. This may sound like an odd way of doing things, but sometimes they needed help. Following the evening ceremony I served some coffee and cookies, then for a wedding gift gave them a quilt and some towels.

### GETTING READY FOR EASTER

Two weeks before Easter the men again decided to redecorate the Chapel. The church had used their last year's Christmas offering money to buy figured building paper and white paint for the chapel walls. It was surely a wonderful change from the old dirty burlap on the walls and the smoky woodwork and ceiling. Everyone seemed so pleased it was so bright. I cooked dinner for the men, gave them some coffee in the afternoon and made a few suggestions. That was all I had to do with it. They were proud of the results and so was I.

We had an interesting program this Easter. In the morning there were regular services with singing by the choir. Then the Eskimos had asked to have dinner together at the Church, after the service. The storekeeper donated some potatoes and the teacher some coffee and sugar. I made over one hundred buns and several loaves of bread, some cookies and tapioca pudding flavored with blueberries and salmon berries. They had been kept frozen in a barrel and had kept well. The natives brought their own kettles of meat, fish, Eskimo ice cream, or whatever they happened to have. So, while I went home and got the boiler of coffee, the men placed the benches around the wall for tables and put wrapping paper over them for table cloths. The men and big boys did the serving and everyone enjoyed the Easter dinner.

At 4:00 P.M. we had our children's Easter program. The boys and girls  sang and the older girls told the Resurrection story using flannelgraph figures. There was a Bible verse quiz, several recitations and then all the children sang together.

The Eskimos wanted to meet again in the evening. Some visitors from White Mountain had arrived and wanted to sing. So we had an inspirational service of song, testimony, speaking and prayer. It had been a full day and an Easter Day to remember.

Mrs. Bowles, who had been a territorial teacher, was with us this year. But she was older and  the school was a little too much for her. She only stayed the one year but how well she had done showed up in the children's behavior and how much they learned.

This time Mrs. Bowles and I went down to the Tuxuk and Teller together with Fred Mosquito and family. Fred's wife had died this last year and he did a very good job taking care of his children. We all missed Mary Ann.

## A BIRTHDAY I WILL REMEMBER — AUGUST 28, 1941

I had returned to the village this fall a little earlier than usual, traveling with one of our native families. I knew the tugboat would be coming any day with our supplies from Seattle and before the supplies and Mission boxes arrived I wanted to pick some blueberries and do some sewing. When they arrived I knew I would be very busy.

It was the 28th of August, my birthday,  I had heard the buzzing of motor boats and knew that the natives were starting to bring back their winter supplies. Some might camp near by to do some fishing on the way back. Then I thought, "What shall I do to celebrate my 45th birthday? — Oh, I'll make some fudge." Before I could start, suddenly two boys appeared at my door. Billy Kopok said, "Can you come down to the Agaypak? Mary, my sister, is very sick." It was almost dark and I knew it would be a long ride, through the sloughs and rivers in the dark, and who knew what might happen there? I wondered, too, if I would be able to help Mary, for I knew she, too, had tuberculosis. But she needed me and that was all that mattered. But how would I get back if I went with them in their boat? So I asked Billy about this. Then the other boy, John Earl, said, "I plan to go to Bunker Hill tomorrow. I could come back with you to Igloo in your boat, if you take it along. Then I will walk over to Bunker Hill." That would work, so I hurriedly got out my sleeping bag, blanket, primus stove, some soup, bread, tea and smoked salmon, along with the medicine kit, motor oil, canvas and my little boat, the "Ark".

They towed it behind their boat. "It will soon be dark. How can we travel then?" I asked. They replied, "We can make it." We did make it, but not without some difficulty. On the way they began to have motor trouble and we finally resorted to my little 4HP motor. At times we had to go through patches of high grass which clogged the propeller. I was glad I had taken my flashlight along for when that happened, we would have to stop and remove the grass. The banks and many bends in the river all looked alike to me and I just could not understand how the boys knew where we were going.

It was almost 2:00 A.M. just beginning to get a little lighter when we saw the tents. Getting in we had to go through a very narrow channel. The motor could not be used. Neither could they row but one of the boys with his high boots merely pushed or pulled the boat. Finally I came into Mary's tent. It was dark, dreary looking and cold so we quickly turned up a small lantern. The patient was lying on the ground with a reindeer skin for a mattress. The father was in another corner with their baby. Mary could hardly speak above a whisper. Her nose, throat and lips were dry. She had a cold, was coughing and had a high temperature. It must be pneumonia. I was told she had been coughing for a long time and had also been vomiting. So I got busy and cared for her the best way I could, cleaning out her mouth and nose, giving her some liquids, putting a warm pad on her chest and other things that seemed necessary for her comfort. She hadn't slept for two nights so I also gave her a sedative. We prayed and talked together, for I knew she felt that she would not live very long. Her husband also had tuberculosis and was trying to care for the baby in the best way he could. It always hurt me very much to see these families for we were so helpless and had no place to send them for the care they needed.

When I left the next morning John Earl came with me and ran the motor. When Mary and her family returned to the village a short time afterwards, I was again called to her bedside. She was conscious although very sick. She wanted to tell me something. "What is it, Mary?" She looked at me then, in a quiet voice said, "I killed my first baby." Yes, she had had a child before she was married and had always felt badly about what she had done. Now she wanted me to pray for her, have communion and know that she was right with her Lord. So in their home we had a quiet service and I gave her Holy Communion. It was not long afterwards that Mary passed away, very peacefully and happy in the Lord. What precious moments those were.

## THE WAR

This was the year of the war abroad when Russia, Germany, Japan and Italy were getting tangled up. We did not know when it might reach our shores but were constantly on the alert. We had new government teachers, Mr. and Mrs. Benson from Mexico, and they were constantly in touch with other radio stations on a government frequency. I shall never forget that Sunday morning, Dec. 7, 1941, when a message came through that Pearl Harbor had been attacked. Soon we were on quite a defense program. The Home Guard was organized and given special orders. Eskimo boys were called into the Army. Air raid wardens, plane spotters and other units guarded Alaska. All windows were to be covered when lights were on, and other curtailments issued. Each day we listened to the news on the radio and sometimes it was frightening.

We heard many rumors. One about the two Russian bombing planes coming into Alaska and how they had been intercepted at Dutch Harbor. Also about submarines approaching the Alaska coast, and tales of Russian men secretly entering Alaska. Some folks were ready to go back to U.S.A. or hide somewhere inland. Somehow, I was not afraid. I was sure the Lord would take care of us, and He did. It was surely a happy day when finally the armistice was declared and the boys came home.

In the meantime, the mumps had been through our village. Several had been quite sick. Then a sixteen-month-old boy developed a serious skin eruption which I had been trying to get under control. Finally, we sent a message to the Nome doctor who sent back some medicine called gentian violet. What a sight that made, with face and head all speckled with the purple medication. However, it helped, and I had occasion to use it several times later. A little boy was brought up from Teller with a similar infection on his body, and how grateful I was I had this medicine supplied by the government. He recovered very soon.

One Sunday night, a few minutes after I had gone to bed, someone rapped on my door informing me that one of the boys had accidentally shot himself in the leg. He was brought over but there was little I could do but put on a hot pack. The next day I again contacted the doctor for instructions but he just told me to continue with the hot packs and if nothing unusual showed up to let him know. The boy did fine and seemingly had no trouble from the pellets lodged in the flesh. In April, Dr. Bower, from the government hospital at Kotzebue, came to our village to conduct a clinic. First he checked the children, did a lot of teeth extractions and other needed treatments and prescriptions. Then he examined eyes, ordering glasses for a few. In the evening older folks came to him with their problems, and more teeth were extracted. Then I took him to the village to see some sick folks there. I was very glad he came for he showed me how to give novocaine when extracting teeth. I often say that I wish I had a dollar for every tooth I pulled. I know I pulled quite a few.

The traders at the village store left for Teller again and turned the keys over to me. There was not much left in the store, but I promised to take care of it, just opening it when someone wanted something. Most of the time it was to trade in their muskrat pelts for shells.

## A BREAK-IN AT THE STORE

One day when I came over to the store I discovered that someone had broken in. The hasp had been filed off where the lock fit in. I knew it had been done within the last three hours. I called Mr. Benson, the teacher, and he said that Arthur, one of the village boys, had asked to borrow a file and screw driver that afternoon. I went to the village and asked him to come over with me. We questioned him but he denied breaking in. He said that he had used the tools to fix a door at home. Although it sounded possible it wasn't probable. Arthur's uncle came over. Just then his sister came, wondering what was going on. They had seen me tracking down the boy. His parents were dead and he was staying with his sister. He was only twelve years old and came from a fine family in our village. I hated to think that he was the culprit. The sister had heard some talk about shells, so asked him where he had gotten them. He said he had worked for Mr. Benson and had earned a dollar. But when Mr. Benson denied this he was trapped and after that he confessed with bitter tears.

The word would get around qickly in such a small village and everyone would know what Arthur had done. I was afraid some might make it hard for him. We talked and I asked him if he wanted to confess what he had done before the congregation the next Sunday. We had prayer and he went home. Sunday morning came and Arthur was one of the first to arrive. I took him aside and asked him how he felt. Did he want to make his confession? He immediately replied, "Yes." After the sermon and the song I explained what had happened and said that Arthur wanted to say something and ask forgiveness. It was hard for him to express himself, but he did and I know he has been a better man for it. Then his uncle gave a little talk in Eskimo and Mr. Benson made a few remarks. All this cleared the air and Arthur felt much better.

### BEING A STOREKEEPER AT IGLOO

Being responsible for the store was quite inconvenient at times but it was certainly an experience. Often I felt that I was really doing the Eskimos a favor. Their only money came from trading skins for shells or the few staples we had in the store. The ice was still on the river so they had no way to get down to Teller. I tried to do the best I could by them. Sometimes it meant many trips back and forth to the store in one day. But it wasn't far and it gave me a little more exercise. My worst problem was to decide the value of the muskrat skins, but Teller Commercial later told me I did a good job. They had done many things for us and I felt this was only a return courtesy.

### THE CONVENTIONS COME TO IGLOO

In the spring of 1943 the Church Convention and Reindeer Convention met at Igloo. Rev. Klyve came up from Teller to take charge of our meetings at the Church, and to give the main talks. There were delegates from Teller, Shishmaref, Wales, Deering, Espenberg and the Old Village. They came for the Reindeer Convention and also attended the Church meetings. They all sang and some of them gave short talks or testimonies. Our various musical organizations, — the choir, Junior singers, and the orchestra played an active part in the programs and I was quite proud of them. The teachers from the other stations were surprised at how well they played and sang.

The first three days the Church Convention had its meetings, then the Reindeer Convention met the next five days. On the sixth day there were various dog races and foot races for men, boys and girls. In the evening natives gathered in the schoolhouse for a few more races and stunts, then all the prizes were given out. At 11:00 P.M. all were at home again, as it was Saturday. Sunday we gathered for our Palm Sunday service. A few delegates left on Sunday, but most of them left Monday, expressing their sincere thanks for the pleasant and profitable days they had at Igloo.

Then we suddenly found out that Mr. and Mrs. Berhard Vogen, who had been running the village store this last year, were packing up and leaving. Mr. Vogen was going into defense work and they were not coming back. We were sorry to see them leave and the village folks were quite worried, wondering if the store would be closed permanently. Later on we found that Bill Munz, a local pilot, had bought the place and that Johnny Kakaruk, an Eskimo from the Old Village, was going to take care of it for him for the time being.

## A VACATION IN WARTIME

In the summer of 1944 I planned to go back home for a vacation. Because of the war, I wondered if I could get space on flights. But because I was a nurse, I had no problem and got my plane tickets quite easily, both going and coming to Alaska. I still remember that trip coming back to Fairbanks. We had been traveling above the clouds and our flight was nice and smooth. For lunch I enjoyed a delicious chicken sandwich. But when we began going down through the clouds suddenly it was quite rough. You can imagine what happened to the sandwich. Near me a mother who was struggling with her one and one-half-year-old baby also became sick. I knew I ought to go and help her but I just couldn't. I was too sick myself. We finally landed and I felt as if everything inside me was loose. In those days planes were not pressurized.

Mr. and Mrs. Lyman Culver met me at the airport. The Culvers had spent some time in the Lighterage Company at Teller, so I was a guest in their home for a few days, visited some friends, then went on to Nome, Teller and back to Igloo.

Strange things happened this fall. During the summer Mr. and Mrs. Benson had been with Al Carey ( a miner close to Taylor). When Mr. Benson had returned, he claimed to be in poor health. It was time to open the school so he wired for his wife who was still working at the mine. She came back but there seemed to be some problems. Before long they resigned and went back  home to New Mexico. At that time, due to the war there were so many jobs open for people that it was quite impossible to get teachers. Then the Juneau government office asked me if I would take over the school. After writing to the Mission Board for their permission I reluctantly accepted. But I wrote them that I was sure I could not put in full time. They agreed to whatever time I could give,— but just keep a record of my time.

## HANDLING  MANY NEW JOBS

However, I soon learned that the school  was only part of the job.   I also had to take over the Post Office work, the radio, checking and sending in the ivory work done by the Eskimos, and prepare the various reports which the government demanded. The boys were being drafted and I would have to help them with their papers. Because of all these tasks, it was very important to keep the school open and keep the radio contacts. There would be fewer students in the school for, because of the war, some folks had moved out of the village and found work on the coast.

That became a very busy and interesting year. The first year I still kept my own quarters heated and going, but the next year I moved into the teachers' quarters in connection with the school. I tried to have most of my classes in the morning and the little children in the afternoon. On account of my own meetings on certain days I would have to cut them short. Since the schoolhouse was heated, most of the evening meetings were also held there. On Sundays we gathered at the Church. This was to save time all around, but I was determined to keep our Church work going as usual.

Although I had my teacher's certificate, I had not taught school since the year I taught at Teller Mission. Therefore, I needed considerable preparation and sometimes I'm afraid I didn't do too good a job. I was really learning many things myself. I had one of the Eskimo girls come over every Friday to wash clothes and so some cleaning in my rooms and in the school. A boy took care of the oil for the motor, carried in water and did other out-door jobs. We had a Delco System for lighting and an oil-burning stove in the kitchen, and a coal stove in the school room. During the real cold weather there were problems with the Delco plant and I would have to get help starting it but, somehow, things worked out. If the Delco plant played "hookie", I sometimes had to use gasoline lamps all day. I had so many different jobs that I burned much midnight oil. I felt that this was one of my war efforts but I hoped it would soon be over.

### SISTER MAGDALINE'S VISIT

After school was out in the spring of 1945, I was again making plans to go down the Tuxuk to Teller, for at this time we had no missionary there. Then I received a wire from Sister Magdaline Klippen who was at Nome. She wanted to come to Igloo then go with me to Teller. She had been asked to help there for the summer, until Bertha Stedje arrived. I told here to come to Hot Springs by plane and we would meet her there. Two days later Mr. Burgher, one of our former Igloo teachers, came to Hot Springs. Fred Mosquito again went there to meet him. He had come from Anchorage to check the radio equipment at the school and to see how things were going.

The next day we all started for the Tuxuk River on the way to Teller, with Fred Mosquito as pilot. Before we had gone very far it started to get very stormy and we had to set up camp at two different places. I had my tent, primus stove, sleeping bag and plenty to eat, so we fared quite nicely in spite of the inconvenience and delay. Instead of taking us about eight or ten hours, it took us two days to reach Teller, but we had a jolly time along the way.

Sister Magdaline, who came to help us in Teller for the summer, pitched right in. Since she had spent three years at Igloo (1923-1927) she knew just what had to be done. Confirmation services were planned for the last Sunday in July, so this was her first responsibility besides the regular services. My time was somewhat divided between Teller Mission, Teller Town and the Tuxuk. We soon discovered that most of the Teller Mission folks were camping on the beach below the Mission. Their usual fishing grounds had been partly occupied by the Army, so the natives were advised to stay away from there. Some of our Tuxuk natives were at Teller and some had stayed close to Igloo, so the picture had changed somewhat. I know my motor boat did considerable traveling. Sometimes I had a stiff arm from pulling that rope to get it started. I guess the motor was wearing out and, of course, the battery had to be replaced from time to time. I enjoyed having Sister Magdaline  with me on the Tuxuk.

Teller had been vacant since Rev. Klyve had passed away very suddenly last spring. So we were glad when Bertha Stedje, our new worker for Teller, arrived. Rev. Dahle came down from Shishmaref to conduct the confirmation services. Miss Stedje came just in time for this. The year before Mrs. Klyve had made white parka covers. With a few alterations,  we were able to use them. There was a very good attendance and it was a nice service.

We all agreed that the living quarters at Teller Mission were very inadequate. Together with Rev. Dahle and the consent of the Mission Board, plans were made to build an addition at Teller. Mr. Vogen, a carpenter living at Teller, promised to do the work with help from the natives. Though Miss Stedje was to be stationed at Teller she would make visits over to Teller Mission from time to time. Although a bit reluctant about it at first she did a wonderful job. I remember I hesitated to leave her when it came time to return to the Tuxuk and Igloo, but God was with her. All was so new and different from what she had expected but she did very well.

Sister Magdaline had to leave on the 15th of August, as she had promised to be back on September 3rd for the reopening of the Nursing School at the Deaconess Hospital in Chicago . She planned to visit her sisters in California on her way back. She had enjoyed seeing her friends in Alaska again, and remembering her past experiences.

The following day I was called up to the Tuxuk. One of our Igloo men, Jim Eyuk was very sick, probably of cancer of the stomach. His wife had cut her leg while trying to chop wood and it had begun to swell, so I packed up everything and went up there. I did what I could and two days later I went to Igloo. The sick folks followed soon, but not long afterwards Jim passed away, Life was difficult in that little village.

But the sun was shining more each day and now it was nice and green at Igloo. The Saw Tooth Mountains to the south looked more beautiful than ever. One of the first things I had to do was to cut down some of the high grass in front of my place. Then I had to thaw out the drain pipe to the cellar, which was still frozen. The swallows had been nesting under the eaves so the walls and windows needed a scrubbing. In some places they had even built two-story duplexes underneath the eaves. There was quite an array of mud huts, perhaps waiting for their next year's return, but I put an end to them.

Although the war was over and Armistice had been declared, I had not heard if there were teachers coming to Igloo. When the word came, asking me to take the school another year, I accepted. The Lord had been with me the last year and I knew He would give me strength for the coming year. Also I felt a little better prepared this year. I did decide to live in the teachers' quarters for that would make my life easier in many ways.

### A TYPICAL DAY AT IGLOO

The alarms went off at 6:30 A.M. I crawled out of bed, turned up the oil stove, then hurried back to bed for another fifteen minutes while things warmed up. Out of bed again, dressed and made breakfast, — usually toast, coffee and a dish of prunes. Meanwhile, I had made many trips into the school room to refill or check the coal stove. At 8:15 I was waiting for a call from Nome, sitting calmly by the radio with my Bible in hand, trying to prepare the evening lesson. The first of a series of interruptions came soon. Someone wanted help to send a telegram. Then Frankie came and wanted some mink-skins mailed and insured. At 8:45 I talked on the radio with Miss Stedje in Teller and Rev. Dahle in Shishmaref. Miss Stedje was waiting for a native to take her across the bay, six miles distant, where she would conduct services for a week, then return to Teller. It was wonderful to have radio and keep in touch each day.

At 9:00 o'clock I rang the school bell and before long our students were busy working. It really was fun trying to help the Eskimos in this way. One day a mother said to me, "My, but the children are learning fast." I was glad she thought so. From 12:00 noon to 1:00 P.M. there was another rush. First I had to check the stove and make sure there was enough coal for the afternoon session.

I would pour some water into my little dripolator and soon my meal of coffee, soup and bread was prepared. Often before I had finished eating someone might come in and want a tooth pulled. I did not mind for a terrific toothache must be cared for. Then someone else wanted to borrow some tools and these must be recorded. The water container must be filled and before classes began at 1:00 P.M. all the smaller children got cod-liver oil. They liked it! We often began the afternoon session by singing. By 2:30 it was getting dark so the lamps had to be lit, or— if it was working, — the electric light plant started. Everyone usually studied hard to accomplish as much as possible before 3:30. Then we would get the school room in order for the next day and I would plan my next day's lessons. Each day passed quickly and, before we knew it, another week was gone, and very soon the school year was over.

Sometimes things that happened would be rather amusing or encouraging. I was pleased by the spirit of our adult choir when they asked for an extra practice period. - In school, when one of my primary pupils looked at a picture, the first thing he saw was the Bible. — My organist, Annie Mosquito, came every Saturday to review the hymns for the Sunday services. — John Octuck came and offered to help with odd jobs, such as filling the oil drums and lamps. — Old Lady Kugzruk had heard me asking for onions at the store and when they did not have any, she brought me some. — Others would often bring berries, fish or a piece of reindeer meat. —Once I was out of coffee, and there was none in the store. One man brought over a pound of coffee and said he had some extra coffee. — When Johnny reported after his trip along the coast and inland, "We had bad luck. —Didn't get any polar bear, no seals and couldn't find any reindeer." —The Junior group had been learning the Bible verses (Matthew 19:14.) I asked one boy to recite the verse. He started by saying, "Suffer the little kids," then stopped , for he knew that was wrong. — One man said about the 23rd Psalm, "Plenty hard to understand. Why can't we just say 'The Lord is my 'herder'?" He knew about reindeer, not about sheep.

## CHISTMAS IN WARTIME

Christmas was approaching fast and I almost wondered how I could get everything done. Fortunately, I had done the Christmas wrapping in September. This year I planned a little pantomime called "A Christmas Candle." It depicted a mother and child putting a candle in the window, hoping that her brother who ran away from home some years previous might accidentally see the light while searching or coming back to his home. When he did there was great rejoicing. There were songs in between scenes, a candle dialogue, the manger scene and some other recitations with a Christmas tree,. The children just loved it. And we had some soldier guests with us!

## GI'S AND THEIR JEEP

Five of the soldier boys from the Army Post at Davidson Landing, about five miles down the river, came over for the Christmas program. They came in their jeep (something new for this part of the country), so it did not take very long to get to the village. The boys seemed to appreciate this opportunity of getting away from their camp for a short while. After the program I invited them to stay and have a little lunch. I also asked Johnny Kakaruk, the storekeeper and his wife.

On Christmas Day many of the Catholic folk from the Old Village came to our Chapel services. Then afterwards they would visit friends in the village.

When some of our village boys came back from the Army, it was hard for them to adjust again. One of them had begun drinking quite heavily and it made me sad to see the change. Of course, there were others in the village who did the same thing — when they could get hold of liquor.

One Sunday morning an airplane landed on the river. Thinking there might be something for me, I went down to the riverbank. A box was lifted off and one of the men said he had ordered a case of milk. But instead it turned out to be "brown" milk and you can imagine the parties a few people had. The next morning I was called over for the storekeeper had been in a fight with someone while drunk. He had a black eye and other bruises. His wife who grew up at our Mission in Teller was in Nome for a few days and he had two fine boys at home. He was very much ashamed of himself, especially for setting a poor example to his family. We talked together for some time, then I suggested we pray about it. He promised to stop drinking. Although he was a Catholic, he often attended our services with his family. His wife was a very fine person.

I wrote to the pilot and asked him not to bring any whiskey to our village, even though they ordered it. I do not know if he paid any attention to it.

## MY LAST YEAR OF TEACHING

Spring of 1947 was approaching. The school children were beginning to get restless. There had been a great deal of snow this year, with high drifts reaching to the roof of our Chapel, and much snow around us on the tundra and river ice below. How quickly this changes when the penetrating heat of twenty-four hours of sunshine begins. Everybody must wear high boots in walking through the snow as there would be water underneath and one would invariably step right to the bottom. The river was fast changing from white to blue as the snow began to thaw. The mountain peaks would turn brown or green when the trees began to sprout. I loved this time of the year and it surely reminded me of God's ever-present love, power and the new life which He has promised to His faithful ones.

It would not be long before I would be winding up my second and last year as teacher in the Igloo School. I had told the Indian Service at Juneau that I could not continue another year and hoped that they now could get another teacher as the war was over.

The natives were now anxious to get to their favorite camping ground near the lake or river, to get some fresh fish or some of the ducks or geese flying overhead. This would be a real treat for at this time of the year their supplies were low or gone.

## END OF SCHOOL YEAR PARTY

Before closing school we had planned a little party. I gave the children some frozen cupcakes left over from Easter. The boys got some ice and we made ice cream from canned milk. How they loved that. On Sunday evening the Sunday School children put on a special little program after our service. The girls in the seventh grace had been studying about Pasteur and Koch, so I had them read a little story about each one of them which they had written. Then I showed some slides of Pasteur and Koch. The Igloo orchestra played some numbers. The two girls who had been taking music lessons from me also performed. One of the girls recited the Twenty-Third Psalm, which she had learned in our catechetical class. The smaller children placed pictures on the board while I told the story of Gideon in pictograph. The Junior Choir sang then the whole group sang some songs. We felt that it had been a very pleasant evening, and everyone enjoyed the ice cream.!

As soon as school closed I moved all of my things back to the Mission house, then I cleaned the school house and teacherage. I had really enjoyed the teaching but knew that all of that was too much for me.

## A NEW TEACHER AND STOREKEEPER

Before school again started in the fall Miss Edna Ottness from Montana had arrived. Usually the government sends a couple to the stations, but the enrollment had become smaller during the war years. They knew I was still there and, if needed, could give Miss Ottness some assistance. She had taught school before and was used to shuffling for herself, so things went very well. I gave her information when needed and we got along just fine.

One Sunday afternoon just before freeze-up, Johnny Kakaruk (Eskimo storekeeper) came over and asked me to come to meet the new storekeeper, Mr. Tex Ziegler. We had heard that Bill Munz ( a pilot) had sold the store. I went over and there, in the kitchen, he was sitting having coffee and something to eat. But what a surprise I had! He looked to be such a young fellow, perhaps twenty-three or twenty-four years old. And such a little fellow, too. He had come from the Old Village via boat and was very cold. He was not dressed for this kind of weather, and was trying hard to get warm. Johnny Kakaruk was trying to tell Tex all he could in a very short time, because he was returning to the Old Village where he had formerly lived. He knew that the river would begin to freeze almost any time and wanted to get there before this happened. It was fortunate that they left when they did, because that night the river began freezing up and it would have been impossible to travel by boat.

Miss Ottness had invited me to dinner that evening, so I went over and told her about the new resident and suggested that she invite him, too. I then introduced her and she asked Tex if he would like to join us for dinner. He seemed quite pleased. But when six o'clock came, then 6:30 and almost 7:00, we wondered what had happened. Finally he arrived and said he had a big secret to tell us. He had been so cold he had been hunting all around in the store for some woolen underwear to put on. Of course, we had a laugh about that. Then he told us that he didn't know what kind of store he was buying. He had merely traded a plane which he had brought from the States for the store supplies. It was, as he called it, a "pig in a poke" affair. Naturally, he was anxious to see what it was all about and, no doubt, was disappointed. He had recently come out of the Army Hospital as a war veteran, knew nothing about the natives, their wares for trading, etc., so he was pretty brave to come into it in this way. Business had been quite good during the war, selling many furs and fur clothing at a high price. But things had now changed. Fur prices were way down and the people in the villages had very little money. But Tex learned many things through bitter experience and he did not give up very easily.

### TEX'S NARROW ESCAPE

One of his first experiences, which might have ended in tragedy, came the next morning when he went down to the riverbank to get some water. It was slippery and as he reached in to get the water he fell in. Even with a bucket in each hand, he managed to keep afloat until he reached a bank he could grab hold of. Then he scrambled ashore, cold and shivvering, but lucky to be alive. No one had seen him and he might have drowned without anyone knowing what had happened. He often spoke of this experience for it was something he could not forget.

The men in the village then got busy pulling up their boats before they froze in. Before long Tex was out, helping too. That gave him a chance to meet some of the men. I had just baked some blueberry upside-down cake when he stopped in. I think he must have smelled it. He certainly enjoyed a piece with some coffee. Then he began asking various questions about the store, village, etc. He was a very interesting young fellow and had big plans.

### THE JINX AT IGLOO

One day I invited Miss Ottness and Mr. Ziegler over to lunch. I had made some jello and wanted to cool it in a hurry so set it on an oil drum right outside the door. A little later when I hurried out to get it, I slipped, my feet went forward and I hit my back against the legs of an upturned bench. For a minute or so I was completely winded and didn't know what had happened. I finally managed to get inside and laid down for a little while/ But it hurt so that it seemed I couldn't do that, either. I then realized I had broken a rib or two, perhaps the large floating rib. My guests had to take care of themselves when they came. After school, Mr. Ziegler and Miss Ottness came over and taped me up, so I felt like a piece of board. By and by I began to feel better.

A couple of days later Mr. Ziegler went for a dog-team ride, fell off the sled and cracked his knee cap. That morning I put a plaster-paris cast on, with the help of Miss Ottness. It was really a bit laughable because two days previous they were binding me and now we were binding him up. But that wasn't all. When Miss Ottness rushed back to the school she was a little too speedy and fell at her door-step, hitting her forehead on the door. Fortunately, she did not break any bones but she did get quite a large swelling on her forehead, a scratch on her leg, a torn stocking and a sickish feeling. So, here we were, the only three white people of Igloo and all in a "jam", or should I say in a "bind."

I was glad that I had a washing machine for there was quite a pile of clothes in the hamper. However, as I could not use my left arm very well, I got one of the girls to come over the next day to help me.   At noon Miss Ottness came over to tell me that she was not feeling very well, I took her temperature and it was 102 degrees. I advised her to dismiss school and come over to my place and go to bed. I think it was a reaction from her fall. In a couple of days she felt better and was able to go home.

Mr. Ziegler got along fairly well although he started to get a swelling in the bottom of his leg and feared a recurrence of the thrombosis condition which he had had in the Army. If there had been some way to get him out by plane he might have gone to see a doctor, but the river was not solid enough for landing. There was no alternative but to stay quiet in bed for a little while. So I had him as a patient, too, for a few days. One of the boys made a crutch for him. Then we also contacted the Kotzebue Hospital for instructions. But he improved so all is well that ends well.

## A COSTLY MAIL DROP

Because of weather conditions there could be no mail, either, and for new folks like Miss Ottness and Mr. Ziegler, this was trying. However, one day, shortly after these mishaps, one of our pilots dropped us a little mail. Unfortunately, that mail drop cost me $7.00. I had ordered two bulbs for my projector and they happened to be in that sack. That was the end of them. If the package had been marked "fragile," they would not have been put in the sack. But we all got mail and that was the important thing.

We often laughed about our mishaps, our series of falls. Mr. Ziegler was quite a jolly fellow, talkative, too, as he told of many narrow escapes in the Army.   He was also a pilot and later brought in his own plane. He told us that he had left the Army Hospital against orders. He had been told that because of the moving embolus he had only two months to live. But here he was, going through the hardships of Alaska, trying to prove that the doctors were wrong. He is still living today, working hard as a free-lance photographer for one of the television companies. He has surely proven his point.

Miss Ottness seemed to be doing fine with her school. The children were making rapid progress and she loved them. Some problems were new to her, but I helped her whenever I could. The new storekeeper had his problems and, since I knew about the store, he would ask me and I was glad to help.

Maggie Topkok  had been coming over to help me with the the washing. I was pleased when I noticed that she had brought her daily devotion book which I had given her last year for Christmas. A little later we had a few minutes to spare, so she got her book and we  had devotions together. We continued our Bible studies on Monday evenings, and Thursday night midweek meetings. They went well this year.

During the week I would make visits in the village with my medicine kit in hand. One day a visitor opened it and looked to see what was in it. Then he spied my little New Testament, took it out and asked, "What do you use this for?' I could have quoted a little poem that I often recalled as I went about my work in the village.

"What will it profit, when life here is o'er, Though earth's farthest corners I see, If, going my way, and doing my will, I miss what His love planned for me?"

### THE SEVERE WINTER OF 1947

We had some very cold weather this year and again I saw the thermometer at 54 below zero. We are supposed to be able to work faster during cold weather, but I believe it works just the other way. The blood seems to thicken and various duties seem a burden. One does naturally rush around trying to get out of the cold and then keep warm. We have had sudden changes, up to 40 to 50 degrees warmer within twenty-four hours. Then I suddenly felt like a wilted flower must feel. Everything seemed to have been drained out of me, and it took some time to adjust again.

### A BROKEN LEG AND A BAD BURN

As usual, there had been some sickness and a few accidents. One morning I was called over to the house of a mother with nine children. Her husband had been laid up for some time with rheumatism and had now gone to Serpentine Hot Springs, some miles inland. He wanted to get some relief by taking daily hot baths. While he was gone his wife, Elsie, had fallen on the ice and hurt her leg so that she was unable to walk. On close examination I realized that she must have broken her leg. I applied a temporary splint and tried to contact the Nome doctor for some plaster-paris and instructions. He merely advised a total splint and to watch for further sympoms and results. About five to seven weeks later she was back on her feet, without the splint, and fine as ever.

Soon afterwards a young boy came with a severely burned arm. He had used gasoline in building a fire and there was an explosion. Almost all the skin had been in contact with the flames. It was a sorry looking arm and took many careful treatments before it was completely healed.

We had a very nice Easter program this year again, with services on Thursday evening. On Friday I showed the Passion Play on an 8mm projector. People came from Teller and Old Village. On Easter morning we had our regular services with a full house. The folks from Old Village were also there. At four o'clock we had the children's program.

### A SURPRISE FEAST FOR EASTER!

Miss Olson, a Lutheran nurse from Fort Dodge, Iowa, then working at Nome, sent us some food for a feast! Some nice T-bone steaks, celery, lettuce, tomatoes and oranges via plane a few days before Easter. So that Easter dinner in the evening was a treat. Miss Ottnes and Mr. Ziegler were my guests and we surely enjoyed it. I think I even took a picture of Edna chewing her chops. In the evening the natives gathered in the school house for a little get-together of games and visiting. They always enjoyed those times.

A few days later, Mr. Starling, the educational director from Juneau, surprised us with a visit. Another day Mr. and Mrs. Wild, teachers from Teller Mission, made a trip to Igloo, coming by dog-team. The same day they were leaving to go to Hot Springs, Rev. Dahle arrived by plane from Shishmaref to conduct communion services and baptisms. He also held a memorial service for Harris Keelick, a veteran who had been in the Portland hospital for some time before he died.

From Igloo Rev. Dahle went to Teller to conduct services for Miss Stedje, first at Teller Town then at Teller Mission,— now called Brevig Station.  Miss Stedje was planning a two months' trip to the States, I was asked to stay at Teller during the summer. I was glad to do that.

### LETTERS

Miss Ottnes helped the children to write some letters in their composition work. She thought the following letter was a good example of their work:

*Dear Friend:*

*The mail plane came today. It lands on the river-ice. In the summer the plane don't land there because it hasn't any ice.*

*In the summer we eat cranberries, salmon berries, blue-berries and blackberries. These things grow in the summer. We put our boat out in the water in the summer. In the autumn we pull the boat on land before the water freezes.*

*In the winter we have a dogride. It is fun to ride on the sled. Before we go, we have to harness the dogs. In the winter we skate on the thick ice. We slide, play baseball, mon-a-mona (an Eskimo game,) hide and seek, Washington poke, sheep sheep my pen and then we play we are dogs.*

*In school we have only one room, because there are not as many boys and girls now. There are 13 now, counting boys and girls. Some went to Teller a little while ago. Our teacher's name is Miss Ottness. When it is time to come into the school, we line up and march in.*

*I wear mukluks on my feet and parka for my coat. Would you like to hear some Eskimo words? Nayak means hair; omiak means boat; okguluk means rabbit; omuluk means wolf; ukluk means hear; timniak means duck; soopun means gun, iskoolty means teacher; ungnak means girl; ungoon means boy; ungnukoo-shuck means old woman; Unglono means pencil; and survick means knife. I can tell you some more sometime if I get a chance. Now I must close this letter.*

*Your friend,*
*Vernon Kugzeuk*

This year has been quite different from the previous two years when I taught school in addition to the village work. Even so, there was plenty to do. Other neighbors as well as the Eskimos called on me when there was sickness. I must have brought spiritual aid too, for.they were both faithful in attending the services; one was a Christian Scientist and the other a Lutheran. They were both helpful to me in many ways.

### BOATING

This summer I had Miss Ottness for a traveling companion so it was quite different from the previous years. On June 14th we started on down the Kuzitrin River to Teller in my boat, the Ark, with its 4HP Evinrud motor. We camped for two nights, about six miles down river, where some of our Igloo folks were already camping. Together with them we went on down through the sloughs toward Salt Lake. The water was so low at this time, that at one place we found ourselves almost on dry land. The boat ahead of us, which was much larger than ours, could not get through to the main river. However, after several hours of digging, a channel was opened and we were in deep water again. A little later we scooted on ahead of the natives, went across the lower end of Salt Lake and into the Tuxuk River, arriving at my cabin about 3:00 A. M., June 17th. There we unloaded our tent, sleeping bags, primus stover and a little of our food supply. We stopped long enough to cook some coffee and had something to eat, before pushing on down about twelve more miles to Teller. We made Teller in about one and one-half hours. I was quite proud of my motor for it behaved very well.

Miss Stedje had been looking for us every day for she had made arrangements with the Wien Airlines for our planned flight to Shishmaref. So that night about 9:00 P. M. we were all on our way to Shishmaref and almost found the Dahles in bed. That was a pleasant and happy visit for us all. On the 28th we were back in Teller and on the 30th Miss Stedje was on her way to Seattle and other points for the summer.

I spent most of my summer at Teller, enjoying Miss Stedje's new living quarters. In July I did make two trips up the Tuxuk where our Igloo natives were camped, three trips over to Teller Mission, enjoying the old sights there. Then I went across to the Nook several times, where some of the Teller Mission folks camped to do their fishing. So, besides conducting services on Sunday morning and once during the week at Teller, doing some medical work, teeth extraction and helping with some social problems in the vicinity, visiting and entertaining friends, the summer went by quickly.

Miss Ottness stayed with me part of the time. But after she made a trip to Nome and Fairbanks, she had a severe sinus and ear infection. She had to stay in the Nome Hospital for some time before returning to Igloo. Both she and I were camera bugs. I had just gotten my new Kodak 35 and was very anxious to try it on my return to Igloo. Previously I had been taking some 8mm movies which I later used many times, both at home and on my trips to the States.

## A VERY SPECIAL WEDDING

When Miss Ottness got back to Igloo following her illness, she informed me that she was engaged and wasn't sure that she would continue teaching. A year ago on the boat coming to Alaska she had met a man who was working at Fairbanks during the summer. He had wanted her to come there. I suggested to her, "Why not have him come to Igloo, be married here and spend the winter with us?" I knew it would be impossible to get a teacher at this late date and I would not think of taking the school again. She agreed to see if it might work out.

It did! In October, shortly before freeze-up, the plane landed right at our door-step and here was Mr. Bill Peterson, her fiance. Since I was marriage commissioner I was able to perform the ceremony in our Igloo Chapel. Mr. Tex Ziegler was best man and Mrs. Josie Octuck was matron of honor. The whole village was present for the ceremony. Since this was the first white couple whom I had married at Igloo, they found it very interesting.

Right after the ceremony Edna Eyuk presented the bride with a lapel ornament made like a small pairs of slippers with the word "Love" sewed in beads above them, a very thoughtful gift. Then the newlyweds came over to my place for dinner. I had baked and decorated a cake for the occasion.

We spent a pleasant evening and then the couple proceeded to the school where Miss Ottness, now Mrs. Peterson, had her living quarters. Now she would not be alone, and she would have help with various other duties while she taught school.

## A DIFFICULT YEAR AT IGLOO

This year proved to be a very difficult year for all. Our storekeeper had to go to Anchorage shortly before Thanksgiving, intending to be back within a week. He left the key with me, which meant, " if anyone wanted something, would you please take care of it?" That would have been very simple, — if the village folks had had plenty of money and could pay for the goods they needed. But it had been a hard year in more ways than one. Trapping was practically nil. There were no deer close by, as there used to be. They were getting far less for their native crafts. During the war there had been jobs for the men or boys, but now there were none so few families had money. Although they had been getting some fish, the natives always needed flour. The store was out of flour, coffee and cereal. The school sold all they could, and gave away some. Something had to be done so shortly before Christmas I ordered 300 lbs.

of flour to be flown in from Nome. The flour cost $18. per 100 lbs but we had to have it. I knew I could not enjoy Christmas knowing there were folks without flour.

### THOSE WONDERFUL MISSION BOXES

That year the mission boxes that had been sent by friends in the States were a Godsend. They had sent cloth for parkas and wearing apparel and many toys. They were always used to prepare gifts for all the children and for some of the adults. Chistmas program plans were moving ahead. Mrs.Peterson had prepared an unusual program which thrilled everyone. One of its features was the play depicting an Eskimo family coming to spend Christmas at Igloo. Five little boys represented a dog-team, pulling a sled with a family of four. Then it showed the excitement of their arrival, talking in the Eskimo language, then in English. It was very well done and it resulted in many interesting comments.

Besides our Christmas Day services in the morning, we gathered for a pleasant hour in the afternoon. I showed the film strip, "City of David," and there was singing and orchestra music. Following the program I was invited over to the Petersons for a delicious ham dinner. I enjoyed being able to relax and have dinner with friends.

The store continued to be a problem. Although the storekeeper returned some time after Christmas, few families had any money and there was so little business he did not stay very long and closed the store. So before break-up the natives had to go down to Teller to get supplies.

### VACANCY AGAIN

When spring came Mr. Peterson left for Fairbanks. He was a heavy duty machine operator and work was starting up there. A little later when school was out Mrs. Peterson joined him. As soon as the river opened up, she went about twenty five miles up river to Hot Springs where the planes landed. She took some of her belongings with her and the remainder was shipped later. Now Igloo was without a teacher again, and I wondered if we would have one the next year.

More of our Igloo families were leaving the village. Fred Mosquito, with his children, had left as soon as the river opened. They were moving to Anchorage as he felt they could make a better living there. Others were preparing to leave to look for jobs elsewhere. Mrs. Eyuk, one of our faithful women came over and asked me if I was leaving. I said, "No, I will be back in the fall." Thank you," she replied. "Then I am coming back, too." Again, I spent most of the summer at my Tuxuk cabin, going down to Teller several times.

### THE MEDICAL TEAM COMES TO TELLER

One day when I was at Teller the big U. S. Cutter "Northland" had arrived from the Juneau office. It brought a doctor, dentist, nurse and various government employees. A smaller boat was sent up the Tuxuk to get those who needed medical attention. Others were gathered from Teller and Teller Mission and brought to the boat, so there was a grand exodus at that time. This was the first time in years that any govenment boat had come to give medical aid to the Eskimos. So this meant a great deal to the natives and to all of us who had been living there and trying to help them.

## WILL IGLOO HAVE A TEACHER NEXT YEAR?

Mr. Dale, from the Alaska Native Service office at Juneau, was aboard the "Northland". He told me there would not be any teacher sent to Igloo this year. The school was getting too small and there was also a shortage of teachers. However, he asked if I was willing to teach, even on a half-day basis, but there would have to be at least ten pupils.

Four of the Igloo families had already decided to move to Teller. Since these families had most of the school children, there would only be four left. Therefore, Mr. Dale's recommendation could not be considered. I did try to do a little teaching on my own, in our Mission class room for a time, but this soon petered out. But I still had lots to do.

## I STILL WEAR MANY HATS

I was given permission to continue the radio contacts with Nome, for that was important in case of emergency. Since I was also postmaster I had to prepare and mail ivory carvings or Eskimo dolls made by the Eskimos. There was also the report to send to the Game Commissioner. In spite of the decreased number of villagers, the regular routine continued, and it seemed that I was almost as busy as ever.

## STORMY DAYS

One Wednesday morning I was trying very hard to get a particular message through to Nome. Reception happened to be good and many messages were going through.  Finally the call "KPXA IGLOO" came and I was able to send my report very quickly. Usually every word had to be spelled phonetically, but that day it was not necessary.

Then I rushed upstairs in my attic to ring the bell which was over in the Chapel. A rope had been connected from my house to the Chapel, so to ring the bell I just pulled the rope in my attic! Though the thermometer registered 35 below zero the five children were soon there. A poker went into the stove almost ruthlessly for it was so cold.

It was after the first of the month and the mail plane was due. People had been bringing in letters, native goods and furs for posting. Suddenly one of the children piped up, "Airplane, Airplane." They had their ears tuned to that sound and often heard it long before I did. We soon discovered that it was the mail plane. Recess was announced and we all headed for the plane. Several boys were there to help with the mail sacks and Mission boxes. These was all brought into my kitchen where we did the sorting. Some of the boys helped with the second class mail, while I sorted the first class. There seemed to be an accumulation of magazines, besides much other mail. But how glad we were to get the mail when it finally arrived.

Suddenly I heard the sound of another plane, and then one more, following right behind as they landed on the river below. Our storekeeper and his assistant, Mr. Scoville, had returned in their plane. Then we discovered that the mail plane was still there! It was so cold that the plane froze and could not get off the ground. The pilot worked with it for some time, but finally had to give up, hoping for warmer weather the next day. It did get warmer the next day but a storm had come up, which made flying impossible. For five days he waited for the weather to clear at Igloo and the freezing drizzle to disappear at Nome, where he was headed.

With all this excitement there was no thought of more school that day. I had been looking after the store, too, while the storekeeper was gone and now I had various reports to give him. For two weeks they had been stormbound in Nome. I had planned to have women's meetings in the afternoon but decided to postpone it due to weather and other interruptions. That is often the case with Alaskan schedules.

## THE BIG STORM

One Sunday morning I awoke to hear a terrific storm raging. It was so stormy we could not have services. All day we watched the snow whirling around the buildings, for this was one of those real south storms. The snowdrifts were getting higher and higher, so no one even thought of venturing out-of-doors. The wind charger on my house had stood the test, but at one time I thought the wind and storm had surely taken it off the roof. That had happened once before. Suddenly I heard a terrible noise. The rope had pulled loose and the wind charger was turning at a terrific speed. With one dive and a jump, I was up in the attic, pulling as hard as I could, to shut it off again, before the propeller landed out in the snowdrift. Finally, after some straining, I managed to pull the rope in, and tie it down again. What a relief that was.

## THE VALENTINE PARTY

That same day I had planned a Valentine party for the young folks. But due to the bitter cold, I was almost afraid I would have to postpone that party for I wondered if the people from the Old Village would be able to get there. I asked some of the young folks and they assured me that, in spite of the cold or storm, they all would come, — and they did! So we had our party in the schoolhouse where there was more space and electric power. First we had some home movies then games and relay races. Musical chairs, our closing game, seemed to be the favorite. Then I served refreshments, chocolate cakes, cookies, cocoa and apples. Everybody had a good time and went home happy, wishing that Valentine's Day would come more often. No bitter cold could stop the Igloo young people.

The next day was clear and beautiful, although still below zero. The sun was now scaling the mountain tops and I was happy to see it once more. Dog teams were out in all directions as the Eskimos hauled wood and checked their trap lines.

### DR. DYBVIG VISITS IGLOO

Dr. Philip S. Dybvig, from the Home Mission Office, was scheduled to visit us the latter part of April. Tex Ziegler had promised to meet him at Nome and pilot him to Igloo, Teller and Shishmaref. Rev. E. Hartje, from Shishmaref, arrived first on the morning of the 28th. Shortly after lunch Dr. Dybvig came. The natives rushed down to the plane, bringing up his baggage and soon I was showing him around, telling of various changes and  that many residents were moving to other villages. In light of this,  should the work at Igloo continue?

Suddenly another plane arrived with a government health team. For years tuberculosis had been the greatest scourge among the Eskimos. Dr. Kirk and a nurse from the Juneau office had brought a portable X-ray unit for taking pictures of the natives. I brought the medical team over to the  school building and had the Delco Motor plant started so they could begin their work. Edna Eyuk was to assist in getting the people lined up and she did that very well.

### FABULOUS FOOD FROM NOME

Wih these guests, some plans had to be made for dinner that evening. Mr. Ziegler had brought a nice reindeer roast and some other goodies from Nome. I appreciated that very much as I had invited the Juneau folks, as well as Mr. Scoville and Mr. Ziegler for dinner. I wondered what I would have for dessert when I suddenly remembered a can of plum pudding that I had been hoarding for a special occasion. This was just the extra touch I needed. Everyone seemed to enjoy that dinner and Dr. Dybvig said the reindeer roast was something special.

At 7:30 P. M. we all gathered in the Chapel for evening services, hoping that everyone would be present. They all came and it was a cozy evening. But I wished that Dr. Dybvig had been there when we had had 150-200 people, instead of today's dwindling population.

We had a delicious lunch the next day, — before the grand exodus. Besides bringing the reindeer meat, Tex had also brought some fresh crab!  Mr. Scovill cooked the crab so  we had a real treat.  Delicious crab salad with fresh tomatoes and avocados! After lunch, Tex Ziegler was taking Dr. Dybvig, Rev. Hartje and me to Teller Mission. The Juneau folks were also leaving that afternoon but Mr. Scovill was going to hold the fort. Later when we met in the States Dr. Dybvig mentioned the delicious Alaskan meals he had at my house, and the kindness of Mr. Ziegler who brought him to our various stations.

Miss Bertha Stedje at Teller Mission was very glad to see Dr. Dybvig for she and the village folks had important questions to raise. Should the old Mission building be repaired or was a complete new building a wiser choice? The decision was to repair it, and Dr. Dybvig promised to send someone to do it. He had Rev. Otis Lee of California and his father in mind, and they came the following summer.

After dinner and an interesting service, we all proceeded to Teller Town where we spent a very relaxing evening and restful night. In the morning, even though it was Saturday, we again had services and Dr. Dybvig spoke. Everybody, young and old, was present. In the States trying to call a service on Saturday morning might not work, but here it was different. In the choir were mothers with babies on their backs and sometimes children alongside them. All this impressed Dr. Dybvig very much and he could see that Bertha Stedje had been doing a fine job. However, it was too much for her to serve both places and he knew that other arrangements should be made for next year.

### SHISHMAREF VISIT

The next day we left early to fly on to Shishmaref. The day was very clear and Dr. Dybvig was surprised when we could see the mountains of Siberia. When we landed, many of the natives were waiting on the ice to meet us. Soon we saw dog-teams coming in from their seal hunting and that always caused a lot of commotion. Dr. Dybvig asked if he might have a dog-sled ride, and one was arranged the next day.

On Sunday morning we again had services at Shishmaref with Dr. Dybvig as speaker. Once more he was impressed with the almost total attendance of the villagers, the good singing by the choir and audience and the many children participating. One thing about which he marveled was the old lady who was so crippled with arthritis that it was necessary for her to almost crawl on hands and knees up the steps to the Chapel which was on the second floor. In spite of this there was a smile on her face. She was determined to get there.

Sunday evening we stopped at Teller Town for a short service, then Tex Ziegler brought me back to Igloo before they returned to Nome. I had enjoyed a wonderful trip to all our stations, a visit with our missionaries and I was very happy that Dr. Dybvig could see our churches in Alaska.

I was also thankful to Tex Ziegler for letting me go along as a free passenger on the above trip. Each time that Tex went to Nome he would bring back our mail. Both Mr. Scovill and Mr. Ziegler were very helpful and accommodating in various ways. He often took me to Nome or Teller. Airplanes had really changed life in Alaska.

### THE BREAK

It was sad to think that Igloo as a Mission Station was gradually disappearing off the map. We had felt it coming for more and more families were deciding to move to Teller. Soon there would only be a few sturdy boys who preferred trying it for another year. Their house was here and there were hunting possibilities. They planned to go to Teller for the summer and return in the fall.

The school was closed permanently.  When the storekeepers realized that I was also closing up the Mission and leaving, they quickly made plans to do the same. I packed together some pieces of furniture and groceries which I felt could be used at Teller Mission. My personal things also had to be packed since I would be going to the States.

The teacher came over to sort out things in the schoolhouse. Some of the school seats were to be used in Teller Town. Some things were to be taken down to the school at Teller Mission and I was asked to get those things together. It was rather sad to see this little village disappearing.

On June 13, 1949 a message came from the Loman Lighterage Company. Johnny Reed was leaving Teller for Igloo, bringing the boat with the scows, expecting that the ice on Salt Lake would be out. Twenty four hours later they were there to load. To get all these things together had been a big job, but many had helped. Before the day was over, everything from the Mission, school and store was loaded on the scows. I knew a big chapter of my life was ending and it was a strange feeling,. This had been my home for sixteen years, and I would not be coming back. I loved Igloo and I loved the people who had been so faithful. I would always cherish the memory of the years spent there. My prayer was that there might have been some fruit from my efforts.

## FAREWELL TO IGLOO

I stood at the door and took a last look all around. I would not see the sun disappear behind those mountains next November, and watch it return at the end of January and then see the days get longer. I said "good-bye"  to the beautiful Saw Tooth mountains, my little house, the chapel, the bell I would no longer ring,  and the many paths I had walked so often. My work may have been far from perfect, but my prayer was that nothing I had said or done or neglected had been a stumbling block or hindered anyone from being in God's Kingdom. Then I hurried down to the boat waiting for me on the Kuzitrin River. Although I rode inside the tugboat cabin it was a long and rather cold ride. We finally arrived at Teller in the early morning hours. Bertha Stedje had been expecting us and had it cozy and warm when we got there. I don't think a cup of coffee ever tasted better than it did that morning.

A few days later when I left by plane for Nome on my way to Minnesota, I doubted I would ever return to Alaska. When Bertha Stedje would leave I felt that there should be a pastor at Teller Town who would be in charge of our Alaska Mission. A tin-mining project was being opened up at Lost River, not far from Teller Mission. Many of our Eskimos were going to work there. Then I felt it was too much for one person to care for both Teller and Teller Mission. Some of our Eskimo families had moved to Nome from Shishmaref, Igloo and Teller so we really needed a worker there and a Lutheran Church. Where I might fit into the picture I did not know. I was leaving that to the Lord. Right now I was ready to go visit my familyl

### VISITING BACK IN THE STATES

My sister, Esther was teaching at Austin, Minnesota so I spent some time there with her and my step-mother.  Then I went on various speaking trips, showing 8mm movies which I had taken at our stations of the Eskimo activities, my travels up the Tuxuk River and camping there. Our friends in the States were very much interested in these pictures and I was happy at every opportunity to show them.  But they also made me homesick for Alaska. Then my aunt at Lomita, California asked me to come out and stay with her. Her husband had passed away and she wanted company.

Right after Christmas I took the train to California. The day I left it was snowing so hard that I had trouble getting a cab for the station.  But I boarded the train and two days later was in sunny California.  What a difference in temperature.  I soon shed my heavy coat and overshoes as I walked from the local bus, trying to find the place where Aunt Nina lived.  When I inquired at one of the homes a lady said that I had gone too far on the bus. She must have felt sorry for me, standing there with two suitcases, holding my heavy coat and overshoes. She immediately asked her son to get their car and take me to my destination. I enjoyed my long visit with my aunt, but most of all I enjoyed that warm sunshine.  For some time I thought of staying in California, getting a nursing job or doing parish work. But I became so restless I knew this wasn't what the Lord wanted. After about three months I returned to Minnesota.

Before long some speaking invitations came and I was once more traveling about, speaking about Alaska missions. One day, when I was in Minneapolis, I stopped at the Home Mission Board office to say "Hello." Dr. Dybvig was there and he told me that Bertha Stedje was leaving the work at Teller Town. Rev. Otis Lee was busy repairing the old Mission building across the bay. He said they needed a worker in Teller Town.

### ANOTHER INVITATION TO ALASKA

Then Dr. Dybvig looked at me and asked, "Will you please go back to Teller Town for a year at least? Perhaps by that time someone can be found to take charge of the Alaska Mission field." I knew immediately that I was supposed to do this,  so I said I would go in the fall. I had a few speaking appointments which I felt I should keep and one of them turned out to be very important!

### VISITS IN NORTH DAKOTA

A friend of mine was married to Pastor Madson at Pollack, South Dakota.  I went there to speak and show my Alaskan pictures at a Circuit meeting. After that I was to speak at a women's meeting near Brookings, South Dakota where my brother Reuben and family lived. So I was glad to visit those places.

When I spoke at Pollack I met Rev. and Mrs. Norval Hegland, the "flying pastor" who had flown to Pollock for this meeting. In my talk I mentioned our need for a pastor at Teller who would help promote other work on the Seward Peninsula. I had no idea that Rev. Hegland or anyone there might be interested.

The next day I planned to leave early in order to make connections for Brookings but that morning there was a very heavy fog which they said would clear before noon. Rev. Hegland told me, "Don't worry. I will take you to Brookings." So that is how I was able to keep my next appointment. Flying there proved to be a thrill in many ways. I thoroughly enjoyed seeing the countryside as we flew over the farms and towns. On the way, Pastor Hegland began asking questions about Alaska, the needs there, and what life there was like. I told him, then I asked him, "Would you be interested in Alaska?" "Yes, " he said, "I would like to make a trip up there," Then I asked, "May I speak to Dr. Dybvig about this?" He replied, "Yes!"

Now I knew why God had led me to Pollock, South Dakota. When I returned to Minneapolis I immediately told Dr. Dybvig about my talk with Rev. Hegland. After that things moved ahead very quickly. The Mission Board called Pastor Hegland and approved buying Mission plane for Alaska. A year later Rev. Hegland and his family flew to Alaska and he became the Superintendent of the Mission!

I always feel there are special times when God guides us to do what may seem to be routine things. But these small things may be important links in very important steps for the future. I certainly felt that way about the conversation with Pastor Hegland. He was to become an important leader on the Seward Peninsula. Working with him was a privilege and a joy. He made a remarkable contribution to the Lutheran ministry with the Native Peoples on the Seward Peninsula.

# GOING BACK TO ALASKA

The night I was scheduled to leave for Alaska I had dinner at the home of Dr. and Mrs. Dybvig. They asked to see some of my Alaska pictures. Then I suddenly realized that I should call and confirm my reservations which I had made a month earlier. My ticket said my flight would leave at 11:00 P. M. but now they told me it would leave at 10:00 P. M. I had only fifteen minutes to make that but the agent promised to hold the plane. Everyone helped me get my things together. When Dr. Dybvig went out to get the car to drive me to the airport, it was gone! His son was using it, so we called a cab. As I arrived at the airport I heard my name being called on the loud speaker and I just made my flight. I could hardly believe I was bound for Alaska again. What a wonderful feeling it was.

Our flight went to Edmonton, Canada then direct to Anchorage, arriving there on a Sunday morning. I took a taxi to Central Lutheran Church where Pastor Odegaard was serving. It did not take me long to realize I was really back in Alaska. There seated in the front pews were about twenty of our Igloo Eskimos! They had moved to Anchorage and now were in that congregation. It was so nice to see them with their children. I was very pleased that Pastor and Mrs. Odegaard and the congregation had welcomed our Eskimo people to the community. We know that some have slipped away but I pray that they may not forget their Lord and what we have tried to teach them.

That Sunday morning I also had another surprise. Sitting in the pew right behind me were Tex Ziegler and Orrin Scovill, our former Igloo storekeepers. They were on their way to the States. That day we had a little Igloo Reunion. While I was in Anchorage I also visited other friends.

## SUMMER OF 1950 AT TELLER

On Tuesday I left for Nome. Rev. Otis Lee met me at Teller and took me to my new home. That night I had a lovely roast salmon dinner at the home of Barney Vogen. There is nothing like fresh salmon. Now I knew I was back in Alaska.

A few days later, when the freighter came in with our supplies, Mrs. Lee and her family came over from the Mission and I was happy to meet them. Pastor Otis Lee had completed the repair work at Teller and everything was in good condition. The Chapel had been repaired and I enjoyed the new living quarters. Bertha Stedje had been a faithful worker, more Eskimos were taking an active part and many problems had been solved. The Lord had blessed her efforts in a community that had seen many changes.

## TELLER – VERY DIFFERENT FROM IGLOO

Teller had grown. There were Catholics and Lutherans, many white people and Eskimos and one Indian woman. There were two stores, and new territorial school with a couple as teachers. It had a radio station, a fairly good-sized airstrip down on the point, and some new houses. Some Eskimo families had moved their Igloo homes and rebuilt at Teller and a few had moved here from Diomede Island.

Teller is located on Grantley Harbor which leads out into Port Clarence Bay and then into the Bering Sea and Arctic Ocean. During the early gold rush days, this place had a large population of white people but now there were only a few prospectors. The Nick Tweets, of Norwegian Lutheran heritage, had lived there for several years, and were interested in our Mission work. The Tweet family did considerable mining a few miles out of town. Their four sons lived in Teller; three were married and one operated a store and helped with their mining activities..

I was glad to see the nice large quonset building that had been added. Bertha had used this for Luther League and women's meetings, classes and other gatherings. I found it was a good place to work on the Mission boxes which were still coming in.

The white folks at Teller were all very hospitable. I enjoyed being invited to dinner by Mrs. Alberta Peterson and Mrs. Ethel Marx, who owned the Teller Commercial Company. Their husbands had passed away some years ago. Mrs. Peterson's sister, Adella Vollmers, was with them. Mrs. and Mrs. Lon Rice were the school teachers.

Igloo had been a quiet and peaceful place, but not Teller. It was a busy place with a lot going on, especially just before freeze-up. The lightering and mail boats were busy on the water front, trucks going back and forth with supplies for the stores, Mission and school. The mail boat always carried other things besides the mail. The surveyor boat came in, other boats were coming back from Wales or Diomede and some coming down from the Tuxuk to pick up last minute supplies. Being right on Front Street, the Mission got the noise of all these activities. But there was work to be done. Before long, I was out making sick calls. In a short time two of the former Igloo Eskimos died. When he could, Rev. Otis Lee came over to conduct the funerals.

But the cold weather was coming. By the last of October solid ice in the Harbor and Bay had stopped boat traffic. Then things quieted down and I could begin my regular schedule with the Lutheran League, play night, religious classes, orchestra practice, women's meetings and visitation work. I also met with the Church Council to discuss various matters.

After freeze-up the government nurse arrived to give immunization shots and T. B. tests. On November the 16th Miss Stoffer, the Methodist missionary at Wales was storm-bound at Teller and stayed with me until the 15th of December. I think she enjoyed helping with the Thanksgiving and Christmas preparations. As we were wrapping presents, I asked what she had up there at Wales to give her children. She admitted they had very few things on hand. Since we had plenty she took boxes of color books, toys and clothing with her when she left.

Our Christmas activities here were very much the same as we had enjoyed at Igloo. The children were always very good about taking part. We had a small orchestra here, and our Junior and Senior Choirs sang at the Christmas Day services. Everything went well.

Our New Year's Services were in the morning of the 31st with celebration in the school house supervised by the teacher and some of the boys. They enjoyed various races and games.

When one of our former Igloo girls, Edna Eyuk, was married to Frank Ahnangetogak before Christmas, we had a little party for them at our Luther League gathering shortly after New Year. Everyone enjoyed this and they were happy to receive some articles for their home.

One Sunday morning, shortly before service time, a boy came with a message from Rev. Lee at the Mission, asking if I could come over as their daughter Becky was sick. I asked William Oquillok to conduct the service and went right over. I did what I thought was right and she improved rapidly. I was thankful and returned the next day.

### THE DOCTOR'S VISIT

Dr. Langsom from the Methodist Hospital at Nome, together with Rev. Amundson from the Swedish Covenant Church, surprised us one morning in January when they flew in to conduct a clinic. The doctor extracted some teeth, treated others and scheduled some needed tonsilllectomies. They then flew over to Teller Mission for the same program. But when they got back to Teller Town, it was too late for the operations, and the necessary supplies were exhausted.

After we had dinner, there were services in the evening. Rev. Amundson offered a religious meditation. Then following prayer and more singing, Dr. Langsom spoke on "First Aid." A few people wanted dental attention and eye examinations. The next morning the men left with the promise that they would be back later to remove the infected tonsils at Teller.

### OUR CHAPEL BECOMES A BUSY HOSPITAL

On March 2nd, about 11:30 A. M., they returned and what a busy day that was. Rev. Lee came over to help with the anesthetics, Mrs. Peterson loaned us several cots which we set up in the Chapel. Each patient was to bring his own bedding. The Tweet boys set up an electric motor for the doctor to use. One of the school girls came to help scrub and sterilize the instruments. Ethel Vogen cooked the dinner so it would be ready when we were done. Within five hours there had been eleven tonsillectomies. The patients needed to be watched, so between various duties I was kept busy, but everything went fine. After dinner, a short service was conducted in the Chapel where the sick children were still resting on the cots.  That night one person from each family stayed with the children. I managed to get a little rest on the cot in the living room, where I could be on call. Ann Vogen and her brother stayed and helped keep an eye on the patients. But they all seemed to sleep quite well.

Though it was very stormy the next morning, by noon it had calmed down enough for the patients to be taken home. Due to the snowstorm, however, it was three days before Dr. Langsom and Rev. Amundson could leave. So we had services one morning and one evening. I was the organist, Rev. Amundson sang and played a little concert on his accordion. The Eskimos liked that very much.

I was quite amused one morning when Rev. Lee and his whole family came over with the little tractor pulling a small trailer on which was a large box. In this box sat his three children. Becky was fine and they were snug and warm for that box really protected them from the wind. Friends at Anchorage had given that little tractor and it surely came in handy. When the ice conditions were just right Rev. Lee could come across the Bay, pick up his mail and then return in a short time. This time they did not stay very long for Pastor Lee feared a storm might come up. Although it was only an eight mile stretch, the ride back could be treacherous. But they got home safely that day.

### REV. SOLBERG'S VISIT

One day Rev. Clarence Solberg, from the Home Mission Office, arrived to visit Shishmaref, Teller, Teller Mission and Nome. He was making a survey and evaluating the future needs. Rev. and Mrs. Hatrje at Shishmaref had asked to be relieved and there were other needs to be studied. Some decisions had to be made about Teller. The government nurse had not wanted to cooperate and felt I should not have any of the medical supplies. However, Dr. Langsom just gave me what was needed for he knew that many of the natives had known me for years and would probably come to me for help.

At Teller I soon realized there were new problems. Teller was not like Igloo. The natives here had come from many villages, moving here from Wales, Diamede, Teller Mission, Council, Igloo and even from Nome. Since there was no real Village Council there was less unity, even among the white people.

Here in Teller our Mission quarters were right in the midst of Eskimo homes. On one side was the street where many of their homes were. On the other side, I was only a few feet away. The Chapel was facing the ocean front, where a great deal of the activity went on. On the fourth side was a large warehouse belonging to Teller Commercial Company. At Igloo the Mission buildings, store and school had been quite a distance from the rest of the village. I only saw the people there when they walked by going to the store or rode by on the river in winter with the dog team or in summer by boat. Maybe here my eyes had been opened to many things I was unaware of before.

There were other problems. With more planes caming in from Nome, it was easy for anyone to get liquor. Also work was scarce and it was hard for some of the people to make a living.

I loved our dear old women like Avarina Kagzruk, Eva Eyuk, Mary Oquilluk, Sarah Okpeok and other sincere women who were much concerned about their children and always active in the church.

When Sunday morning or evening services came, and I would be standing before them delivering the message I had prepared, I seemed to forget about any of these problems. I knew that God was speaking to them through His Word. When I went to their homes to visit, especially in time of illness, I felt very close to them. God had given me a task to do and I was going to do it. Some of the white people would also call me for help in time of illness and, whenever possible, I gladly responded.

One widow, Olive Miller, whose husband had been a white man, was a great comfort to me. For a number of years she had worked for some teachers at Wales. Later, while I was at Igloo, she worked for Mr. and Mrs. Burkher, who were teaching there. I often went down to Olive's house at Teller and talked to her. She had five children and was doing a good job bringing them up in the fear of the Lord. Although she could not read very well, she often interpreted for me. She understood English very well and was able to say what I was trying to tell the audience.

Olive's mother, "Annie", as she was called, was also a very dear soul, and faithful in coming to church. It was quite a way down to Olive's house and a long walk for Annie. In the winter you often saw the boys pushing her on a sled to Church. In the summer they would pull her in a boat along the shore. Seeing her coming always gave me a thrill. In fact, most of these old women were very faithful and, rain or shine, snow or storm, they were at church. I surely missed Mary Oquillok when she died, for she had long been a favorite of mine. She was a good soul and she prayed with such sincerity. She had many adopted children to pray for and was always concerned about them.

### TWO VISITING SCIENTISTS

Some unusual things happened at Teller. Two scientists had been working at the cemetery on a special project related to the influenza epidemic of 1916-1917. They had been digging in the frozen ground where the 72 Eskimos had been buried during that epidemic. They wanted to see if they could get frozen specimens to isolate the influenza germ. It was the last day in June when Rev. Lee brought the two scientists back to meet Otto Guist and two other doctors at Teller. After they met they flew on to Nome with those specimens. Rev. Lee came over to the Mission and asked if I would like to go back home with him and spend the night with his family. I quickly picked up some things and jumped into the boat. He had been working hard on the old building but there was more to do. He wanted me to look at it and give suggestions, since I might be the next worker there.

### THE HEGLANDS ARE COMING

Word had come from the Mission Board that Rev. Norval Hegland and his family were coming to Teller Town that summer. This was exciting news to me for I had met him in South Dakota and he told me he might be interesting in coming to Alaska. Now everything had worked out.  He was to fly up in the new Mission plane and will be the Superintendent of the Alaska Mission.

### A SURPRISING REQUEST —A DIFFICULT DECISION

Then one of the boys brought over another telegram which had come from Pastor Hartje at Teller after we left. It was about Shishmaref. Rev. Hartje wanted to be relieved in two months and asked if Rev. Lee could go to serve at Shishmaref when he had completed the carpenter work at Teller. After Rev. Lee read the telegram he thought for a few moments then turned to me and said, **"I think you had better go to Shishmaref.** My work here is not done and when I do finish  we want to go back to the States." That really surprised me and I needed time to think it over. First I thought of many excuses as to why I couldn't go to Shishmaref. That night I didn't sleep much as I fought the idea and could not get if off my mind. Suddenly, during the early hours of the morning, someone seemed to say to me, "Helen, didn't you promise when you went to Alaska that you would go where the Lord wanted you?" I knew then the Lord had spoken to me in a special way. Almost immediately I said, "Yes, I'll go to Shishmaref and You will help me." The strangest feeling came over me and there was peace. I went to sleep, and in the morning I told Rev. Lee I was willing to go.

When Rev. Lee answed the telegram, he suggested to Dr. Dybvig that I go to Shishmaref when Pastor Hartje left. Dr. Dybvig approved so I had two months to get ready. I felt now that God was leading me to go to Shishmaref, for as soon as I gave in I had peace in my soul. All the problems I had worried about, He took care of in time.

### GETTING READY TO MOVE TO SHISHMAREF

In those weeks of waiting some interesting things happened. The territorial school had their eighth grade graduation exercises and I was able to attend. The children of all the families attended this school.  I had not seen an eighth grade graduation, for I had been on furlough when the first was held. Since Mr. and Mrs. Rice, the teachers at Teller Town were leaving we had a little farewell service for them in our Chapel one evening.

### A Death and a Funeral

About a week later there was a death in the village. An Eskimo man by the name of Washington was found dead in his house. It seemed that he had had a stroke and fallen on the floor. The men quickly got busy making the coffin and digging the grave. This happened on Saturday. We had our regular services Sunday at 11:00 A. M. and the funeral at 2:00 P. M. It was rather difficult to officiate at that funeral for I knew so little about this man.

By the last of August, I was busy opening Mission boxes and recording donors and contents. Then came the sorting and wrapping of Christmas gifts, giving out some of the left-over clothing and storing away the rest. I had a list of families and ages of the children, but that was all I had to go by until I knew them better. I had to get this done before our religious classes and group meetings started, for I was working in the room where these classes met.

### Preparing for Winter

In September the natives were busy hauling up their fishing gear and tents, fixing up their houses for winter, and hauling ice as soon as the lake was frozen. If they had a sod house it often meant almost a complete rebuilding. However, there were only a few sod houses left. I enjoyed looking out from the Chapel tower for I could see the village with the ocean on one side and the lagoon on the other. Shishmaref was on an island about two and one-half miles long and a half mile wide. Before long I had fallen in love with the village and the two hundred or more people living there. I thanked God for sending me here. My prayer was that I might be faithful to His calling.

### Rev. Hegland Arrives in the Mission Plane

On September 13th we received word that Rev. Norval Hegland and his family had arrived in the new Mission plane furnished by the Lutheran Daughters of the Reformation. In ten days with perfect flying weather they had flown all the way from South Dakota, along the Alcan Highway to Fairbanks, then to Nome and Teller,. Pastor Otis Lee and family were at Teller to greet them when they arrived.

I had left some of my things in Teller, all packed and ready to go,. The next day (Friday) Pastor Hegland and Pastor Lee brought these things up to Shishmaref. Then Pastor Hegland asked me if if I could to be ready in half an hour to fly back with them to Teller. It did not take me long to pack. Due to the fog, Pastor Hegland had followed the mail plane up there and he also wanted to follow it back. He needed to get acquainted with the route and the mountains.

### Our First Staff Meeting

We had a wonderful time together at Teller. I told them how I had met Rev. Hegland now they was here! That night after our dinner we had our first staff meeting and made plans for the installation service on Sunday. We also talked about the possibility of attending the Alaska Circuit Convention at Fairbanks on September 20-23. This was to bring our Eskimo Mission Congregations closer together with the rest of our Lutheran work in Alaska. That Mission plane was going to change the way we lived and served in Alaska.

Here is an article I wrote for our national magazine, the Herald about his coming.

At left, the Hegland family. Prairies of South Dakota are exchanged for the snow of Alaska

Below, installation service. Left to right are Pastor Hegland, Pastor Lee, and Miss Frost

"FLYING FAMILY"

BEGINS WORK AT

TELLER, ALASKA

(Story on next page)

VOLUME XXXV      MINNEAPOLIS, MINN., OCTOBER 23, 1951      NUMBER 43

Missionaries in Alaska: Pastor and Mrs. Otis Lee (back row, left), Pastor and Mrs. Norval Hegland, and Miss Helen Frost.

# Air Parish in Alaska

Helen Frost

**O**n September 13 at five P.M. the Reverend Norval Hegland and his family arrived at Teller, Alaska. They had travelled all the way from Newell, South Dakota, along the Alcan Highway via White Horse, Fairbanks, and Nome, to Teller in ten days, using the plane furnished by the LDR. According to their reports, it had been a wonderful trip, with perfect flying weather. Pastor Otis Lee and his family were at Teller to meet them when they arrived. I am sure the mission quarters resounded with much glee, happiness, and thanksgiving for their safe arrival.

A service was conducted in the chapel that night so that the Eskimos, too, could meet their new missionary and his family and join in the thanksgiving and prayer.

The next day (Friday) Pastor Hegland and Pastor Lee

brought some of my things up to Shishmaref. Pastor Hegland then asked if I would come along down to Teller. I had come to Shishmaref August 2, and on August 4 the Hartje family left for the states. It did not take me long to decide that question, but I had to be ready in half an hour. Due to the fog, Pastor Hegland had followed the mail plane up there and also wanted to follow it back in order to get acquainted with the route and mountains.

It was surely fun to be together this way at Teller, and that night after our dinner we had our first staff meeting. Plans were made for the installation service on Sunday. The possibility of attending the Alaska Circuit Convention to be held at Fairbanks September 20-23 was also discussed. We hope thus to unite our Eskimo mission work together with the rest of our Lutheran work in Alaska.

**S**unday morning (September 16) also marks a definite point in our Alaska mission work. Pastor Hegland was then installed by Pastor Lee as the pastor at Teller. He will also be the superintendent of the Eskimo mission. It was a very wonderful service. Pastor Lee spoke on what it meant to be a servant of the Lord. I gave a greeting of welcome, using an interpreter so that all might understand. This was followed by the installation service. Pastor Heg-

Hegland children "packing" for a trip.

Miss Frost, author of this article, ready for take-off in plane furnished by LDR funds.

land then responded by telling of his call and of the responsibility in connection with a call from God. We also had special music by the choir, a song by the missionary children (six children in all), and a vocal duet by Mrs. Lee and myself. All joined in the song, "O Master, Let Me Walk With Thee." After our dinner and a little more visiting, Pastor Hegland brought me back to Shishmaref. These had been wonderful days and something quite unusual. We are thankful for the coming of the Hegland family and thankful to the LDR for their efforts in making it possible for us to have the use of a plane in this manner. May it all redound to the glory of God and the furtherance of His Kingdom among the Eskimo in Alaska.

## INSTALLATION SERVICE

The church was full for the wonderful installation service. Pastor Otis Lee installed Pastor Hegland as Pastor at Teller and also as Superintendent of the Eskimo Mission. Pastor Lee spoke on what it meant to be a servant of the Lord. I gave a greeting of welcome, using an interpreter so that all might understand. Pastor Hegland then responded by telling of his call and the responsibility in connection with a call from God. We also had special music by the choir, a song by the missionaries' children (six in all) and Mrs. Lee and I sang a duet. All joined in singing, "O Master, Let Me Walk with Thee." After our dinner and a little more visiting, Pastor Hegland brought me back to Teller in time for our evening service. I told the folks about our Installation Service at Teller.

## FLYING TO FAIRBANKS

Flying to the Circuit Convention in the new Mission Plane was exciting. With our own plane, the Seward Peninsula staff now could get to these meetings. On the 19th at 8:00 A. M. Rev. Hegland came up to take me along to Fairbanks. At Nome we picked up Rev. Carlson, the Swedish Covenant Pastor who had some business to take care of in Fairbanks. Since he was a pilot and knew these airways very well, Rev. Hegland was glad to have him along. That evening when we arrived at Tenana we stayed in an old-time roadhouse, all sleeping in the same room. An Episcopal pastor and his wife were also there, on their way to Candle. For breakfast we had oatmeal, fried potatoes, bacon, bread and coffee.

Then we took off for Fairbanks, arriving there about 11:15. Rev. John Maakestad came out to the airport to get us and we arrived just in time to join the rest of the guests for lunch. The Maakestadt home seemed to be a hospitality center for travelers. I enjoyed this fellowship very much and learned to know our other Lutheran pastors in Alaska. A week later we flew back and I was back at Shishmaref. Many more Mission boxes had arrived. I wanted to start our religious classes, but a flu epidemic broke out and our classes were postponed. This gave me more time to prepare for classes and meetings and I needed that. I had more classes and meetings to prepare for than I ever had before — and many more people to deal with. I soon realized it would take time to get acquainted with everything.

Somehow, Shishmaref seemed very peaceful. There were no automobiles, trucks or trailers shooting by. There were no traffic accidents on the one and only street running from the airstrip at the end of the island, past the Mission and down to the store. Almost all of the outdoor activities centered around the school and store at the other end of the village where most of the people lived. The mail plane came in twice a week for a time, then later just once a week. Usually the plane landed some distance away. Some folks might have been lonesome, but not me. I had too many interesting things to do.

On October the 7th Rev. Hegland brought his family up for the morning services and I was installed. Our teachers, Mr. and Mrs. H. C. Bingham, were also there for the services. Then all of us were invited to their home for apple pie a la mode. They were always generous, hospitable and helpful to the Mission. I had many enjoyable visits with them later on, at my home and theirs.

There was one other white family, Mr. and Mrs. Goshaw, in the village, and they invited me for dinner a few times. Although they did not attend our services, they had been very helpful earlier when Rev. Dahle was putting up the Mission building. For a number of years Mr. Goshaw had been running a trading post there and he also had a fox farm. Two years later they sold out and left for Nome.

One day a Wien's airline DC3 landed on our beach with five men from the Geodetic Department. Few planes that large ever land here, so this was quite a surprise. They stayed in the National Guard building and set up a cute little tent outside the building. This was their observation tent and they were to do what we called "star gazing." They only stayed about a week, then the Wien's plane returned to pick them up. We wondered how much information they had been able to learn about the stars.

### THANKSGIVING

Before I knew it, Thanksgiving Day was upon us. At the morning service an offering of $56.74 was received for Lutheran World Action. After service the natives had their Thanksgiving dinner in the school house. Each family brought something and I baked eighteen loaves of bread. They took care of serving themselves. I had dinner that evening with the Binghams.

One day I received a wire that Rev. Hegland would be up with Tex Ziegler as soon as the weather cleared. Tex was making movies for himself and also a film for the LDR. He had the equipment for both inside and outside photography. One day he took pictures of the children as they were practicing for our Christmas program. Another day Bessie Moses and Mary Eningowok displayed their old ivory and Eskimo artifacts and mukluk sewing. He also took pictures of our evening services. When Rev. Hegland returned, Tex Ziegler took pictures of his plane landing and being greeted by the Eskimos. This film was very good and the LDR used it quite often.

### A TYPICAL SUNDAY AT SHISHMAREF

Sundays were busy days at Shishmaref. When my alarm went off at 7:00 A. M. I first checked the thermometer outside the window. It often was 25-30 below zero. I would hurry out of bed and turn up the oil stoves. I knew that I must get the fires going in the Chapel, both in the oil stove and the coal stove. At 8:00 o'clock I might be having my morning coffee, some fresh bread and jam. Then I began going through my sermon which I had prepared earlier in the week. I would make one or two quick runs upstairs to see how the fires were getting along. Then I'd start the oil stove in the classroom so it was warm for our Sunday School classes. At 10:30 I turned on my radio and listened to the sermon of Rev. Mjorud at Anchorage. Usually the interpreter would come in to go over the morning Scripture lesson. At 10:50 one of the Council members would put on a religious record in the Chapel for our prelude music. At 11:00 someone would ring the bell and our service would begin. Our Sunday School classes followed the services.

Lunch was usually prepared on the run, for that afternoon I wanted to visit a few of the isolated tuberculosis cases or other sick folk who were unable to attend the service. At 4:00 P. M. several of the young folks, or perhaps the men's chorus would come up to practice some songs for the evening services.

Our evening services were at 8:00 P. M. and young and older folks would gather. I was using the flannel-graph story from the book, "Pilgrim's Progress" and people seemed to like that very much. They loved to sing so on Sunday nights we had quite a bit of singing.

For the monthly women's meetings I also used flannel-graph pictures. I tried having these meetings on Saturday afternoon but I soon found that they brought along too many children and it was very noisy. So we changed our meetings to Friday afternoon when many of these children were in school. The children were disappointed to miss the cake or cookies which I served. Friday was much better for that left my Saturday free to prepare for the busy Sunday.

At our meetings the women often sang their Eskimo songs. I enjoyed hearing them for they seemed to sing those songs with so much more feeling and understanding than the English hymns. That wasn't really strange, since many of the women could speak very little English.

Once a week before choir practice we had adult Bible Class. We had some very good voices and they could sing all four parts. I had to play the organ so I could do very little leading. I often thought what a wonderful choir this could be if they could have a real director. They loved to sing so much that they all came, even in cold or stormy weather.

One of the Council members led our mid-week service, usually in the Eskimo language. Each service included volunter testimony and prayer. I played the organ for the singing and was happy just to sit back and listen. The congregation at Shishmaref was very strong and they loved to worship together, — as long as they could sing their beloved hymns and songs.

Every day after school a group of children would come up for an hour's Bible or catechism study then enjoy a short period of games. We had been given several kinds of table games and the young people enjoyed them. I usually stayed right in the room with them during this period in order to keep them from getting too noisy.

Our men's group met once a month in the evenings, and they loved to meet together. They would play some of these games, look at magazines, play the record player or enjoy a game of miniature shuffle board. Then we would have refreshments,-- usually a doughnut, cookie or cupcake for each one, with some coffee or tea. While they were at the table we had our devotions and prayer.

It was hard to find a time when all of our orchestra members could come. There were guitars, mandolins, a few ukeleles and even one or two violin players. By this time I usually stuck to the mandolin, to help carry the melody and sing along, too. Then others could follow the rhythm better and sing at the same time. Our orchestra included men, boys and girls and occasionally I enjoyed playing with them. It may not always have been the best sounding music, but they enjoyed it. It was an outlet and pastime for them, at practice or in their homes.

### CHRISTMAS AT SHISHMAREF

Christmas parties started at least two weeks before Christmas! It seemed early but it would be impossible to prepare for all the events in just one week. To practice for the program, prepare lessons, do the baking, the necessary cleaning, handle the mail, get the remainder of the packages wrapped and the regular work all in one week was impossible. But even if our first party was on the 12th of December, no one protested. The older boys and girls liked it, —we had "fourteen days of Christmas."

The table was set with a little Christmas tree in the center, candles, cup cakes, an orange for each one and a small surprise package at each place. But first we went through our Christmas parts. Then we sang, "O Christmas Tree." It was hard for them to keep their eyes and fingers off the table, but it was fun to see their enthusiasm when the time came to enjoy their packages and treats.

When the choir met on the following Friday night for a regular practice in the class room, they surely worked hard. A quartet and men's chorus also practiced. Then for the first time we used our new wire recorder to record their singing. While I was preparing coffee and re-heating some frozen doughnuts, they listened to the recording. They were certainly surprised, wondering how their singing could be recorded and heard immediately afterwards. We had felt the same way.

At 3:00 P.M. on December 18th the children in the two younger groups gathered for a little Christmas party. This time I had whipped up some jello and put some fruit into it. With this and cup cakes, candy and a little surprise gift for each and the games, they had a great time.

On the evening of December 21st the choir again met, but this time we practiced in the Chapel. Following the practice the boys decorated the Chapel and our brand new Christmas tree was set up. Instead of the usual dried branches stuck into a 2x4, as had been done in previous years, I had sent to Sears for a green artificial tree with electric lighted candles. It surely made a pretty sight. There were many "A h s" and "Akikas" (meaning "pretty") when the folks and children saw the lighted tree. To them it was a picture made real.

On the evening of December 23rd everybody gathered in the school house for the children's program. Mr. and Mrs. Bingham had done an excellent job of putting on seven different scenes of the Nativity. On the wall was wrapping paper painted blue to represent the night skies. A donkey had been carved from wall board and painted to help tell the story. The one who read the Gospel story could be easily heard with the amplifier. Children from the school took the parts, representing Joseph, Mary and their journey to Bethlehem, the Shepherds and the Wise Men. As the story unfolded carols were sung with music on the psaltery in between. This was all very beautiful and something new to the village folks. Mr. and Mrs. Bingham were certainly to be commended for this presentation of the Christmas Story.

On Christmas Eve we all gathered in the Chapel. Here I used the strip film called "Holy Child" and as each scene was flashed on the screen, various children or groups of children told the story in scripture, verse or song. The Choir sang a beautiful number called, "Wonderful Star." Then there was a song by the men's chorus, and two women sang "Silent Night" in the Eskimo language. Then after more songs by the children, and two numbers by the orchestra, the audience sang songs as words appeared on the screen.

At various intervals the Christmas tree lights and a lighted star were put on. We closed by singing "O Christmas Tree," then gifts and candy were passed. It was hard for the children to wait to open their packages, but they did this in their homes afterwards, with their friends. It was so much fun watching their excited and beaming faces as they received the gifts. When the service was over and the people had gone home, the Binghams joined me downstairs in opening their gifts and we had a little snack before they went home. It was a lovely Christmas Eve.

During the night a storm came up and I wondered if there would be any service on Christmas Day. However, it seemed to calm down before morning, but some families found their chimneys down the next morning. That time of year it was usually dark so I was glad my motor man came over at 10:30 A. M. to start the motor for our lights. But that day he had trouble starting the motor, so he told me that we would have to use the lamps. That meant a grand scramble to fill and pump up the gas lights and lanterns. I was just trying to find hooks and nails to hang them up when on came the lights! Although our service was slightly delayed, we had a nice Christmas service, with singing by the choir and various other groups. Our Christmas offering of $58.56 went to Foreign Missions. I thought this was very good at that time for many of the people received welfare aid, or A. D. C. or old-age pensions. A few had earned money through trading to give for this special offering.

Between Christmas and New Year, the Village Council put on various kinds of races and indoor sports. But the first day was dampened by a terrific south storm that had come on during the early morning hours. The ocean had risen, broken up the ice, washing out one of the boats and smashing others. Other boats were covered by the ice and water. Losing their boats was a great loss to the Eskimo as they are dependent on them in the early spring for fishing, seal hunting and the walrus catch. Now a great deal of repair work must be done when the warmer weather came.

Rev. Hegland came up shortly after New Year and conducted our New Year's services and the Communion service.

In February we borrowed the film, "King of Kings," which I showed one evening. This made quite an impression on them, and perhaps brought out things they had not thought of before. I had various Bible film strips which I used from time to time. Sometimes we ordered films from Anchorage. We had to rent these, so I placed a little box at the entrance so anyone who wanted to donate toward this cost could put an offering in this box. I had an 8mm film called "Passion Play" which I had used at Igloo. I used this during Easter, together with music on the record player.

During March Mrs. Hegland became ill and had to go to Seattle for treatment. This made it rather hard for Rev. Hegland at Teller. Once when he came up with the children, I asked him to leave them here for a few days, and he did. So for about a week I had a jolly household.

**THE ESKIMO COOK BOOK**

One day Mrs. Bingham asked if I would mimeograph the little Eskimo Cook Book that the school children had prepared. They had made their first copies on the mimeograph while the Hartjes were there. It now needed to be revised and another edition made. This was quite a job, but an interesting project. When the Alaska Crippled Children's organization in Anchorage saw it they liked it and bought the rights to it. Many copies were sold and the school did get some royalties. This was used to buy a projector, later a record player and a few other things. I thought this was a very fine thing, for now we could use various educational films or travelogues. Every Friday evening we showed a film or two and almost the whole village came.

Then we received the sad news that Mr. and Mrs. Bingham were to be transferred up north and would be leaving us at the close of the school term. The Eskimos did not like this very well, nor did I, but we didn't have much say about it. On the 23rd of June we saw them take off for Fairbanks on their way to the States for the summer. In August on their way to their next school at Kivalina, they stopped off and stayed with me for a few days. The new teachers for our school had arrived, but their quarters were too small to welcome them and I had more room.

**SPRINGTIME**

Springtime activities were quite different at Shishmaref than at Igloo or Teller. We had a great view from the tower and enjoyed watching the men and boys as they got ready to go on their oogruk (sea lion) hunts. They took many things with them for they never knew what might come up. The ocean ice usually froze up from eight to ten miles out. They would then go out to the edge of the ice by dog team and do their hunting among the ice floes, sometimes using a kayak to bring in the seal. If the ice left the beach, they used only their skin-boats together with their kayaks.

## DANGER ON THE ICE

That spring I leavned how dangerous life can be in the Arctic. Some men had gone out with the dog teams to the edge of the ice where there were many ice-floes from the north, —some broken off and piled up along the edge. Suddenly the wind changed and a heavy fog rolled in. They hurried to their sleds and were about to start home when they realized that the ice was moving. They knew that the ice had suddenly broken off from the beach and they could not see where to go. So now they were stranded on the floating ice. Their families at home realized what had happened and became very much concerned. The teachers wired Nome and they called the Rescue Squadron from Fairbanks who tried to get in and find them. But the fog was too heavy and they had to return. However, they returned the next day and just as they were flying in the fog lifted. Then the wind changed and began pushing the ice back to shore at various points. The Rescue Squadron found the men, dropped them some food, then directed them to the closest beach. They all got home safely, thankful for their safe return. Life here can be very exciting.

I often took a walk down along the beach with my camera in hand. One day I saw some of the men returning with their boat and watched them unload thirteen oogruk and seven seal! This made a lot of work for the women during the early and late hours of that day. I would find them busy with the seal or oogruk, cutting the skin and blubber off at the same time, then separating the blubber from the skin and cutting it in two or three inch strips. This was put in containers or seal pokes and later rendered for seal oil, so necessary for the Eskimo diet. The meat would also be cut up and hung on racks for drying. The remainder of the seal or oogruk was used for dog-feed. The valuable skins were then cleaned, washed and stretched on frames or fastened with pegs in the ground for drying. From these skins they made parkas, fur pants, mittens, slippers or mukluks (Eskimo shoes) either for themselves or to trade at the store. The oogruk, which has a rather heavy skin, was very often used for the bottom of mukluks.

## SKILLED SEWERS

From the reindeer sinew the women would make their thread used in the skin-sewing. Sometimes the Eskimos made seal pokes in which to store the dried meat, blubber, berries, leaves or even certain kinds of flowers that they picked. To make a seal poke, they must take everything out through the head portion, then turn the skin, clean off all the blubber, wash the seal skin on both sides, which is now like a bag. Then they blow up the seal skin, flippers and all, through the head opening. Many times I have watched them do it and still think it is quite a feat. I can't even blow up a ballon, to say nothing of blowing up a seal poke. A piece of string or sinew is wound around the opening and it is placed to dry. This is called a "seal poke." When dry it is filled with whatever is to be stored away. Sometimes I have seen the women place up to eight pokes into a big hole cut into the ground. Even during the summer the ground is usually frozen about fourteen inches below the surface. When covered over with boards and moss this acts as a deep freeze. Who invented the deep freeze, the Eskimo or white man?

One day I saw a little boy with several ducks dig a hole in the ground and place them in it. They had too many to use at this time, so he put some away to use later.

### FINDING A WALRUS

I saw one man busy scraping a walrus skin which he had procured from a dead walrus found on the beach. He knew he could use this skin for many things. His oomiak (boat) had been damaged in the terrific winter storm and needed repairs. He would use some of the skin for a covering for his boat and to make rope to use for his boat or his sled. The men used their boats to go to the mainland or up the Serpentine River for fishing or game hunting. So a walrus skin was a valuable find.

As the snow disappeared and the weather became warmer, we looked forward to some rain. Our drinking water made from the lake ice would soon be gone. Many times, in order to save on the ice stored in my ice house, I would go out to a fresh snowbank and fill my boiler or tubs with snow. That is what the Eskimos used most of the time. The ocean water was too salty. But before the rains came, I would get one of the boys to help me clean out all the water barrels and troughs leading to the roof. I collected many barrels of water in this way. Later on, a tin roof was put on instead of the malthoid paper and then we had very good water.

As the snow disappeared, I enjoyed looking down the street from the Mission to see the children playing on the dry spots on the ground. Here and there I could see the children playing marbles on the path. In front of the school I saw them playing croquet. This game was new and was one thing they bought from money received from the sale of their cookbooks. The school had even ordered two bicycles, but these did not last very long. Everybody wanted to use them on the beach or on a path, and they were soon worn out.

When it was warmer the children would try out their pet dogs, hooking them to their home-made sleds. When the snow disappeared the children could see berries that had been frozen beneath the snow. The children liked to pick these berries. The warm sunny days would soon bring out a variety of wild flowers. Then the little girls would bring me bouquets, knowing that I would be pleased and give them a piece of candy or a cookie. I soon had to stop this or I would have flowers all over the place.

## A PUZZLING PARADE

One day I wondered what was going on when I saw women and men walking by with their shovels on their shoulders. I had no idea what they were doing. Later I found out that they were going out to the end of the island where many hundreds of years earlier there had been an old Eskimo village. For many years it had been buried under the sand. As it thawed out in the spring, they would dig down very carefully. Sometimes they would find some valuable ivory pieces, ivory carvings or things made from bone. Some of the pieces, when deciphered, told a real story concerning the early life of the Eskimo, Of course these things could be very valuable.

As soon as it was warm enough I fixed up the little garden in the green-house and also the window box in the kitchen. I hoped that I might have a green thumb like the missionary wives often had, before I came there. Spring also meant it was time to clean house. I often asked one or two of the girls to come up to help me with that, especially cleaning the Chapel. The floor there was quite large and each spring it needed a good coat of varnish.

I wondered what could be planned for a Fourth of July celebration. Then I decided to make some popcorn and put it into bags with a little candy and a cookie for each one. I showed some of my old movies. But by July, many native families were already camping up the coast, so not everyone was there for the celebration.

## A FLIGHT TO LOST RIVER

One July day I had a pleasant surprise. Rev. Hegland flew in and invited me to go with him to Lost River. That was something I had been wanting to do for some time. I had heard much about Lost River, the only tin mine in North America and it was then operating all the year round. They also said it was the windiest place in Alaska. To go there in the winter was quite a problem for there were frequent storms.

We struck a beautiful day and I enjoyed the trip. Many of our Eskimo men had found work there, and this was a wonderful experience for them. We wondered about the future of the mine operation, and hoped that we might establish a church there.

The next day we flew back to Nome. Here we met many of our people who had moved there from villages where we had worked. We hoped that a Church could be built there and definite work done. Starting a congregation for Nome had long been a matter of great prayer and our highest priority.

Coming back I stayed at Teller for a couple of days, visiting with old friends and the Heglands. I was happy that Mrs. Hegland was home again and apparently quite well, after her long siege of illness. She still had to be careful and not overwork, but she is such a cheerful and happy person that it was good to be with her.

Coming back in the plane, I could see where our Eskimos were camping on the island. At this time of the year most of our families were out fishing, living in tents, —

some on the lagoon side and others on the highlands at the end of the island. Although I continued to conduct services every Sunday morning and on Wednesday evenings, the audience would be somewhat smaller. Perhaps that was because of the distance, or they had to concentrate on hunting and fishing. When the fish were running everyone was busy! From the middle of August to the first part of September, there would be almost a complete exodus. After fishing, everyone went inland for berry picking and more fishing. Usually they returned with barrels of blueberries or pokes filled with salmon berries. They also picked moss berries (blackberries) and cranberries if the season was right for them. Each year that might vary.

### NOREEN PAULSON COMES TO TELLER

Late in August I received a letter from Mrs. Hegland saying the Rev. Lee and his family had left Teller Mission and that Miss Noreen Paulson, a parish worker from Mankato, Minnesota was coming to help at Teller Mission. That was good news. Then in the same letter I received a letter from Rev. Hegland who described his survey trip down into the Kenai Peninsula. He said that he was bringing two carpenters back with him from Fairbanks. They would finish the Chapel at Teller Mission and do some other jobs. He also told me that he would be up to Shishmaref to get me on September 1st. He wanted me to go back to Teller Mission and cook for the carpenters. This proved to be an interesting change, though it was a bit strenuous. While I was there, I also did some cleaning and painting at the Mission so all would be ready for our new worker, Miss Paulson. The carpenters stayed from Sunday to Thursday, working full days and into the night. They came as volunteer workers and we appreciated their help. Then Rev. Hegland flew them back to Fairbanks. It had been an unsual experience for them to see the Mission work.

Miss Paulson arrived on September 9th and was installed that evening. Rev. Hegland, Miss Paulson and I then went over to help complete the painting at Teller Mission. Then on Friday, September 12th, Rev. Hegland took Miss Paulson and me up to Shishmaref. Here I told her about our various activities, especially caring for the Mission boxes, opening, sorting, wrapping Christmas presents. Then preparing the family boxes from any extra clothing.

People had been so generous that we had extra clothing to distribute. One day we had the big girls come over and pick out coats for themselves. The next day I asked the women to come, then when classes were out, the school girls came and did the same thing. We had received so many fine clothes that I was amazed at the generosity of the people.

Miss Paulson stayed with me for about two weeks, and was excited to be introduced to a new and interesting life. She also attended some of our meetings and met some of our Eskimo folks in the village. Then she returned to her post at Teller Mission.

Our new teachers, Mr. and Mrs. Derringer, had arrived and were busy getting acquainted, putting away their supplies and getting settled. As yet I had hardly seen them, but after Miss Paulson left I decided to go down and get acquainted. Mrs. Derringer was to be in charge of the school and her husband was to help her. Usually it was the other way, but Mrs. Derringer seemed to be the experienced teacher, having taught Indian children in the States.

## THE NEXT CHRISTMAS — 1953-54

Our Christmas preparations and activities this year were much the same as last year. However, the teachers were not prepared to put on the same kind of a program that the Binghams had put on. They wanted more of a Santa Claus program and wanted it on Christmas Eve. That posed a bit of a problem for the Mission had always had their program that night. But after the Church and Village Council conferred with them, Christmas Eve was reserved for us.

We had some excitement, too, for one Sunday morning just before Christmas I had built a fire in the large pot-bellied stove. Being cold and windy, a pretty good fire was going, and soon the stove was red hot. Then I discovered that a small crack in the stove had suddenly gotten considerably larger, I became frightened for fear the stove might buckle and start a real fire. I called some of the men who watched it during the service. We did not have services that evening and the next day they replaced the stove with a smaller one. This, of course, did not give as much heat so we had to also fire up the little stove in the front. The next year we got a double oil-burning stove, and what a relief that was. The men who put it in for me did a good job. Now I could start a fire in the evening, leave it on low, and in the morning it was fairly warm.

## FLU HITS AGAIN

Shortly after Christmas we again had quite a flu epidemic, resulting in a few deaths. One of the men, Carson Tingook, passed away. He had been a staunch worker in our Church and also in the village. He had been in charge of the cooperative store for some time. He was quite crippled and had a chest and back defect. I do not know what had caused it, but the flu was too much for him and he went very quickly. Although I was called upon for medical help at times, I did not have as much to do with it at Shishmaref. The government and Miss Keene, the traveling nurse, preferred that the teacher and a native helper take that responsibility. Sometimes it resulted in a little tension as the Eskimos would like to ask me for help and, in emergencies, often did. However, if they had a bad tooth and Miss Keene was not there, they would be right up, knocking on my door. I would get out my pliers and novocaine and do the job.

One morning a big and husky man came to me, saying he had a tooth which pained him very much and wanted me to pull it out. I looked at it and really didn't think it was necessary. I put my forcep on it but just couldn't budge it. I was afraid I might break it as I had done when trying to pull one for Rev. Klyve at Teller. So I told this Eskimo I couldn't do it. All he said was, "That's okay." The next day he came to me and said, "No more toothache!" So I figured I had jerked a nerve loose or killed it. I don't know which.

### SHISHMAREF CIVIL DEFENSE

Walter Nayopuk was the first director of the Civil Defense program at Shishmaref. He had been in the army during the last war and was very active and a leader in the village. Later he had charge of the welfare program, was the secretary for the Lighterage Company when it was organized and recently he started a store of his own. Since he did, others have taken over the other positions.

He wrote a very interesting article in the little school paper telling about the National Defense program at that time:

*"Throughout Alaska and United States, Civil Defense organizations have been authorized by Territorial and Federal government, so that all civilians will be prepared to protect themselves and their property, in the event of a national emergency. In isolated villages such as Shishmaref, there are Alaska National Guard companies, men and boys who are assigned to certain defense duties in their immediate areas will assist if there be fire, floods and other emergencies. Civilians must assume certain duties and fulfill them should emergency become necessary. Shishmaref is divided into two defense zones — The East Area and the West Area. The Federal school house is the center and dividing point."*

*"The different officers were given duties, such as reporting immediately to the radio operator anything unusual in the air or on the water and listening for the Shishmaref alarm, which would be the rapid ringing of the school bell.*

From this we see that the village was organized to report anything unexpected that might come up. The National Guard men also had training meetings on procedures, exercises and instructions. These men were paid by the government and were quite proud to be members. They were given special uniforms, guns and ammunition and a separate building had been put up for them to use.

### AN ESKIMO CELEBRATION

One day William Allockeok came home with two wolverines and Ray Ningeolook with one. Wolverine is considered a very valuable catch as they use the skins for ruffs around the parka hoods. Due to the vacuum inside the hair, this kind of fur does not frost like others. When an unusual catch was made, their custom was for everyone to celebrate. Now they had three reasons!

At 5:00 P.M. William Allocheok's house was full of guests enjoying some fruit, cookies and tea. At Ray Ningeulook's house there was reindeer meat and soup, as well as cooked ptarmigan and tea. Then in the evening everyone in the village gathered in the guard house for Eskimo dancing and fun. At Shishmaref the people knew how to share their good fortune.

This winter the hunting seemed to be unusually good. Later in the spring John Kiyutelluk shot a polar bear, tracking it out on the ice with his dog team. His first shot did not kill it but after three or four shots, the bear fell. He then skinned it and cut it into pieces. It was too large for him to take all of it home at the same time, so he returned the next day for the rest. When a bear is shot the natives usually share with the rest of the village. So that night there was another celebration. I was given a piece, so I invited Mr. and Mrs. Derringer for a roast bear dinner. This was their first taste of bear and they seemed to enjoy it very much.

In the early days the Eskimos used spears and bows when hunting seal and other game. It really must have seemed strange for the older men to see how easy hunting was for the younger men after guns were available. It is the same with their motor boats. In 1926 when I came to Alaska they used kayaks. We did see some sail boats on the lakes or rivers. Later when motors were available, very soon all of the natives had motors of various makes. At first some did not know how to take care of them or repair them, but they learned very quickly. The natives were kind to me and always checked my little boat so the motor ran smoothly.

When spring came I could look out in the early morning and see the natives fishing on the ice. Men, women and even children were out there on the ice, hooking fish — smelt, tomcod, flounders, or even little crabs.

## A SPECIAL "THANK YOU" PARTY

We had such dependable, dedicated leaders at Shishmaref I wanted to show my appreciation for their faithful services. So I had a little party at home for the Sunday School teachers and Council members and their wives. When the day came it was cold and stormy but that did not them keep from coming. We played some games and had various contests with prizes. But they enjoyed most the "one-man show." Each person took a slip of paper from the basket describing some stunt they had to do. It was something silly; sing a song; perform an Eskimo dance; tell a story or a joke, play the drum; crow like a rooster; make a sound like a cat; count up to ten in Eskimo; whistle a tune; shake hands with someone across the room, or comb someone's hair. With twenty-two people it became quite a circus and everyone had a good laugh. Then I served refreshments, —sandwiches, dill pickles, cookies, prune upside-down cake and coffee. There was a small gift for each one, then we had devotions and closed with prayer. As they left everyone agreed it was a happy evening.

## AN ESKIMO WEDDING

Every once in a while wedding bells would ring. The young gentleman would usually come in the evening, announce his plans, and then, as marriage commissioner, I would help them fill out the necessary papers. Three days later he would bring his girl friend and witnesses and I would conduct the marriage ceremony. Most couples wanted a private wedding, — usually in the evening. Rarely did they have any visitors with them. After the marriage, I usually took a picture of the couple, then served coffee and a special cake made for the occasion. I usually had a gift — a blanket or quilt, with a pair of pillow cases and possibly a towel or two, wrapped and ready to give the wedding couple with my congratulations. Afterwards they would go to their parents' or friends' homes for some feasting and celebrating .

## A Tragic Flight

Early that spring we had a tragic incident in the village. A plane from Kotzebue flew in and landed in a slight snowstorm. Catherine Moses, daughter of James and Bessie, was going to Deering to stay with her grandmother who was ill and needed help. The weather didn't look very good when the plane left, about 1:30 P.M. I believe that the pilot expected clear weather a few miles from Shishmaref. The natives said later they heard a plane at different times that afternoon, but the last time anyone heard it was about 5:30 P. M.

The next morning Kotzebue called to ask about the plane which had not returned as scheduled. From the roof-top with a spy glass, someone thought they saw a dark object some distance up the coast. Some of the men with dog-teams went up to investigate and there they found the plane with the pilot and Catherine killed. The pilot must have flown around and around, trying to see enough to land in the snowstorm. He may have been trying to land when he hit the bank. The ground was white with snow and he was unable to see through the falling snow. Another plane came from Kotzebue to remove the bodies from the wreckage and to take the pilot's body to Kotzebue. Catherine's frozen body was brought to the Mission and prepared for burial. It was a sad funeral. I remembered that Catherine had recently memorized the Twenty-Third Psalm and had underlined it and other verses in her Testament. Her mother found it in her belongings and kept it as a treasure in her memory. We were sure that Catherine was in God's hands. Later on, Bessie and James Moses made a trip to Deering by dog team to visit Bessie's mother and see how she was getting along.

## The Days Get Longer

During the month of May the children would begin to get very restless. The days were lengthening and soon there would be the 24-hours of daylight. It was getting warmer and the snow was beginning to melt. At this time I often took different Bible groups out for a picnic on the snow. They loved that, and I enjoyed getting out. Except for going out to make visits, I felt I had been staying inside too much. So all of us enjoyed getting out in the fresh air.

## Mice are worth a Penny!

One day I noticed that the little mice were coming out of the snow, and many were around the Mission building. Melvin Olanna, one of our little boys living close to the Mission, came over and offered to trap some of them. I was so pleased that I said I would give him a penny for every mouse he caught. This suited him fine and he got busy. I don't remember how many pennies I gave him, but he must have done a good job. I didn't see any more mice around the Mission.

## THANKING OUR FRIENDS

"Eskimo Land" was a little paper I would mimeograph and send out from time to time. I wanted to tell people what we were doing up in far off Shishmaref and thank our friends for sending those wonderful Mission boxes. Sometimes I asked various individuals to write a letter or story to put in our paper. Here is one of these stories:

*"My name is Flora Eningowuk. I have been resting in bed at home for approximately eight and a half months. I tried my best to do what the nurse had advise for me. My mother is taking good care of me. I spend some of my time reading, knitting, writing and sometimes doing a little bead-work, as well as memorizing the catechism which I recite when Miss Frost, our missionary, comes over to visit me. It's my favorite subject, because I didn't seem to have the opportunity to memorize it or the Bible verses while I was at White Mountain School. I hope to be confirmed this spring. May God help me get well. Flora Eningowuk."*

Flora was bedridden with tuberculosis, which became active while she was away at school. When I visited her, I was interested to observe how she passed the time. She didn't lie idle but busied herself in various ways. On the table by her bed was a typewriter which the teacher had brought over. Then there were beads, sewing, yarn, books, her Bible, Sunday School papers, writing paper and, on the wall, her guitar. She was later pronounced well and the tuberculosis arrested. Rev. Hegland confirmed Flora and later he performed her wedding ceremony.

## MY TRIP TO SOUTHEAST ALASKA

I had mentioned to Rev. Hegland at one time that I would like to go to Juneau, Haines and Sitka, to see how our students at Mt. Edgecumbe were doing. Rev. Hegland was going to Seattle in May so plans were made for me to travel with him part way. On the 19th of May he was coming to get me. I knew his plane was already on wheels since the snow had already melted so rapidly I feared he would not be able to land up here as snow conditions up here called for skis. So I wired that I thought we had better cancel the trip. But the Heglands thought it would be too bad for me to miss out on this trip. There was a small place close to their beach at Teller with snow and ice, so he switched back from wheels to skis. I was surprised when he landed on our snow field out on the ocean ice. So we took off and before long landed on their little snowfield at Teller. I stayed in Teller from the 19th until the 23rd, when we left for Fairbanks. Rev. Hegland was such a good pilot, that I never feared flying with him. He always had his plane in tip-top condition, was very careful and never took any risks. How wonderful to have this opportunity. We arrived in Fairbanks the next day and were guests at the home of Rev. and Mrs. John Maakestad, attending their services in the morning. After the service, Mrs. Maakestad had a delicious luncheon for a friend who was leaving for the States. In the evening their Luther League gave a program and put on a play called, "How the Story Goes." We enjoyed our visit for Rev. and Mrs. Maakestad were always gracious hosts.

From Fairbanks we left for Palmer, where Rev. Hegland would leave his plane for an overhaul. The mechanic flew us to Anchorage where we visited Pastor and Mrs. Mjoruds. Then Rev. Hegland flew by commercial plane to Seattle. Mrs. Mjorud drove me around to visit some of our Eskimos now living in Anchorage. I was happy to see them but disappointed in one home. The father was intoxicated and I felt the mother had also been drinking. When I came in they were quite surprised to see me. The mother, who had been at our Eskimo orphanage when I was there, came running to me and put her arms around me. She seemed to be ashamed. I did try to talk to them, but right then there was little I could do. Rev. Mjorud told me later that he had been trying to help them in various ways, financially and otherwise. Just why that happens is a puzzle. I feel Satan is surely busy everywhere.

From Anchorage I went to Juneau where our good friends, Dr. and Mrs. Rude, lived. Dr. Rude has a beautiful boat and he took Mrs. Rude and me for a lovely ride around the islands. We saw the gorgeous Mendenhall Glacier. One evening I spoke in the Lutheran Church, showing slides of our Mission.

### CHECKING OUT SITKA

On June 1st I flew to Sitka in a pontoon plane. It felt strange to be taking off from the water and then landing in the water again, with the water splashing all around us each time. Flying in a Gruman Goose was a real adventure. Pastor Knebel's wife met me at the dock.

The next day the Knebels took me over to Mt. Edgecumbe Government School to see our students. I also visited the sanitarium where some of our Eskimo folks were patients. I was glad to see them all and they seemed pleased I had come. In the evening I showed slides to a group of women at the Lutheran Church. Clara Eyuk, one of our Igloo girls, who had graduated that spring, came and asked if she could bring her boy friend over to meet me. He was working at the school and she was proud of him. He seemed to be a very nice man, so I was happy for her. Rev. Knebel was to marry them a little later when the man could get a job at Bethel, Alaska.

While I was at Sitka I saw many of the possibilities for our students and for work that I might be able to do. Pastor and Mrs. Knebel had been very kind to our Eskimo folks, making sacrifices to help the students and patients at the school and the hospital. But just caring for the congregation kept them busy and they had little time to visit the students at the school and patients in the sanitarium. Also some folks from the north were living in the Pioneer Home very near the Church. For some time we had been hoping that more of our students from the Mission might complete the high school program and get their diploma then do additional study. I wondered what was the best way to acomplish this goal. Should I move to Sitka, or should we work with the Swedish Covenant Church and establish a closer school at Unalakleet? We did not know so we just kept praying.

From Sitka I went back to Juneau then up to Haines to visit Mrs. Edna Peterson, the teacher whose marriage ceremony I had performed at Igloo. Mr. Peterson was not at home for he was working on the road some distance away. But I had a wonderful visit with Edna and her two cute little girls and some of her friends. She also drove me out so I could see the beautiful countryside. A week later I returned to Juneau and then flew on to Palmer to meet Rev. Hegland. He had been checking his plane and it was ready. On the 18th we were back in Fairbanks and flew on to Teller the next day. It was too foggy to land at Teller so we flew on to the Tweet Mining Camp where we had an interesting visit with the miners. We managed to get into Teller the next day but could not land at Shishmaref until the 26th. Rev. Hegland made three different attempts before we could get in. Once as we flew right over Shishmaref we could hear people's voices and dogs barking, but the fog was too thick to land.

We finally made it and this had been a memorable trip. I can't begin to describe the beautiful views I had of Alaska. First flying over the Nulata Hills, then where the Yukon and Tanana Rivers meet, to Fairbanks, past Mount McKinley, over the Matanuska Valley and into Anchorage. On the trip to Juneau the mountains and glaciers were beautiful. So were the snow-capped mountains and islands around Sitka, located on Baronoff Island. One cannot really imagine the wonderful scenery and sights of Southeast Alaska until you visit there. For this trip I was thankful to Rev. Hegland and the L.D.R., who bought and sponsored the plane for the Alaska Mission.

## SPRING CLEANING

The congregation at Shishmaref had wonderful leaders. While I was gone the Church Councilmen had led the services, even though this was the time for their spring seal hunting. The building at Shishmaref was excellent but quite large so now I had to get busy and do some cleaning. Miss Paulson came up and helped for a few days. My kitchen linoleum was a plain dark brown battleship linoleum. I was tired of it so Noreen painted a block design on it. From certain angles this did look a bit dizzy but it certainly broke the monotony. Some of the Eskimos asked. "Where did you get the new linoleum?" Two of the girls helped me clean the Chapel. Some of the boys worked outside for me, chopping wood for kindling, straightening the oil drums, and filling the ice barrels. I was very pleased when all of this work was done.

## THE DIOMEDERS

One day a Diomede skin boat with several passengers arrived. They reported that they had found a whale along the beach and had pulled it into the lagoon. As soon as the wind stopped and the lagoon was calm, almost the whole village went across to help carve it. Yes, that night there were strong smells of whale blubber as everyone feasted in the houses and tents. Some of the whale could not be used for eating but that was buried in the ground for future dog-feed. I do not know how the natives could judge whether it was good or not, —but they knew!

### "WHALE ON THE BEACH!"

Another time a large whale was spotted some distance out in the ocean, seemingly driven toward our beach by the wind and tide. The men who were working on the new school house were watching it very carefully. Suddenly I saw several of them rush down to the beach and use their ropes to anchor the whale until they could work on it in the evening. By winding a rope around it and turning it at the same time, the men pulled it up on land. Everyone, men, women, and children took hold of that rope. Then with long sharp knives, they cut through the skin and blubber, removing it in large pieces about two feet square and placing them on the ground up from the shore. Very soon all of that whale was cut into pieces and placed in piles so that each family got a share. Nothing was wasted, —even the sinew was carefully divided among the skin sewers. I had my camera and took pictures as that whale disappeared. I enjoyed seeing it and felt that it surely showed the true spirit of sharing. The people of Shishmaref always shared their bounty.

### GOOD NEWS AT NOME

I had just finished baking about fifty cupcakes and fifty drop cookies when Rev. Hegland and Sam Ailak flew in unexpectedly. Rev. Hegland wanted Sam to check our light plant, which was not working as it should. Rev. Hegland reported good news, —that the first services had been held in the quonset building in Nome. It now was set up with a Chapel in the front and small living quarters in the back. Last Sunday he had taken his wife along to Nome to attend the first services there. Eighty people came, so the Chapel was full and that day he had eight baptisms! This wonderful response made two things clear. First, a permanent worker was needed at Nome. Second, though the quonset hut was helping us get started, we needed a real Church building for a larger program. Next summer Interne Curtis Johnson and his wife Ruth came to Nome and were there for one year. With their help the Nome Mission started to moved ahead. They were followed by Rev. Thomas A. Knudsen and his wife. The Home Mission leaders then hired an architect to start making plans for a new church building at Nome. The whole Church began a funding effort they called "Dollars for Nome". Sunday School children brought their pennies for everyone was helping. This was another milestone of the Lutheran Church ministry with the Native congregations in Alaska. We had prayed earnestly for this and now the church was giving strong support.

### MOVING THE IGLOO CHAPEL TO LOST RIVER

Another major change was under way at Igloo. A new mission was to be started at Lost River, about 25 miles from Teller. The Tweet boys at Teller were going to move our Igloo Chapel and living quarters down to Lost River before the spring thaw.

Rev. Hegland had been giving valuable help. After they started, Rev. Hegland would fly to the work site on the ice, — where they were pulling the buildings with their tractors. If they had a breakdown, perhaps needed parts to make repairs, he would quickly fly to Nome, get the parts and fly them back. That way there were no major delays. The plan worked! They were able to get the buildings off the ocean-ice onto the beach before the ice started cracking. We gave thanks when we heard that the buildings were now in place in Lost River. That Chapel could tell quite a story! Those first Christians at Igloo really had faith. They built that Chapel before they had a pastor. Now at Lost River the old Chapel would again ring with hymns of praise and thanksgiving.

Many of our people from Igloo, Teller, Shishmaref and Wales had moved to Lost River to work in the tin mine. I was very happy when I heard that Rev. A. Tastad, from Lynwood, Washington was coming in November to serve as pastor there.

Shortly after Rev. Tastad arrived, Rev. Hegland brought him up to Shishmaref for a short conference to discuss future possibilities and needs. When he came up on August 27th he said, "I want you to see your Igloo buildings in their new setting." I think he said *my buildings* because after living in them for sixteen years I almost felt they belonged to me. We had hoped work at the mine would continue and Lost River might become a permanent village. But this did not happen for the price of tin dropped later and the mine was closed. But the government feels that there still is a possibility it may reopen.

On August 28th Miss Paulson surprised me by giving a birthday party for me at Teller Mission. Four of the white ladies from Teller Town and the teacher at Teller Mission came, and we had a very cozy time. As soon as we entered Noreen proudly took us around the old Mission building to show us all the redecorating and painting that had been done. Then she served a delicious ham dinner, fit for a king, then a birthday cake. Later we saw some picture slides Noreen had taken at the Mission.

The fog was so heavy my trip to Lost River had to be postponed for a few days. Then Rev. Hegland received a message asking him to bring to Nome the boys who were going to Mt. Edgecumbe School. Finally we got to Lost River and it was surely fun seeing some of those Igloo buildings in a new location, in among these hills. Edna Eyuk, one of my Igloo girls, was married to a fine young man who had charge of the local store which the Tweets of Teller owned. The tasty lunch Edna made for us tasted very good. She had a neat clean-looking kitchen and bedroom in the back of the store building.

We got back to Teller from Lost River just in time, for there was another little storm brewing that delayed my return trip to Shishmaref. But that delay gave me a chance to spend a few days visiting the Teller folks.

## A NEW PROGRAM FOR YOUNG GIRLS

Back at Shishmaref one evening I called the larger school girls together and suggested we start an LDR group. I explained what that meant and some of the things we might do. A president, vice president and secretary were elected. Then we made some plans for future meetings and studies that we might have together. Looking back I believe I hoped to get closer to the girls and help them become a close fellowship like I had known when I was their age.

We did need something to help these young girls. Just a short time before, two of the older girls had delivered babies out of wedlock and this bothered me a great deal. I tried to talk to the girls, their parents and also the Church Council, but somehow it did not seem to make much of an impression. I had hoped to be able to reach these young girls some way. Our new group did have a few very fine meetings.

One day one mother sent a note down to me saying that one of the girls was not in school that day. The previous night she had been sleeping with a certain boy and was still at his home. "What shall I do?" I decided to go and find her, then talk to her. She was in his house but the boy was not there. This girl was quite easy to talk with and she told me that she intended to marry the boy. To her what she had done did not seem wrong. Then I asked her to send her boy friend down to the Mission when he came back, which she did. After we talked for a while, the date was set for their wedding. But not all problems were settled as easily as this one.

One evening two little girls came in and asked if they could stay for a little while. They looked frightened, so I asked what the trouble was. Their father was drunk and their mother wanted me to come over. I knew that I couldn't do very much as long as he was drunk, so I said I would wait until their father felt better.

One day Mr. Kelleher (traveling deputy) and another representative flew up on Alaska Airlines to see me. He wanted to see how they might get the fathers of two of these illegitimate children to support the mothers instead of their depending on welfare to care for them. Since neither of these men were in the village at that time, I don't believe they were very successful. Still I told them I thought this was a step in the right direction. It might make others who were promiscuous think more about what they were doing.

## BUSY FALL DAYS

Each fall we save time for opening Mission boxes, acknowledging the donors, beginning classes again, preparing for Thanksgiving. Then Christmas plans had to be made. Somehow I seemed busier than ever. That Fall there was considerable illness in the village. Our very fine interpreter, Roy Avessuk, became ill, was taken to Nome Hospital, and later was sent to Seattle. But when he returned I learned it was terminal cancer. We really missed him when he died.

One woman gave birth to a beautiful baby that died a few hours later due to internal bleeding. I had been present at the birth of many babies and whenever this happened I always felt badly. Each time I wondered what I should have done that I didn't do? I will never know. Perhaps there wasn't anything that could have been done. I was just a nurse, we had no clinic and we were many miles from any hospital.

## TIME FOR A CHECK-UP

With all of these various problems and the pressures of work, I developed a stomach condition. I was not feeling well and did not have my normal energy so I almost took the plane to Nome to see the doctor. But with Christmas so near and so many things to do, I knew that I would just have to wait. When I mentioned this in a letter to Noreen Paulson she told Rev. Hegland. As a result, shortly after Christmas both Rev. Hegland and Miss Paulson came up. He felt I should go soon to Nome for a check-up. He had brought Miss Paulson up to stay at Shishmaref while I went to Nome. I appreciated their concern so I agreed, packed my things, then Pastor Hegland flew me to Nome.

I must have been in Nome about ten days, staying at the quonset building. The doctor gave me various tests, but could not find anything particularly wrong. After a few days I was feeling fine again. When I think of it now, I know it was nothing else but a nervous stomach. I had been pushing myself too hard or possibly worrying too much. Being all alone at a station as large as Shishmaref had been a little more than I could master. Before there had always been a couple at the station.

However, while at Nome I did keep busy. I conducted services in the quonset building, showed some of my slides to the Eskimos, and visited old friends. Rev. and Mrs. Amundson, the Swedish Covenant pastor and family, were very kind to me. It was pretty cold staying at that metal quonset for the stoves did not heat it properly. One exceptionally cold night the Amundsons insisted I go over and stay with them. One evening I showed slides at their Church and attended midweek services. One morning Rev. Amundson was making a tape for a devotional service to be broadcast later that morning. He asked me to say a few words of greeting for he knew that some of our people in Nome and at Shishmaref would be listening. I enjoyed doing that and later learned that some of our people had listened to that program. Then Rev. Hegland flew me back to Shishmaref and brought Miss Paulson back to Teller.

## BITTER COLD BRINGS NEW PROBLEMS

I was glad to get back to Shishmaref but I found it had also been very cold up there. It was 40 degrees below zero my first night back and the next morning I discovered that the water tank in the shed had frozen solid. Alex Weyiouanna (my handy man) moved the water tank into the kitchen. The next night I kept the door open to the shed and slept in the living room where it was warmer. My wind charger also needed attention, for there was heavy snow and ice on it. Then I found that the burner on the kitchen stove had burnt out and had holes in it. Alex fixed that by putting in a new burner. At times the wind could cause other problems. During a terrific wind storm, the chimney would sometimes blow down or the malthoid roofing get loose. Fortunately, someone would come to help, usually without thought of pay.

About the middle of January Rev. Hegland brought Rev. Tastad up for a few days. While there he conducted worship services with holy communion and confirmed our young people. Then he visited various families who could not get to Church due to illness or the cold and gave them communion. While there he presided at a funeral service. If he had stayed longer, he might also have had a wedding, for soon after he left a couple came to be married.

## A CRISIS AT SHISHMAREF

One cold day one of the men came to tell me that one of our council men had been severely beaten in a drinking brawl then had gone outdoors. He was found lying in the snow, partially unconscious. It was very cold and if he had not been found in time he would have frozen to death. He had received some bad bruises and so I went to look at them. At that time I could not say very much to him for there were too many in the room. A little later I saw a young boy staggering down the street and knew then that someone had brought in liquor.

Things seemed to be piling up on me. This had seemed a good and peaceful village, but as I learned to know the villagers better, I was finding conditions which I did not know existed. It wasn't just drinking. There was gambling, adultery, slander and stealing. I became quite burdened with it all and wondered if I was to blame. I asked myself, "Hadn't I made it clear enough that these things did not belong in a Christian life? Was I taking too much for granted?" I went through a physical and spiritual battle and even wondered if I should give up and let someone else try. But God again seemed to speak to me. "I sent you here, speak the Words." The Church Council met and we talked about what had happened. We wondered if this man should still be a member of the Council. Perhaps they should talk to him. It was decided that I should talk to him first, and then they would decide.

When this man recovered he came to the Mission and we had a very good talk. I explained to him what the results might have been if he had died out on the ice, the results of such a sin to himself and others. What was his responsibility as a member of the Church Council? He said he had been thinking about it and realized his position with God and was very much ashamed. I referred him to Hebrews 7:25 and John 1:9. "If we confess our sins, he is faithful and just to forgive our sins and to cleanse us from all unrighteousness." We talked some more, then prayed together. According to the schedule, it was his turn to lead the next midweek service. What was he going to do about it? He said he wanted to confess his sin before the congregation, promise to abstain from liquor and ask forgiveness.

I realized that I had a great responsibility for my next Sunday and chose Galatians 5: for the text, speaking on the fruit of the spirit and the fruit of the flesh.

The condemnation that lay upon those who continue in their sins, and the difference between false peace and true peace. I spoke especially to the older folks, asking them if they wanted this to continue and to think of their children who were growing up. Here they were, most all going to Church and confessing to be Christians. Surely these things did not belong to a Christian life. Then I tried to show them what God says about it.

The following Sunday sermon was a sequel to this one, but I had also done considerable visiting in some of the homes. I don't know just how it happened, but the Holy Spirit was surely working in our midst. One young widowed mother was the first to make a confession. There was no prompting on my part but suddenly, after the message had been given at our midweek service, she got up with tears in her eyes, confessed her sins and asked for help. Then she knelt at the altar, praying most fervently. I wished that I could have understood her. She later explained what she had said. What happened was all so unexpected and so sincere. Then before I knew it others were doing the same thing, husbands with their wives and sometimes the children. Others started coming to me during the week and wanted to talk to me, confess and have prayer. I had not expected this but realized this was a time of renewal for all of us.

It was during this period at Shishmaref that Miss Arna Njaa, the National leader of the LDR, came to visit us. I told her what had been happening. She could see that it was not just an emotional revival, but a genuine, spiritual awakening. The people had become burdened with their sins and many knew that they were guilty and it was brought to light. In private they were confessing and asking forgiveness of one another for certain wrongs that had been kept secret.

I remember visiting one home. Here was a young girl (just married because she was pregnant) sitting in front of her grandfather and mother, weeping and talking to them. She had been disobedient in more ways than one and fallen into sin. Then each of them prayed.

This did not only touch actions. It touched inner attitudes. One mother said, " I have been so cross and mean to my children and the neighbors' children, too."

One by one the Church Council members confessed their sins, too. One of them said, "I would get up here and talk, but it didn't mean much because I didn't live according to it." Another said, "I have been trying to walk two roads, but now I'm going to walk only one."

## A NEW JOY AT EASTER

Easter was different that year. It was a Happy Easter in the Risen Lord. I was so glad to have had Miss Njaa with me the last week, to share some of the blessings and see that the many sacrifices and efforts and prayers made by the LDR, our Church and other folks had not been in vain. God was blessing us at Shishmaref.

I asked Miss Njaa to give the Easter message. She spoke of the Resurrection then tried to show them what belongs to the new life of a Christian. We happened to have a visitor from Nome. He felt that he had received a special message that he needed in his life and his work as a Council member of the Nome Lutheran Church.

Many things seemed to be changed, even the offering! After the morning services, the Council had counted the offering, and found it was almost twice as large as usual. I had invited the Council downstairs for a cup of coffee, some home-made-ice-cream and cake. Miss Njaa again spoke about their responsibility as spiritual leaders of their congregations. I was always very thankful to this group of men and the excellent leadership they gave in the Church.

### A THOUGHTFUL THANK YOU

That evening the Sunday School and choir presented an Easter program. At the close of the program Walter Nayokpuk (the interpreter) got up and spoke first in Eskimo and then addressed Miss Njaa. He said, "We know the folks in the States have Christmas parties in the summer in order to send presents to us for Christmas. Now we Eskimos want to have a Christmas party for you." He then pointed to a small tree that was on a little table up in front. "Each family has brought you a small gift and placed it on the table. We just want to say 'Thank you.' "

Of course, Miss Njaa was surprised and pleased. She thanked them. After the program we enjoyed some refreshments — cupcakes, popcorn balls and Kool-aid, served in the class room. That gave Miss Njaa another chance to visit with the Eskimos for she was leaving the next day. That was a memorable Easter at Shishmaref.

### EASTER JOY CONTINUES

The days that followed Easter were days of rejoicing and spiritual development. People showed their new stand in Christ in various ways. Some made public testimonies at our evening services; others wanted to sing certain songs that had special meaning to them, either as a solo or with someone. I was told there was no more gambling and drinking, —at least for the time being. If someone brought in liquor, it was immediately reported to the Council and they would do what they could to stop it. Many who had never taken part in prayer now prayed openly. The choir enrollment became twice as large. We had wonderful Bible classes. And how they sang!

I often found groups together, singing songs. I came into one home where one woman was interpreting and telling the Bible story we had studied in Sunday School. One day one mother asked if she could borrow my sermon notes and share them with her husband, for he was isolated at home with tuberculosis.

To me it was both a great joy and a challenge. I was thankful that God had given me the opportunity to serve at Shishmaref and that I had gone there. It certainly convinced me that my twenty-five years in Alaska had really been worthwhile. I was ashamed of some moments when I was discouraged, ready to give up. Now I was convinced that the only way was to trust and to follow God. "Stand still and see the salvation of the Lord" was God's command to His people of old. I knew, too, that the devil would be busy and that nothing would be perfect. But how good to know that God is ever present and will not let His own be lost. When Miss Njaa got back to Minneapolis she sent us several copies of the song, "I look not back." It became very precious to us all as we practiced and sang it again and again.

## A NEW SCHOOL HOUSE IN RECORD TIME

The month of July became a very busy and profitable month for the Eskimo. When the government boat "North Star" came they brought the lumber and supplies for the building of a new school house and teacherage. Mr. Hobson, an Eskimo from Point Barrow, came to be the foreman of the project. Sixteen men from the village were hired to work on the building. Some representatives from the A.N.S. Construction Bureau came from time to time. One day two doctors and a nurse from the Public Health Office arrived to look things over. Then some of our folks from Nome came back, possibly to see what was going on. The team worked hard, did a very good job and the school house was finished about October 1st. One of the inspectors who came said, "This was the first time a school house in Alaska had been built by only Eskimos and it had been completed in the shortest period of time." They had done a very good job and they were very proud.

## WE WELCOME THE JOHNSONS

On the 25th Mr. and Mrs. Curtis Johnson arrived from Fairbanks via Kotzebue to stay with me for several weeks. They were new to Alaska and I was supposed to orient them before they went to their new station at Nome. I was glad to have Mr. Johnson conduct our services and I am sure the Eskimos enjoyed the change.

We had received a new 16mm movie projector from the LDR and we used it often. Our first films were "Desert Sand" and "All That I Have." Everybody enjoyed the films. There was a box at the door and anyone who wanted to put in a donation toward films would slip something in. The LDR office sent us some very good films and occasionally we rented films from Anchorage, depending on how much money was in the little offering box on the wall.

Another day Alex came over to put in our new two-burner oil stove in the Chapel. A platform for the oil drum was made and fastened to the wall outside the Chapel, with a pipeline to the stove inside. Now we didn't need the little wood stove. In the evening we started the fire in that new stove and next morning it was warm and very comfortable. We could not have it too warm for most of the folks wore their parkas in church.

When our Delco motor was not working well one summer, Charlie Okpowruk offered to go over it. He had helped Rev. Dahl overhaul it, so he felt that he could do this. He did a good job and we had no more trouble. The Eskimo people were very capable. They easily learned many new things and quickly mastered new skills.

Our fall and winter season seemed to go very rapidly that year. I know there was much more enthusiasm and more help with various programs in the Church. Whenever something needed to be done, the Church Council men were always willing to do it. No wonder things went well at Shishmaref.

### STATION VISITS

One day in February Rev. Hegland came. He wanted to take me to Nome so I could visit the Johnsons and see how the work was progressing. A little house next to the quonset building had been bought and the Johnsons and their new-born baby boy were living there. It was good to see the program getting under way. They now had two services in the small quonset building. We surely did need a Church building. In the evening all tried to squeeze in to see some slides I had taken at our other stations. To my surprise they had also planned a little party in my honor, serving cake, baked by one of the Eskimo men, cookies baked by Mrs. Johnson, some Eskimo ice cream made by some of the women and then the conventional tea. Believe it or not, I had some Eskimo ice cream and enjoyed it, too. But it was dreadfully crowded in the quonset building. Some of the serving was done from inside the altar railing. Many of the children sat on the kneeling bench of the communion rail or on the floor. Despite being crowded, everybody enjoyed getting together.

Later I enjoyed visiting the homes of our Eskimo folks now living in Nome. Mr. Johnson walked around with me as I made these calls. It was quite cold but we managed very well. I was so happy to see how the people from our villages up north were now active members of this new congregation.

On Monday when Rev. Hegland returned he flew me to Lost River, where I spent one night. All our Eskimo folks got together in the old Igloo church building and I showed some of my movies there. Though they had seen many of them before they enjoyed seeing themselves in their earlier quarters which reminded them of the "good old days."

Following the evening meeting, Rev. Tastad invited all to come over to the class room near their living quarters. There I had a chance to visit with some more of my friends as we enjoyed a cup of cocoa and cupcakes which he had made. That night I slept in the same bedroom where I had slept many times before, when the buildings were at Igloo. It surely awakened many happy memories of my years at Igloo.

From Lost River Rev. Hegland dropped me off at Teller Mission where I visited Miss Paulson. Many changes had taken place here since I came up in 1926. Rev. Hegland had just finished putting in the electric wiring so I could again show some of my pictures. One evening one of the Eskimo boys showed some slides which he had taken. Then on Sunday morning I spoke to some who had been there when I first arrived on the Mission field. In the evening after the services, Miss Paulson served cakes and tea for everyone as we enjoyed another little get-together.

On Monday Rev. Hegland arrived to take me back to Shishmaref, but when we got within seven miles the fog was so heavy we could not see the skyline or the snow-covered ground below. We had to return to Teller, where I had another chance to visit with the Heglands and friends.

While at Teller Rev. Hegland received a message from Rev. Maakestad of Fairbanks. "I am coming to Nome on a certain day. Could Rev. Hegland meet me? I have decided to accept the call to Shishmaref." That would mean I would be leaving Shishmaref and now could make some plans for the following summer. After a short furlough in the states, I wanted to go to Sitka.

Rev. Hegland did meet him and we finally got to Shishmaref. But we again had bad weather, so Rev. Maakestad had to stay longer than he had planned. But this allowed him to get better acquainted with some of the people, learn more about the village and the general schedules. He even was able to speak to the congregation on Sunday. Then we had men's meeting one evening, quartet practice and the movie, "Hand of God," another evening. I believe he was quite elated about it all and was looking forward to coming back with his family during the summer.

## A BUSY SPRING

I started packing my trunks in April, sorting various things and cleaning at the same time. But I also had unexpected visitors. One day two Army Air Force men came to our village, preparing to set up a radar relay station. What excitement and what a sight we had, when one of the huge Air Force planes (C124) using parachutes dropped 8,000 lbs. of equipment. Two light plants (motors) weighing over 2,000 lbs. each were dropped in the same way. Then five men were sent to take care of the equipment. This was extremely interesting and new to us all. Of course, that resulted in extra activity in the village. But that location did not prove to be a logical place for the relay station. Better locations had been found. I believe the equipment was removed a year or two later.

We had a very fine Easter Day service with a great deal of singing in the morning and the evening. There was a strange feeling coming over me as I realized that this would be perhaps my last Easter at Shishmaref. Words cannot express my love for these people, their faithfulness and all they meant to me. How thankful I was for having had the opportunity of being here. It has indeed been a blessing to me, especially when I thought of the wonderful revival or rededication period we had just a year ago. I knew that I could never say, "Mission work does not pay," as some are tempted to say at times. I know that God has spoken to me in a special way and reprimanded me for times I had been discouraged.

Since many families would soon be going to their fishing camps, the Sunday School classes were closed May 8th and I conducted my last regular service on May 14th, 1955. In the evening we gathered again for a song service and devotions. I was very surprised at the close of that service. The parishioners had set up a table in front. On this the various families had placed a variety of gifts, some ivory carvings which they had made, beaded lapels, Eskimo dolls made from reindeer horn, artifacts, and other native treasures. Some had even placed an envelope with a small money gift in it. Walter Nayokpuk (our interpreter) gave a little talk of appreciation on their behalf, saying that although many of them had very little to give, they did want to be remembered in some way. They wanted to thank me for what I had done for them in various ways, and hoped to see me again, if not in this life, then in Heaven with God. I was touched by their kindness and would cherish their gifts.

While I would miss these wonderful people at Shishmaref, I knew that soon Pastor Maakestad and his family would be there and provide leadership. I was excited to be going to Sitka to work with our students studying there at the High School.

Two days later Rev. Hegland came to bring me to Nome, on my way back to the states. As we left, almost the whole village was standing on the field, waving farewell and singing "In the Sweet By and By."

While it was not easy to leave Shishmaref, I was looking forward to going to Sitka to work with the students at the school. But first I would enjoy a furlough.

**133**

# SITKA YEARS

I was looking forward to some visits back home, seeing my family and friends. That interesting summer passed very rapidly. My first stop after leaving Nome was Anchorage where I saw the movie "The Man Called Peter." It was a long time since I had seen a real movie and I surely enjoyed this one. The next day I left for Juneau and Sitka, where I spent two days visiting our students and the hospital patients. I also looked for an apartment for September but had no success. Rev. Knebel promised they would keep looking for one.

On May 24th I arrived in Seattle, then for some days I visited relatives, spoke a few places, and did some shopping. I spoke to a Women's Federation Meeting in Tacoma and was very surprised when the faculty at Pacific Lutheran College presented me with a Citation honoring my service in Alaska. That was very kind.

I arrived in Minneapolis on the 11th of June, attending an LDR meeting on the 12th while visiting my friend, Petra Bly in St. Paul. On the 15th I left for Austin, Minnesota where my step-mother and sister Esther were living. Next I visited with Gerhard and his family in Decorah, relatives in Spring Grove, Minnesota, and Rev. and Mrs. Dahle in Chester, Iowa. After some speaking engagements in North Dakota I attended the 50th Anniversary of Pingree Lutheran Congregation as one of the speakers. This was interesting as father had started the congregation while serving in Sheyenne, North Dakota. Rev. Hartje, then at Harvey, North Dakota, came and picked me up as I had several other speaking engagements not far away. Of course I had to visit Sheyenne, North Dakota where I had oodles of cousins on my mother's side. My own mother was buried there. The Church where I spoke and showed pictures was filled. In fact the people were standing in the hall and even outside. Many had come from nearby towns where father had also served or was known. That response was an inspiration to me.

## A BIG SURPRISE AT BIBLE CAMP

The LDR had made reservations for me at the Alexandria Bible Camp in July. Petra Bly, Hazel Richardson and Mrs. John Bly were also going, so I rode with them. I expected to be asked for a little talk or perhaps answer some questions about Alaska. Instead I had the surprise of my life. I went to the auditorium and the program started with singing. Then they asked me to come to the platform. First they began asking me various questions about our Alaska Mission field, my work, one question leading to another. Suddenly, looking down at the audience, I saw my sister, Florence and Rev. John Kronlokken with their family. This surprised me and I began wondering what was happening. The LDR leader then turned to me and read a letter from Miss

Arna Njaa, Executive Secretary for the Lutheran Daughters of the Reformation. She had been unable to attend and her letter addressed to the LDR Friends at Mt. Carmel closed with these words:

..........................................

*"As one who has observed Helen at work, I surely would like to be present today to speak a special word of appreciation to her. Actually we are not honoring her for herself, but rather we are honoring God who chose Helen and appointed her to go and bear fruit, and gave her the power to draw on, for every need.*

*"As an LDR group we have prayed much that souls would be saved among all those whom we serve. We have prayed that God would give wisdom, insight and power to the missionaries to teach the word faithfully so that the Holy Spirit could take the word and apply it to the hearts of the flock.*

*"It was that fruit I had the privilege of observing when I visited our Shishmaref Mission last year. Through all the years since that work started, the Word has been taught and lived. One sowed; another watered and it was God who brought forth the increase. In a sense we can say that none of us does anything; it is only God who has done His good and perfect work. God has made good use of Helen. He created her to be sympathetic and understanding, in His school has taught her to be selfless so that as she has walked in and out of the Eskimo homes she has left a part of her dedicated life in every life.*

*"In Sitka when I called on patients in the T. B. hospitals and students at Mt. Edgecumbe, faces were blank until I said, "I want to greet you from Helen Frost." Then a warmth flooded their faces and immediately they wanted to talk. We had something precious in common.*

*"The girls of the LDR want to give you a lift today, Helen, a lift that is a gift from the LDR girls throughout the Church. You have served all these years with far too little salary to give you an opportunity to build up any kind of a retirement fund. You've known that God never forsakes His servants. It is He who has prompted this gesture and guided us to attempt to provide you with a little extra.*

*"So with gratitude and praise to God we give you this check, Helen."*

*The Lutheran Daughters of the Reformation*
..................................

This wonderful gift was indeed a great surprise. I was very touched but certainly did not feel that I deserved it. There was even a telegram from my brother Gerhard and family and some other greetings. This was a day that I shall always remember with Thanksgiving and praise. It is because of this gift that I am now living at Carlsbad Retirement Home.

## ON NATIONAL TELEVISION

I also made a trip to Cleveland, Ohio, to visit my brother, his wife and other relatives there. Then I was asked to stop off at Philadelphia and New York where Tex Ziegler's mother and aunt live . Tex and his wife were in New York.  It was interesting to see them all, but I did not know until I got to New York that I had been scheduled by Tex Ziegler for an interview on television, sponsored by the TIDE Program, called "For Her Sake." First they questioned me on my Alaska experiences, then asked some other questions. For this I received $300.00, which with some other gifts helped me get settled in my new home in Sitka. Being on television was an interesting experience. That afternoon I left for Minneapolis and two days later, while shopping at the Penny store, a lady stopped me and asked, "Were you on the 'TIDE program' two days ago?" She had recognized me. I thought that was rather exciting. Later when I got to Austin, a few people there said they had watched the program and recognized me. Many must have seen that program!

## STARTING AT SITKA

I arrived at Sitka September 8th, 1955 and took a room at the hotel for a few days. Rev. Knebel then brought me to the little house he had held for me. It needed a great deal of paint and some repairs, but for only $45. a month I couldn't expect much more. It was a fine location, only a half a block from the Lutheran Church, close to the shopping area and in the center of town. I would have a fairly good-sized kitchen, bedroom, living room opening wide into another little room, which I could use for the office. I decided that this would make a good gathering place for my students and we would not be disturbed nor disturb anyone. Mrs. Luella Smith, a Presbyterian, owned the house and lived close by in the Photo Shop Studio. She became a good friend. I then went over and told her I would take this place. I was glad when she said her father would help with some of the repair work and papering.

## PREPARING MY LITTLE HOUSE

We then went to the paint shop and bought the necessary paint and brushes. Rev. Knebel also offered to help, bringing over his paint roller. While he did the ceilings and large spaces, I followed with the brush around the edges. Then we did some papering and painted the woodwork, some old bedsteads, dresser, chairs, cupboard. Next we did the floors, using the conventional grey in the bedroom and kitchen. But for the living rooms I used tile-red which really made it look quite cheerful. I had oil-burning stoves but this I was used to up north in Alaska. Here I would have regular electric lights, a frigidaire and hot and cold running water. I really appreciated that!

Some things came from the LDR office, — cretonne, curtains, pillows, blankets, sheets and other needs. I had also ordered a ready-cut bookcase and music stand from Sears. With a little help from one of the school boys these were put together and varnished.. I had brought my own sewing machine, cooking utensils and dishes. By the time everything was in and finished, the old house really looked cozy and comfortable.

It was a great day when I had an Open House to display my little living room, office, bedroom and kitchen to the house-warming party that came one evening. The ladies from the Lutheran Church with Pastor Knebel and his wife commented on the transformation, — especially on the red floor of the living room and office. Though it was only linoleum painted and waxed, it really shined. The kitchen had a grey floor and green woodwork. A few scatter rugs were added later. The students were delighted to see how nice the place was. My home was to be sort of their home away from home, and they were welcome at any time.

Now I felt that I was ready to do something I had longed to do for some time. I wanted to encourage the Eskimo youth to continue their education. I wanted to help them see more of life and its needs than was possible in their own little village. Hopefully they would then find a place in their own State to do something to help their people.

I loved to watch the Eskimo teen-agers as they crossed the channel from Mt. Edgecumbe to Sitka on the ferry. Some proudly carried their Bibles as they came to attend Church on Sunday morning. At first it seemed strange to them to be seated among so many white people, but they were so warmly welcomed that soon they felt at home in the congregation. I wanted to keep them interested in Church while they were away at school.

## SITKA TOWN

Sitka was indeed quite different from Shishmaref. Both Sitka and Shishmaref were on an island. But Shishmaref was quite barren and for three-fourths of the year it was surrounded by snow and ice. Around Sitka the mountains were covered with trees with foliage in a variety of colors. Beyond and above were the snowcaps. One of these is called Cross Mountain, because the snow there seems to lie in the formation of a cross.

The Mt. Edgecumbe School and Indian Service Hospital (owned and operated by the government) is nearby on Japonski Island. Each time when I crossed over by ferry, I could not help but marvel at the beauty. Here the waters never freeze, so the ferries went back and forth every day. There were other little islands with a cause-way between Alice and Japonski Islands. These Islands have a rich history, serving for years as a coaling station and during World War II as the Sitka Naval Air Station. Not needed after the war, the buildings became the school and hospital.

Sitka itself was an ideal American community. In addition to a grade-school and high school, there was Sheldon Jackson Junior College, started by the Presbyterian Church in 1895 for Alaska's native children. There were churches of fourteen denominations including Sitka Lutheran Church, — the first Lutheran congregation on the Pacific coast. Sitka had a daily paper, a radio station, modern stores, a new seven-story apartment building, docks for boating and fishing, and a cold storage plant. There were clubs sponsoring cultural activities. Many early Alaskans now lived in the large Pioneer Home.

### SITKA LUTHERAN CHURCH

Sitka Lutheran Church has a rich history going back to the Russian years. Finnish Pastor Uno Cygnaeus came with Governor Etholen and his wife on the Ship Nicolai with other Lutherans coming to work for the Russian American Company. Services in Finnish, Swedish and German were held in the Governor's home until the Lutheran Church building was dedicated in 1843. It had the first organ in the West —a gift from the Governor! In 1848 Finnish craftsmen completed the Greek Orthodox Church which has many valuable icons and art pieces. The Lutherans held important positions with the Russian American Company as engineers, physicians, navigators, seamen, carpenters, metal workers, ship builders, teachers and musicians. After serving for five years, Pastor Cygnaeus returned to Finland where he later achieved fame as the founder of the Finnish Public School system. Two other pastors followed Cygnaeus, serving this congregation during the Russian years. But when the Americans took over, for many years the Lutherans had no resident Pastor. But some chaplains and pastors often led services in the church. After their historic building was torn down in 1888, the members would meet in homes. In 1941 the United Lutheran Church sent a pastor and a second building was erected on the same site, with a second floor apartment for the Pastor. The Knebels showed me their view of two little islands and we enjoyed watching the fishing boats coming & going. The fishermen often visited the Church for many of them were Lutherans.

### ALASKA'S PIONEER HOME

The Pioneer Home was an interesting place with over 200 residents, many of them pioneer miners, fishermen and men from other interesting walks of life. In front of the building stands a bronze statue of heroic size called "The Prospector." At night when flood-lighted with colors of the Northern Lights it is very impressive. When you look over the narrow waterway to Japonski Island and beyond you can see snow-capped Mt. Edgecumbe, an extinct volcano.

In the early days under Russian occupation Sitka had the first boat yard, the first sawmill, the first flourmill and the first iron, bronze and brass foundry in Alaska. The flour mill and iron works became extinct, but while I was at Sitka a large pulp mill, owned and operated by the Japanese, was started. In a short time the city population increased from 2,000 to 4,000.

Sitka was a busy port, and the waterfront was crowded with trollers, seiners, halibut boats, launches and cruisers. Each year there was a fishermen's festival and the Lutheran pastor had a service to bless the fleet. Huge quantities of fish were canned or frozen; and up in the mountains there was hunting for deer, bear and goats.

Skiing and tobogganing in the winter was grand sport. Sometimes there would also be skating on the lake, but only for a day or so, for it seldom stayed that cold. When an unusually cold spell froze the lake, the school would usually close for an afternoon, so the children could go skating.

Sitka had a long history, from the Russian occupation, the transfer to the U.S.A. in 1867, and finally statehood in 1959. It had a gorgeous location and moderate climate with some snow and a great deal of rain at certain times. I enjoyed Sitka..

## BEGINNING THE WORK

The work became more and more challenging as I became acquainted with the Church and its surroundings. Of course my main purpose for coming was to establish a Lutheran Center for our native students attending Mt. Edgecumbe School. They were far from their home villages and enjoyed having someone they knew to visit and worship with on Sundays.

## VISITING THE STUDENTS AT SCHOOL

Every Tuesday night I went over on a ferryboat to Mt. Edgecumbe School to hold Bible study for sixteen to twenty students attending the high school. Most of the students were from our Misson stations up north. Two or three came to us from the Swedish Covenant Church for they had no worker there. On Sunday morning most of them attended Bible Class and services at Sitka in the Church where Rev. Knebel was pastor.

On Saturday afternoon the students would get passes to come over to my place at Sitka. There they would sometimes spend up to three hours, playing games, looking at pictures from the north, listening to the music records, or just visiting. It made them feel as if they were closer to home, for sometimes they would get a little homesick. To suddenly travel five hundred miles to Mt. Edgecumbe was not easy. They suddenly were among total strangers, in a new environment, with other kinds of food and clothing. Then the school had rules and regulations they had to follow. That often became a problem. So it seemed to make them feel happy to meet with some of their friends. As one boy said, "I feel different after I have been here." Of course they enjoyed it when I served coffee or tea with cookies or cake. Occasionally I had a group come on Sundays, too. Or they could drop in on other days if they came over to town. I enjoyed having them come, for I almost felt that I was back up north with my Eskimo friends.

## VISITING PATIENTS IN THE HOSPITAL

Some of our folks were in the T. B. sanitariums so on Sunday and Thursday afternoons I would visit them. Some were in the hospital wards and others in the convalescent wards on Alice Island. I also made some visits at the Pioneer Home. One day I found two old timers from Nome in one of the large wards. They were always ready to talk and glad to have visitors for they had very few. Another day I came into a double room and saw a fur parka on the bed. I wondered whose it was and found it belonged to Lap-Hans, as he had been called up north. He was acquainted with our Mission and even spoke of Rev. T. L. Brevig, our first missionary to the Eskimos. He had herded many reindeer in his life and had also worked with the Lomen Company when they drove some deer thousands of miles across Canada in the early days. There was one old man who was blind. When I visited him he wanted me to read his Norwegian letters to him and sometimes write letters for him. Then I found two men who had lived at Teller, —one of whom had been married to an Eskimo. I remember the delicious smoked salmon we used to buy from him. The other Teller man had been a fox farmer, a miner and later, when I was at Teller, worked for the Lomen Lighterage Company. He had been married to one of our workers at Teller Mission Orphanage, who died about two years later. Sad to say this man, while at the Pioneer Home, had become senile. He was always determined he was going back to visit his mine. He tried one night and walked out into the water and drowned. I was happy to visit these various residents, try to cheer them up, perhaps do a little shopping for them, write an occasional letter or do whatever I could for them.

### CHRISTMAS AT SITKA

I taught a Bible Class at the Lutheran Church for our students and sometimes a few others. The Sunday School was to present a Christmas program at the Lutheran Church. On the Saturday before Christmas the students helped me trim the tree at my house. This time we had a lovely spruce tree, — quite different from the artificial trees we had had up north. Getting a tree here was no problem. There were trees everywhere! I put up other decorations, too, so it looked very festive for Christmas. For that Christmas program our Eskimo students sang "Silent Night" in Eskimo and it sounded very familiar to hear them.

On Christmas Eve, after the program at the Church, the students came to my house for a little get-together. We heard a Christmas recording of the St. Olaf Choir that was broadcast over the radio. I had prepared some gifts for the students and patients from donations sent for them. The Mission stations up north had also sent gifts. These were given to them, besides a little money gift which they were always glad to get. Sister Ruth Poetzsch from the Philadelphia Motherhouse, who was acting Administrator at the New Sitka Hospital, came over and helped me serve refreshments. The group had to leave to get back for the party in the dormitories. It was a pleasant evening for all the students and helped them feel less homesick on Christmas Eve.

Then Sister Ruth and I opened our gifts. Just then a call came from Rev. and Mrs. Knebel, inviting us to come over to see their gifts, then they would come over and help us open ours. We did and that made a very pleasant Christmas Eve.

On Christmas Day I went over to Mt. Edgecumbe to visit the dormitories. Each one had a display of decorations made by the students. Some of the beds resembled little booths surrounded in green spruce or pine branches. In other corners there were little nativity scenes with various lighting effects. There were Christmas cards and pictures all over. In the large reception room of the girls' dormitory a model Church about three feet high had been made by some of the boys who were taking carpentry. Following my rounds in the dormitories, I visited the hospital patients. It was interesting to see how some of them had drawn colored Christmas scenes on their windows. Mrs. Hegland at Teller had sent a small Christmas gift for each one of our Lutheran patients, and I delivered these.

The various denominations had prepared a gift package for each one of their patients, but four days before Christmas a call came to the Ministerial Association. There were forty patients not yet taken care of. So I was given $30. and asked to go out and purchase something I thought might be suitable for each one. We went shopping and each one got a package of stationery and some stamps. The women or girls also received a bottle of hair tonic. There had also been a call for gifts for students who were not being cared for. The women of our Church and other organizations took care of this need.

I also visited the patients at Pioneer Home at this time. All of them had been remembered very well through donations and from Territorial funds. Some trees had been set up and some decorating had been done. But to many of these old men Christmas was just another day. How I wished that I could have done something tangible for them. Some were blind, some crippled, some moved about in wheel chairs, some passed the time by reading or playing cards. Many of these men had really pioneered in Alaska and done a great deal to build and develop Alaska.

One day while visiting in the Pioneer Home, an old Norwegian began talking Norwegian to me. I struggled along trying to answer him. Yes, I even tried to pray in Norwegian, but it was difficult as I had not spoken it for many years. How I wished my father had been there. Older people always want to pray in their Mother Tongue!

### MEETING THE NURSES

I also enjoyed getting to know different nurses who came from the states to work at the hospital or sanitariums. Some were very fine people but they felt a little lonely and isolated on the islands. Some were Lutherans and they came to our Church at Sitka. I would invite them over from time to time for lunch or for an evening and we enjoyed getting together.

One day one of our nurses had a birthday and asked if she could come over with six of the nurses for supper. They would bring the birthday cake and fresh oysters for stew. I made individual cranberry salads and some cookies and we had a delightful evening. I think I also showed some Alaska pictures from up north and they enjoyed seeing films from the Seward Peninsula.

Sister Ruth Poetsch had charge of the opening of the New Sitka Hospital and had put in much hard work before its opening in April. She would come quite often to talk over her problems and have lunch or supper with me. She seemed to appreciate getting away and talking. Then sometimes I would take a walk with her out to the hospital, about a mile out of town. Once I was asked to help on an emergency case for a few nights as there was a shortage of nurses. I felt a little outdated, but with the help of Sister Ruth I managed to care for the patient and was glad for the opportunity to brush up on my nursing. Some time later, I was asked to help out at the Pioneer Home, and took the night shift two or three nights a week. This gave me a chance to raise my Social Security and I could take care of my other work during the day. As a member of the Lutheran Church and also of the Women's Group, at times I did some visitation for the Church. I enjoyed being a member of this congregation and I met many fine people there.

The following summer, Rev. and Mrs. Knebel left for Argentina and for quite some time we were without a pastor. We managed to carry on our women's meetings and Sunday School classes. Perhaps I felt the responsibility more than was necessary. A pastor from Sheldon Jackson would come and conduct the Sunday morning services, but we did miss having our own pastor.

### THE SECOND YEAR

For my vacation that summer I took a trip down into Washington, Oregon and California, visiting friends and relatives. My brother Reuben was at Eugene, Oregon for a year's study, so it was fun visiting them at the University. In August I was back on the job and there were many things to do before school started again. That year all the students had been sent home to their villages for the summer. The first years, the students stayed at the school in the dormitories but later they decideded going home was better for them.

That year before school started there was a meeting of the Ministerial Association at Mt. Edgecumbe. Various matters were discussed. How to cooperate better with the Superintendent of the School, and coordinating work of the ministers with the students. Certain religious groups who had been doing considerable proselytizing were advised that this was forbidden. Each denomination should take care of their own students. Then on Sunday there were transportation problems. On Sunday right after breakfast the ferries were crowded and the students could not get to Sunday School or Church at a particular time. They had to take the ferry across the channel and only a certain number could cross at one time. The Saturday passes which the students received had to be considered, too. It would not be possible for all of them to come over every Saturday. The dormitories tried to cooperate with us in the best way possible. It was a helpful discussion.

It was encouraging to see our returning Lutheran students and meet the new ones. I was glad to be there to contact them, then encourage them to come to Sunday School and worship services. They were not always able to attend both, but I felt that they did very well. I continued to go over for our Tuesday evening Bible classes at the school. This year for our studies I used the theme, "If God Were King." Last year we studied the Gospel of Matthew.

As we did not have a pastor, I soon found myself doing more at the church. At first I did not offer to help, for I did not want too many responsibilities. But gradually that seemed to change. I was asked to serve on the Church Council, then teach Sunday School, be the organist for the Sunday School, then vice-president and program chairman for the Women of the Church. It has been said that the longer one stays in a place, the more one finds to do. But I enjoyed doing these things and learned a lot from these new experiences.

Rev. J. Luthro from Petersburg came to conduct services one Sunday. He was very interested in the different phases of my work. I took him over to Mt. Edgecumbe to see our students and patients there, also to Pioneer Home, Sitka Hospital and the Orthodox Church. He visited at the Sheldon Jackson School, saw the Museum and met some friends there. Then he was at a friend's home for dinner one evening. When bad weather closed the airport, he also was able to conduct one of my student Bible Classes at Mt. Edgecumbe. The next Sunday Pastor Coovert from Juneau, Alaska came and conducted communion services. So we did have some help from other Lutheran congregations. The rest of the time one of the pastors from the Sheldon Jackson School came and held the morning services for us. We appreciated their help.

My second Christmas at Sitka was somewhat different from the first, because we still did not have a resident pastor. However, the women of the Church, Sunday School teachers and Mrs Sylte, our organist, all were very helpful. Mrs. Spiegle directed a nice little skit for our Women's Christmas party, depicting Christmas in other lands where our missionaries were working. Then each one brought a gift for the Mt. Edgecumbe students or patients, besides some little goodies for the refreshment table. I played a tape from Rev. Knebel, the former pastor, with his greetings to all the members.

Our Sunday School program turned out nicely with the use of a filmstrip called "Around the Christmas Tree." Three of the students together with Mr. Lee Raefeldt, the music director at Mt. Edgecumbe, gave us some orchestra music as a prelude. The Junior Choir sang some Christmas songs.

On Christmas Rev. Coovert from Juneau was sick and could not come and conduct the service. But Mr. Fred Kuehn, the Chairman of the Church Council, led our Christmas service.

I had my usual party for the students with a little gift for each one, followed by refreshments. Thursday after New Year I attended a very interesting graduation exercise at Mt. Edgecumbe auditorium. Eleven girls had finished their practical nurses' training and two of them were girls from our Mission. I was very happy to see this and hoped that more would complete this training. A very nice lunch was served by the Home Economics Class. Both of these girls now have positions in the Alaska Native Service Hospitals and are doing well. There are many openings for students with training in Alaska. We must somehow encourage our young people to come and study here.

The number of students coming down from the north increased and sometimes I had twenty or more students in my home. For one of these sessions I served sandwiches sent from a teachers' reception at Sitka. The students enjoyed this change from their usual fare. The two hours went rapidly and I remember some of their remarks when it was time to go. "I wish I could stay longer....Thank you for everything."

There were times, however, when I became worried about our students at the government school. These students came from all over Alaska and some of them were not the best influence. There were reports of drinking bouts and immorality. The staff did their best to keep the situation under control, but with five hundred or more students, that was not easy. Most of the teachers were fine, but a few were not. Even so, it was important for the students to be in school to receive the training they needed for a brighter future. Here students had an opportunity to see how other people lived and worked. Coming here was certainly a test of their home training and their Christian faith. My prayers were that some of our students would go on to college and become Christian leaders among their own people. I had also hoped that some day we might have our own Chistian Academy or college in Alaska. But this was a far-off dream.

## THE NEW DRIPOLATOR

I woke up one night in February to find that it was snowing again. We had had our snowy season earlier and I thought it was finished. However, the sun was again shining in the afternoon when I took the boat over to Mt. Edgecumbe for my usual round of visits. I had been invited to Mrs. Rider's home and enjoyed my visit there. The Riders were Lutherans and attended the Sitka Church. On the way home when I stopped at the Post Office for mail, there was a large package for me. My coffee dripolator had come! I had sent in some bands from four pounds of coffee, given to me by friends, plus a little extra money. The students were delighted because they could handle this coffee pot.

The landlord had recently put in a new oil stove in the living room and connected it with the tank outside, so I didn't need to fill the tank inside any more. That was much easier for me.

One week I showed my Eskimo movies to the T. B. patients in the different sections. Later a nurse in the occupational therapy department asked if I would show them to a group of children. "Please show especially those of the children playing in the snow, the dog teams and ice-skating." I did and it was surprising how quietly the patients sat, looking and listening. Another time the nurses and staff asked if they could see the pictures. So I felt I was making good use of my far-north pictures, even in Sitka.

### THE SLIPPERY ICE

Christmas preparations did not go smoothly for me this year. Just one week before Christmas I fell on the slippery street, broke my right arm and it was put in a cast. I was glad that I had already finished wrapping the gifts for the students and done some baking. But friends helped and brought in cookies and cakes for the Christmas parties. The students were not permitted to come on Christmas Eve so our party was held on Christmas Day, following the morning services. The girls sang two songs at the services, directed by Mrs. Gaenslen, wife of our new pastor. The Anchorage Lutheran Church had sent sweaters and billfolds for the boys and slips and scarfs for the girls. The Petersburg women sent corsages for the girls and there were some nice things from the LDR office. All the students knew they had been remembered in a wonderful way.

After Christmas there were other parties. One day I invited three ladies from the Pioneer Home, together with their matron. Another day three ladies from our congregation came for "Coffee-Ann" as Rev. Mjorud used to say. It was rather a stormy week so with my fracture I did not venture out much. But with some friendly help I managed to do the necessary work. Miss Lindeland, the matron at the Pioneer Home, was always helpful in time of need.

In the spring I had the pleasure of having Rev. Alton Halvorson and Rev. Zephania from Madagascar as guests for a few days. Rev. Halvorson was preparing a film on our Lutheran work in Alaska and wanted some pictures of the students at work. I took him to Mt. Edgecumbe to one of the class rooms and to the hospitals. One evening Rev. Zephania showed a movie from Madagascar, telling the story of his life, conversion and work. The students were all given permission to come to hear him. This was an eye-opener to them and I was glad they had this opportunity.

### BACK NORTH IN 1958 FOR NOME DEDICATION

I heard the good news: the new building of Our Savior's Lutheran Church in Nome would be ready for dedication on April 27th. Many of us had been praying and looking forward to this day for a long time. I was invited to attend the dedication so I left for Nome on the 24th. A room at the hotel had been reserved for Miss Alice Sanne and me. Dr. Schiotz, the ALC President, Dr. H. L. Foss, Pacific District President, and Miss Noreen Paulson, the welfare worker at Juneau were there. Then on the 26th chartered planes from Anchorage and Fairbanks arrived with Pastor Mjorud of Anchorage and Rev. Groth of Spenard, and members from their congregations. They had given generously to the building fund of this Mission. Mr. Gordon Dufseth from Anchorage had directed the building project and he also came. We wondered where all of these fifty-seven from Anchorage and forty-two from Fairbanks would stay. But the Nome families generously opened their homes. Even the prison manager said he had some vacant beds if anyone wanted to use them, so everyone had a place to stay.

## A JOYOUS CELEBRATION

The Dedication Service was beautiful. Dr. Schiotz delivered the main sermon; the choir was magnificent. Six plaques for the new Church made by the talented Eskimo women from the various villages were dedicated. Two women from Shishmaref, Teller and Nome had sewed skins to represent Christian symbols: God the Father, God the Son, God the Holy Spirit, Baptism, the Holy Communion and the Word of God. These were presented and placed on the front wall after the service. The Eskimos were proud to know that some of their creative art work would always be there in their Church.

Many of the Nome ladies helped prepare a light lunch that was served in the quonset building following the Dedication. All gathered again in the afternoon. Short talks were given by the workers from the various stations. The main speaker being Miss Alice Sanne, the Executive Secretary of the Women's Missionary Fellowship. That group had generously supported the new church by seeking "Dollars for Nome." Thanks to the mission plane, Rev. Hegland had also brought the Maakestads from Shishmaref, his own family and Bertha Stedje from Teller. Although the folks from Anchorage and Fairbanks had to leave early in the afternoon, we were grateful for their presence at this historic Dedication.

Rev. and Mrs. Knutson hosted the out-of-town guests at the Polaris Hotel for a dinner. All in all, it was a day long to be remembered. Prayers had been answered. We now had a fine Church in Nome!

## RELIEVING THE MISSIONARIES

Following the dedication at Nome I returned to Sitka to be with my students who were graduating from high school. One girl planning to take up nursing had been recommended to a school in Philadelphia. One boy was interested in bookkeeping studies. These  eighty graduating students— Indians, Eskimos, and Aleuts —were from all over Alaska.  Many of them were going on to other schools, helped by scholarships from their church denominations or from the government. It was thrilling to see them graduate and it was my hope that many of them would continue their studies and become leaders in Alaska. Soon all the students at Mt. Edgecumbe left to go home for the summer. Sitka Lutheran Church now had a new resident pastor, Rev. R. A. Gaenslen.

That summer all of the missionaries at Teller, Shishmaref and Nome were going on furloughs. I had been asked to relieve them, so on the 19th of May I flew back to Nome. The Knutsons were leaving and after their summer's furlough the Maakestads were to move from Shishmaref to serve at Nome.

Rev. Hegland of Teller and Rev. Knutson met me at the Nome airport. After a delicious lunch with the Knutsons we flew to Teller. There I found Bertha Stedje busy teaching Vacation Bible School. Mrs. Hegland was sewing summer dresses for her girls, getting ready for a trip to the States. When I smelled a duck roasting in the oven, it reminded me of the old days.

I noticed there were some major improvements at Teller Mission. One was the well underneath the house and the electric pump that supplied hot and cold water. Even for a hot shower, if you please! I had never thought this possible. Then Rev. Hegland had added a quonset building for a living room, small bedroom and work shop. This pleasant and useful addition showed Rev. Hegland's ingenuity in improving conditions for more convenient living. Workers in Alaska could always use those skills.

I noticed Rev. Hegland kept busy making sure his plane was in first class condition. His Piper Cruiser was taking the whole family to the States via the Alaska Highway. It was a good thing all the Heglands were slender so all five could fit into that small plane!

The next day we were to leave Teller for Shishmaref but a heavy fog kept us from going. That afternoon one of the Eskimo women teased me, "You were like Jonah, trying to get away from us without talking to us." True enough. I had not taken time to visit in the homes, for I knew I would be coming back later to stay for a few weeks. That night after the mid-week service, I showed slides of Mt. Edgecumbe and Sitka, showing their children at school and telling about our student activities.

### BACK AT SHISHMAREF

Next day it was clear so we were finally able to get into Shishmaref. The Dahles were away on furlough. It was thrilling to return, see the smiling faces and hear the Eskimos say,"We are glad you came back." One man said, "I thought I was dreaming when I saw you walking down there on the beach."

Sunday morning was a beautiful day with almost a full house at the service. I almost wondered if I, too, were dreaming. The same interpreter, Walter Nayokpuk, was there, helping wherever he could, as did the others. Alex Weyiouanna, whom I called my right hand, was there to start the electric motor and get things going. At 4:00 P.M. a group of singers came to practice for the evening meeting, just as they used to do. They enjoyed it when I showed slides of Sitka, Mt. Edgecumbe and the students at their studies. The students, back from school for the summer, were glad their parents could see their school, some of their activities and Sitka Lutheran Church.

I had only been there a few days when I was called upon to treat a sick baby. There was one with a running ear and another with an infected hand. Old man Koonuk was gradually slipping away. Measles had also crept into the village. Since the teachers had left I had to find Jack, the caretaker of the school, in order to get some medicines. I came to his house just as they were having coffee and sourdough hot cakes. When they invited me to join them, I eagerly accepted. Jack said, "It's a good thing you came to be with us while the missionaries are gone. Now you are back at your old job, taking care of the sick." "Yes," I replied, "I'm glad, too, that I could see you all and help again."

This year had been a very profitable one for the Eskimos. That year the ice broke off from the shore earlier than usual so the men had been very busy hunting and bringing in the oomgruk and seal. In their omiaks they had been out to the main ice coming from the north and there they found their catch. Consequently, the women were kept busy skinning oogruk, cutting blubber for seal oil and meat for drying. Many of the skins had been cleaned and stretched and were drying in the sun for future use. Plenty of game and fresh eggs were in evidence, so I was sure there would be no famine. With the coming berry season their seal pokes would again be filled and buried in their deep freeze, — a hole in the ground above the perma-frost.

The Shishmaref Mission had some added improvements, too, both inside and out. Rev. and Mrs. Maakestad had added a dryer and refrigerator,— a real luxury compared to the old days. A beautiful red dossal was now hanging behind the altar in the Chapel. The new tin roof and electric light plant, both badly needed, were a great improvement. I could also see that Rev. Maakestad was handy with a saw and hammer as well as a paint brush. It takes a great deal of time and energy to keep buildings like these in good condition.

While visiting one of the homes I was told of the narrow escape of William Allokeok, one of the older men. He and his grandson Clifford had been crossing the ice with his dog team and going up the bank. Suddenly the ice broke and the sled got caught underneath the ice, leaving Allokeok standing in deep water up to his shoulders, not even touching the bottom. Finally Clifford managed to get hold of his hands and pull him up on the bank to safety. Fortunately they had some matches in a glass jar so they could build a fire and dry out before returning to the village. I know that other Eskimos could tell similar experiences. Hunting on the ice was often very dangerous.

## TO NOME

I stayed at Shishmaref about a month, then left for Nome on the 17th of June. Bill Munz, a fearless pilot, also went by way of Wales to pick up a hunter there on a very windy and foggy day. I am sure the Lord was with us that day. The pilot could hardly hold the door of the plane open until the hunter, with his big walrus skin and other trophies, had gotten into the back of the plane. I sat with Bill in front. When we finally got off the ground I was sure he was going to hit the rocky points of the nearby cliff, but suddenly there was enough speed to ride above and away from them. However, because of the thick fog on the ocean he had to follow the coast line.

Suddenly the pilot made a very quick turn, then pointed to another plane coming out of the fog in our direction. Fortunately, we cleared him safely.

It was a good feeling to finally land safely at Nome. I went to the "little parsonage" as it was called, — the small house next to the church. This had become a convenient place for the parish worker and the visiting missionaries. While in Nome I tried to call on all our Eskimo folk, conduct Sunday services and mid-week meetings. It was interesting to see so many familiar faces in this new place. The Midnight Sun Festival and parade representing various fairy-tale characters was celebrated at this time. Some friends invited me to go along with them downtown to see the activities. Of course, I took pictures. I was invited several places for luncheon and dinner. Rev. and Mrs. Amundson of the Swedish Covenant Church always had open house.

## BACK TO TELLER

After about four weeks in Nome I went to Teller again and, on arriving at the Mission quarters, I found that the door to the class room entrance had been broken open. Since nothing of importance seemed to be missing, we decided it had been done by an intoxicated person who didn't know what he was doing.

I had only been in Teller a few days when I was called to Teller Mission to conduct a funeral of a baby. Most of the Eskimos from Teller were out camping and doing their summer fishing. It was interesting to see the place where I had first landed upon coming to Alaska. Since then, many things had happened. A few of the Eskimo children who had been at the orphanage were still living and three of them were married and living in the village.

On the Fourth of July the storekeeper's wife, Mrs. Blodgett, had a "Johnson Picnic" on the beach for the Eskimos, That meant that everyone who used a Johnson motor for their boats was invited. This was the brand they were selling so it was also an advertising affair. But I noticed that people with other makes of motors were there, too, —including myself.

It was a such nice warm day that some came from Teller Mission. Mrs. Blodgett served salad, hamburgers on buns and coffee, a great treat for all. I enjoyed visiting with many old friends. The day ended with some Eskimo dancing and a few racing games.

While at Teller Town I was called to the delivery of an Eskimo baby. I had not done that for a long time. The next day a sad report came that the body of Roy Okie, one of our mission boys, had been found. Some time before he had fallen out of a boat and drowned. Then Miss Berglund, the government nurse, came by and wanted to go over to Teller Mission to conduct a clinic. One of the Eskimo boys took us over, That evening I led the memorial service for Roy Okie. The next day we returned to Teller Town and conducted a clinic for the Eskimos. Miss Berglund was a Lutheran and a very fine person. I enjoyed working with her.

Besides the services on Sunday and Wednesday evenings, I also invited the women and older girls to come over one afternoon for a devotional hour and refreshments. Another day I had a little party for the children. Then the freighter came in with the supplies for the store and the Mission. Although many of the people were up the Tuxuk River for berry picking, when the freighter arrived the men and boys came back quickly to take jobs unloading the supplies.

One day Olive Miller came over about 8:00 A.M. and said she wanted to make sourdough hotcakes for me. Of course I was pleased with that idea. I knew Olive and enjoyed her very much. Before she was married she had lived at Igloo, working for the teachers. We also went out blueberry picking, for her family was camping some distance out on the road.

On the 31st of July the Heglands returned from their trip to the States. Then we again went up to Shishmaref for the Sunday services. The people were told that Rev. and Mrs. Dahle would soon be back. So on the 5th of August I started on my way back to Sitka. On the way I stopped at Anchorage a few days and visited the Eskimo folks there. Then I spoke at the Sunday morning service at Juneau and visited with Noreen Paulson a few days. She had been a missionary at Teller Mission and now was the welfare worker in Juneau. Then I returned to Sitka. I thanked the Lord for many wonderful experiences and the opportunities to help while up north.

**BACK TO SCHOOL.**

It was nice to be back with my students again. Pastor Day, the chaplain at the school, gave me the names of twenty-two Lutheran students. Five were from Shishmaref, eleven from Teller, four from Nome, one from Unalakleet and one from Kotzebue. I was pleased when many of these students were in Church the first Sunday after their return. Then the following Saturday I got passes for them to come to my place. I planned a Sunday dinner for the girls one Sunday and the boys the next Sunday. This helped us all get better acquainted and I encouraged them to come to our Tuesday night Bible classes. This year I used the course from LBI, "Salvation Made Plain," which I believe proved a great blessing to all.

When I went over to the hospital to visit our patients, I found there were only three Lutheran patients, compared to thirteen the first year. Many patients were now being sent to the new government hospital at Anchorage. Through the years the number of T. B. patients had also decreased because of better follow-up work done in the villages. Doctors and nurses used X-ray units to check everyone in a village. If any were found to have T. B. they were taken to a sanitarium, —either in Seattle or Alaska, wherever there was room. Since tuberculosis was being detected in the early stages, it was very much under control. Through a number of years government nurses had conducted classes in the villages and given instructions in the schools. By movies and literature the people have been made aware of the situation and how they can cure, arrest or even prevent this dreaded disease.

## ALASKA STATEHOOD

In 1959 Alaska finally became a state and the 49th star was added to our U.S. flag. This was something Alaska had been working toward for a long time. There were great celebrations and bonfires at Sitka to celebrate this event. Our first Governor was William A. Egan. We listened very closely to our radio that day, hearing the speeches from Juneau, telling of the festivities there in our Capital City. Alaska stamps and Alaska dollars were issued to commemorate the event.

## ALASKA DAY IN SITKA

For years Sitka had been celebrating Alaska Day on the 18th of October, commemorating the 1867 transfer of Alaska to the United States by the Russians. Colorful pageants depicted the history of Sitka from its initial establishment in 1799 by Alexander Baranof, manager of the Russian American Company. For these celebrations men would let their beards grow and the women would don their early American dress costumes. Some of them were very beautiful with ruffles and lace. There were many Tlingit Indians in this vicinity and they would put on their colorful robes. They represented Indian chiefs who attended the original event when Princess Maksoutoff and the Russian governor lowered the Russian flag and the American flag was raised in its place. Eskimos with their fur parkas appeared. At Christmas time the million dollar pulp mill was opened up with great celebration. The Japanese who were financing this were hiring people from Sitka and the United States. These new jobs brought so many people to Sitka that in about one year the population had increased from 2,000 to 4,000. Our Church membership also increased.

Pioneer Home had added a women's addition and now they could care for women. Arline Lindeland, the matron from Oregon, became a very good friend of mine. She joined our Church and sang in the choir. At Christmas she helped set up a beautiful nativity scene in front of the Pioneer Home. This caused a great deal of interest among the residents of the Home and those who passed by. One summer I relieved the matron for two weeks while she was on vacation. In the summer I did not have the students to care for and it was a change for me. This was interesting work and I enjoyed it.

There was a very active women's group at the Lutheran Church. Mrs. Gaenslen, a former missionary to Argentina, was a dedicated person and she helped stimulate the programs in the Church. So, in addition to my own specific endeavors, there were fine programs at the Church and I enjoyed helping there whenever I could.

## EASTER AT SITKA

I have told about my Christmas parties for the students but not much about Easter. This year it was a beautiful sunny day and the Church was packed. Many Mt. Edgecumbe students came over on the ferry to attend their respective Churches. It was thrilling to see all twenty of our Eskimo students filling up the two front benches and part of another. They looked nice, too, dressed in their Sunday best. (Some had been Christmas gifts from the WMF friends or dresses I had sewed for them.) The girls took part in singing "He Lives," and they did it splendidly. But they admitted later that they were nervous when they got up in front of so many people.

Following the services all the students were invited to my house. Ham sandwiches, cross buns, doughnuts, cakes, cookies and coffee had been prepared. On the table was a little white bunny surrounded by Easter candy eggs for decoration. It was warm enough so that we could even use the front porch. That day there were students all over the place, enjoying themselves. Following the refreshments, some even went out doors in the little yard and played handball. Incidentally, some of the boys had come over the day before and raked the yard. There was a very good movie in town and I arranged for them to go that afternoon. This had been a pleasant day for everyone.

## THE PASTOR LEAVES FOR ARIZONA

This year Pastor Gaenslen accepted a call to Ajo, Arizona. That summer I made a brief visit to Minnesota and North Dakota. and when I returned they were gone so once more we were without a minister. I was elected Sunday School Superintendent and chairman for the Lutheran Church Women. Though I knew I would be busier than ever, I enjoyed the work in the Church and there were many good helpers.

We usually had Rev. Armstrong from Sheldon Jackson College conduct our Sunday services. The Church Council had to solve a few problems, and letters of call were sent out to pastors recommended to us by the Synod President. All the members joined hands again and helped to keep things going.

## THE FLU EPIDEMIC

I had just barely gotten over the Christmas rush, answering letters and acknowledging gifts when the flu epidemic was upon us. This fall I was so busy with the Church work, visitation and my student work, that I had not done any relief nursing at the Pioneer Home and Hospital. But when two of their nurses fell sick the Home called to ask if I might be able to help. In Sitka there were no extra nurses on a waiting list, so getting help was difficult for them. It was Saturday night and I knew Sunday would be a busy day with little time for sleep, but I said I would try. I went on duty Saturday at midnight, worked until 8:00 A. M. then took the ferry over to Church. Being Sunday School superintendent and also teaching a class, I could not go to bed until after the morning service the next day. After Church I had promised to practice with our Senior Girls' singing group which I had organized. I had a nap, then at 6:00 P.M. we had a pot-luck supper at the Church and later a congregational meeting. At midnight I went on duty again and by morning I was very tired. It took some time to get settled down. I did not go on duty Monday night, but did on the next three nights. I liked the nursing services, but with some very sick patients, we were very busy. Very soon two of them passed away.

One evening some time later I was invited over to the home of the Episcopal parish worker for a get-together for the two Salvation Army girls who were leaving. They asked me to bring some of my Alaska slides and speak about my work among the Eskimos. We had a pleasant evening.

Two of our Eskimo boys, one from Shishmaref and one from Nome, were attending the Sheldon Jackson Junior College this year. But before the year was over they gave up. I do not know what their problem had been, but I was very disappointed. I had hoped they would finish there and perhaps go on to one of the Lutheran colleges, but this was not to be. Instead they both decided to go into the Army.

Without a pastor various problems can came up in any congregation, but at Sitka we managed to survive. We knew that when one did come there would be much work for him to do. Many new people had come to town and I tried to visit and contact them. But without a car this was difficult for many lived a distance from the main part of town. Then for about three months the arthritis in my knee hampered my activity, but I hobbled about in spite of it. The Lord was good and gave me strength for each day.

### SORROW AT SHISHMAREF

One day in April Rev. Hegland sent a telegram announcing the sudden death of Rev. Dahle at Shishmaref. Would I go up to Shishmaref until a pastor could be sent there? This was quite a shock but I knew that my responsibility to the needs of the Mission came first. Therefore, I asked Mr. Lee Raephelt to take the Student Bible Class on Tuesday nights and I managed to delegate some other jobs to various members of the congregation. Then I flew to Nome.

Two weeks before Easter Rev. Hegland again flew me up to Shishmaref Island. It was a cold day and they were recovering from a severe storm. At the church the wind had blown out the oil-burning stove in the kitchen, sending a deluge of soot all over the kitchen and even out into the living room. This was a sorry sight but with the help of one of the Eskimo girls we finally got the rooms cleaned.

Everyone was sad because of the sudden loss of Rev. Dahle. Mrs. Dahle had gone to Nome to make funeral arrangements and she had expected to come back to Shishmaref. But her children wanted their father to be buried in Minnesota, so plans were being made for that. But even with the shock of his death and our sadness, the life at Shishmaref had to go on. It did help that I knew everyone.

Many stopped by to greet me. One of my first duties was to finish the Bible Classes using the material they had been following each week. The children were eager to meet again for study.

Easter was almost upon us so there were more preparations to make. All were helpful in planning and presenting the Easter program. I was "back home again" and pleased that I could help.

Then another task came. Mrs. Dahle sent me a list of the personal things which she wanted packed and mailed to her. Two trunks were to be filled and sent by boat. So as I went through everything, I cleaned house and packed at the same time. With the help of Alex Weyiouenna, we finally got their packages ready and sent them off. I know this was a sad and difficult time for her and the children.

One day Rev. Hegland asked if the Thirtieth Anniversary Celebration at Shishmaref might be held the 17th of July. I was happy to help and found some notes which Rev. Dahle had made for this event. He had started the regular work there in 1930 and had directed the building of the Church and living quarters. The Women of the Church had raised all the funds to build this Mission so their work should be recognized. Sister Anna Huseth had prayed and worked for years to have this Mission approved by the Mission Board. But we felt it was sad that Dr. Dahle would not be there for the celebration since he had been pastor there most of those years. He would be missed at this historic event.

## THE ANNIVERSARY CELEBRATION AT SHISHMAREF

On Friday before the festival Rev. Hegland arrived with Rev. Maakestad and family, Arna Njaa, Bertha Stedje and Elvira Bergendahl. Elvira was a friend of mine from Mt. Edgecumbe who had asked if she might come while I was here. On Saturday the Hegland family came and it was wonderful for us all to be together. Each group brought some of the food for the gathering. The program went well.

Rev. Maakestad spoke on Sunday morning, telling of the beginnings of Shishmaref, when Rev. Dahle and his family had arrived thirty years ago with the building material and necessary supplies. For some time they had lived in a tent. In the early years there had been many willing hands and much work had been accomplished in a short time. We gave thanks for "thirty years of grace," to the people in the past and looked ahead to the future. Rev. Hegland led the liturgy, the choir sang "How Great Thou Art" and Bertha Stedje and Rev. Maakestad sang "God So Loved the World." I was pleased when four babies were baptized at this service. Walter Nayopuk was our faithful interpreter.

The afternoon meeting was more informal and several of the Eskimos participated. Ray Ningeulook led in prayer. The choir sang "The Book That Never Grows Old." Miss Arna Njaa gave a beautiful message on "The History of the Individual." She told how this book may contain three chapters, the first one "Living with God." If we have strayed, the second one might be called "Life Away from God," and the third chapter, "Back to God." It contained a message for each of us. Some of the little girls sang, "His Yoke is Easy."

I was asked to reminisce a little, telling of early days before we had this station, visits by the missionaries and my first trip here. I spoke of the requests of the Eskimos for a permanent missionary and Sister Anna Huseth's deep concern that someone might be sent there. I told how she prayed and finally succeeded in getting the LDR to take Shishmaref as their project so that work could be started. Because of her faithful work, this station is called the Anna Huseth Memorial Mission Station. Mary Eningowuk, one of the oldest women, showed us a book she had made containing Bible verses in picures as they had been taught to her by Rev. Dahle with the help of an interpreter. The pictures that she had made told the story and the meaning. Then she and Mary Seetomona, another elderly person, sang in the Eskimo language two songs that they had learned long ago.

Each of the Council members brought a greeting, telling how thankful they were for this day and all that had been done for them by the Church, the LDR, missionaries and friends in order that they might have the Gospel. It was inspiring to hear these expressions of the natives.

Letters were read from Dr. Foss, the District President, Dr. Schiotz, the President of the American Lutheran Church, Dr. Dybvig, Rev. Hartje and the Lutheran Daughters of the Reformation. Our service closed by singing "Blest Be the Tie That Binds" then refreshments were served to everyone. It was such a beautiful warm day that the children were served out of doors. In fact, Anna Njaa said that she didn't think she had ever been so warm in the States. The older folks were served upstairs in the Chapel in somewhat of a hurry for Miss Njaa was to speak that night at Nome. Rev. Hegland would take his passengers back. It had been a wonderful anniversary festival that the Eskimos would long remember. I was so happy that I could be there for this Anniversary.

### BACK TO SITKA

On the way back to Sitka I again stopped and visited a few days at Teller, Nome and Anchorage. When I visited Noreen Paulson at Juneau, I was surprised to hear that Sitka's new pastor, Rev. G. Holmquist and his wife had arrived. So I was able to travel with them to Sitka the next day. I fell in love with them right away and felt that he was a man of God and how thankful we should be.

Some of the folks from the congregation met us at the airport. Later we were taken to the pulp mill where Elaine Sharpe served coffee and doughnuts. That made a pleasant introduction to Sitka. Everyone was happy to have a resident pastor once more. I noticed that much had been done to the Church building during the summer. Members had put in a new furnace, fixed up the Sunday School rooms, painting, laying tile on the front entrance to the Church and cleaning and remodeling the Pastor's office. There must have been many volunteer workdays and the women had served dinners for them. It was good to see that everybody had been working together to make things more pleasant for the new pastor.

**A WELCOME FOR THE NEW PASTOR**

The following Sunday a reception was held to welcome Rev. and Mrs. Holmquist and their fine young son, David. Rev. Holmquist was a talented violinist and he favored us with a number, accompanied by Mrs. Sylte, the organist. Rev. Armstrong, who had helped us during the year, was our speaker. Pastor Steinhoff came later from Juneau to install the new pastor.

**MY LAST YEAR AT SITKA**

Before long I was back in my usual routine with religious classes at Mt. Edgecumbe, visitations at the hospital and Pioneer Home. I also helped Rev. Holmquist as he got acquainted with the work.

**ANOTHER FALL AND MORE BROKEN BONES**

Shortly before Christmas I again fell on the icy street, breaking a bone in my foot and hand so that I had to have a cast on both. I sometimes wondered if I had any more bones to be broken. But again my friends helped me with the Christmas plans and the lunch for the students after the services. Some brought sandwiches, cakes, cookies, candies and nuts. Arline Lindeland baked and decorated some square cakes with peppermint sticks underneath to look like sleds. So with their help, the gifts and the lunch, the students had a wonderful time. At 3:00 P.M. they had to return to the school.

At 4:00 P. M. our Church choir sang at the Pioneer Home when Rev. Holmquist conducted a service in the Chapel for the residents who were able to come.

At 5:30 P.M. I enjoyed a turkey dinner at the home of one of our Church members, and this was a rare treat. The hostess, Mrs. Dronen, was a wheelchair patient and a true Christian. Her daughters had helped her with the dinner. They asked me to show some of the Alaska movies.

How glad I was when I could discard those heavy casts. For a time I had a pain in the back of my head, probably caused by carrying those casts around and trying to work. But soon that pain was gone.

As spring approached I began wondering where I would be going from here. I knew that this would be my last year. The students had become used to the idea of going down to Mt. Edgecumbe for high school. A vocational school was being developed in Nome and many probably would go there for training. The practical nurses' course at Mt. Edgecumbe was being transferred to the new Alaska Native Services Hospital at Anchorage. That was becoming an important Medical Center and many of our Eskimos were being sent there when they were sick.

My arthritis was beginning to bother me more and more, possibly due to the wet and rainy weather at Sitka. Then I could see that Rev. and Mrs. Homquist were very much interested in our students and they could possibly do as much for them as

I had tried to do. So I wrote to Rev. Hegland and told him I felt my work here had been successful and that I felt I should retire. He submitted my request to the Mission Board and it was granted. Now I could make plans to leave at the end of this term. I wanted to stay for the graduation exercises at Edgecumbe.

## A Gracious Farewell

The pastor and the congregation gave a lovely farewell party, presenting me with a money gift and a book of many letters of commendation and appreciation. There were also letters from various people in Sitka, Mt. Edgecumbe, the missionaries with whom I had worked, Church officers, pastors and students. Many guests from various Churches came. All of this was very touching and I realized more than ever that I had made many friends in Sitka. I had much to be thankful for. But I knew that leaving then was best for me, as various ailments had begun to appear. I also felt that the work that I had been doing would be continued by the local congregation and the new pastor. So I left Sitka and headed back home to see my family again.

## In Retrospect

As I look back my heart is filled with gratitude. I cherish the memories of my years in Alaska. My work as a nurse, first with the orphan boys and girls, and later at Igloo, Teller and Shishmaref. The many sermons I have preached, the religious classes, men and women's meetings, girls' and boys' meetings, orchestra and choir practices. I know that my work wasn't always the best, but I was using the abilities and education God had given me. The medical work was always challenging and a means to better reach the Eskimos. Alaska had become my home; the Eskimos my people.

As I look back I also think of the many enjoyable times I had with the Eskimos at Thanksgiving, Christmas, Easter and other festive gatherings. Then I remember the many cakes, cookies, doughnuts, popcorn balls I made, the gallons of coffee, tea, Kool-aid or cocoa I brewed for various events, the many presents I wrapped, candy and nut bags prepared and the joys this all brought. And the sparkling eyes and happy smiles of the children. Busy years, and great fun!

We have God's promise that His word shall not return void. So when I think of the wonderful spiritual awakening we had at Shishmaref while I was there I am tempted to ask,"Was the Lord giving us a little glimpse into the results of our work?" We are prone to ask ourselves, "Is there any fruit as a result of our efforts?" I know there was — and it continues today.

Always in Alaska we had the wonderful interest, love and cooperation of our beloved Lutheran Church and the Home Mission Board. Many friends had prayed for our work, sent dozens of mission boxes and helped us financially and spiritually. I had worked with many dedicated missionaries and learned to love them for their dedication and strong faith. I will always cherish the memories of those years with the Eskimo people. I will never forget them.

In all humility I can only say, "I tried to do what God wanted me to do, when He called me to Alaska as one of His servants." No doubt He was disappointed in me many times, but He knew what I was able to do and expected nothing more.

# *A P P E N D I X*

## Contents

# Crown of Joy
### Based on the life of Helen Caroline Frost, 1896-1986

Helen C. Frost's niece is a prize winning poet. This poem, a tribute to her aunt, was published in the book, *Skin of A Fish, Bones of A Bird* (Ampersand Press, 1993). Influenced by her aunt, she also went to Alaska and taught in an Athabaskan village school in the Kuskowin River Valley for three years. She also visited the villages where her Aunt had served and took recordings which she sent to Aunt Helen at Carlsbad. She now travels extensively, giving readings in schools and workshops for writers. Grants from the National Endowment for the Arts fund these journeys, One early photograph shows her with her Aunt Helen. The other is a recent picture of Helen M. Frost, author of this poem.

### 1910 *No Choice But to Believe*

To a girl fourteen in 1910,
no doctor could prepare, nor father
console. Her mother couldn't really
speak to her from heaven.
No choice but to believe
the gentle, kindly men.
"Lie down here. Breathe this."
She woke to an absence
ever after present. One breast
growing on alone, into, she must
have felt, no chance of marriage.
How could she speak of this
to any man? How could she not?
God and her father would love her.

### 1926 *The Tangled Voices Stretched*

God and her father would love her
but how could she unbraid their voices?
Father, in the pulpit, all her life
the voice of God. To picture
God: a fearsome, loving father.
Then, a third strand, too -

the voice of her desire, stronger, clear.
When the letter came, "You are needed
in Alaska." "Do you want to go?"
the tangled voices stretched
and all sang "Yes" together.
Father said, "Remember, Jesus said
'Lo, I am with you always,
Even unto the end of the world.'"

### 1927 *Before She Knew Her Home*

"Even unto the end of the world."
her father said, not knowing how close
he was to death. When the letter
came to her, by train, by boat, by dog-team,
that first year, she sat alone, months
since he was buried, she not knowing.
Months before she knew her home
was here, her love, her work.
That world could have fractured then
like spring ice, sent her floating
off alone in freezing water, no land in sight.
But people there were watchful, wanted her
to stay. They reached, she held -
days, weeks, seasons, years.

## 1975  *A Yellow Flower*

Days, weeks, seasons, years of love and
labor,
she remembered them to Maury, his love
a gift she'd not had time to dream of.
Out together, walking, taking pictures,
a yellow flower would make her think of
Shishmaref.
"As soon as there were patches of dry
ground
we'd take our picnic out. One year, I made
seventy-four doughnuts." Evenings,
playing scrabble, she might put down
"gangrene," tell about the man whose leg
she'd saved,
the beaded mukluks his wife made for her,
to thank her.
She'd show pictures. "This dog-team took
us five hundred miles." "Seal-pokes store
the frozen berries."
Maury smiled, touched her shoulder. "Oh,
my."

## 1979  *Softly Breaking at the Edges*

She smiled and touched his shoulder. "Oh,
Maury, listen. My niece went to
Shishmaref, They made  this tape..."
 Organ music filled two rooms.
In one, the harmony of someone cooking
hotcakes,
dogs outside, a baby. She knew this time of
year that sea was freezing into silence, while
here she heard its liquid rhythm all year
round,  softly breaking at the edges of this
room.  Maury's room. She could use his
tape recorder any time she liked.
"Listen to him play that organ.
He must be as old as we are. I taught him
how,  and think of that, he still remembers."
"There is a green hill far away" she
hummed along,

## *As the Ship Went Out*

Climbing to the top and gazing out
from the mission to the freighter
coming in each year, she never knew
what it would bring. She knew what she
had ordered and she liked to see that,
stacked against the winter.
Then, as the ship went out she sorted
through the unexpected gifts -coats and
sweaters, stuffed toys, mittens.
Once a furnace for the orphanage,
radiators, pipes, and all the fittings.
Sometimes something odd, you wouldn't
know  what it was for,  but someone
always found a use for everything.
So much thought and human goodness,
so much love.

## *To All of Us*

She thought of all the love and human
goodness
and about the question someone asked,
"Did you ever think you might be
interfering,
destroying what you didn't understand?"
Yes,
she wondered about that sometimes.
You do what seems right,
but you never know. Maybe it was like the
doctors doing the best they could to save
her life, so long ago. Today, they wouldn't
do that, they know more. But life refuses
to be diminished by our limitations.
It takes whatever we can give
and gives back more. To all of us, as
to a girl fourteen in 1910.

---

# A TRIBUTE TO THE NATIVE PEOPLE

Helen Frost's Memoirs reveal her love for the Native People of Alaska. The correspondence of other Lutherans who served there shows they also admired the Inupiat who live in that Arctic region. While this is Helen Frost's story, it also describes the Inupiat who "became so very dear" to Helen that she soon decided, "Alaska is my home, the Eskimo my people."

In 1972 the Lutheran Church asked a respected scholar, Henriette Lund, to study that ministry and help plan for the future. Her study led to two reports, *Of Eskimos and Missionaries* and *Arctic Children of God* which include stories of gifted Inupiat leaders and pays tribute to their gifts and abilities. Unfortunately these reports are out of print. These quotes are from those reports:

*"The gifted Itupiaq live in a world of ice and snow — about 5,600 square miles of it, inaccessible without dog sled or plane; no roads, no telephones and the nearest tree is ninety miles away. But there is much on which to build. A people who could choose willingly to live permanently in the Arctic country and who succeeded in doing so through the centuries, have something valuable to offer their country. Theirs are wondrous qualities of endurance, ingenuity, bravery, honesty, good humor, extraordinary kindness and the spirit of sharing. This is what makes them a challenge, a responsibility and certainly a joy to work with.*

*"A bare account of lives of Eskimos and missionaries, such as has been given in these books, does not do justice to any of them. To do so would take a better writer and one who has shared more continuously their experiences. Many noteworthy natives have received no mention for lack of information. Sacrifices have been great, and rewards have been the inner satisfaction rather than worldly goods or renown, not to mention the comforts and conveniences to which most of us are addicted.*

*"That the Christian faith has enriched the lives of many Eskimos who have adopted it is without doubt. In addition to that, the missions have made an outstanding contribution to all of us by witnessing to the fact that the Eskimos are a people in their own right as fully as any other on earth. We, the technically advanced, are not their benefactors; we have been the takers, not the givers. We are truly their beneficiaries in having learned from them something of the agonies involved when one culture overrides another.*

*"In understanding and acting on these truths, the missions surely have helped us to understand more fully our responsibilities as children of God."*

The readers will learn about Helen Frost, and the Inupiat with whom she lived for many years. Some pioneer Lutherans served before Helen came; others continue this ministry today. Income from the sale of this book will go to the Lutheran Foundation which supports the continuing ministry of the Alaska Native Congregations.

If you would like to receive the Newsletters of the Alaska Native congregations, please write to the Alaska Synod, 1847 W. Northern Lights Blvd., Ste.2, Anchorage, AK 99517-3343. Ask to be on their mailing list.

# NOTED ALASKAN ARTIST, GEORGE AHGUPUK

George Aden Ahgupuk, one of Alaska's finest artists, was born in 1911 in the village of Shishmaref on the Seward Peninsula. He was the second of four children of John and Mary Ahgupuk. His sister, Mary, married another outstanding artist, Kivetoruk Moses.

Paper was scarce when George was in school in Noorvik. When he drew pictures on his lesson sheets his teachers called him a "paper-waster". George's father became ill when he was in the fourth grade. George stopped school so he could hunt seal, walrus and other game and gather wood for their family. Although he had no time to draw, all the sights and scenes of Eskimo life were being stored up for later use.

In 1930 his Uncle Kim took him 135 miles by dog team to Nome to visit a dentist. On his way back, hunting ptarmigan with a friend, George was injured when he slid down a cliff, hit the rocks at the bottom, and fractured a bone in his leg. That evening Ahgupuk managed to hobble back to his Uncle Kim's dog sled and ride back to Shishmaref.

In Shishmaref there was no doctor or nurse to treat his injury. His leg continued to bother him and finally in 1934 George was taken north to the Alaska Native Service Hospital at Kotzebue. There the doctors discovered he had a tubercular infection in the fractured bone. They operated and in time George would be fine, but he had to remain in the hospital for eight months. There he had lots of time to draw but had no supplies. He burned big wooden matches and drew charcoal sketches on tissue paper. Each day he would draw Alaskan scenes then destroy his work.

One day his nurse, Nan Gallagher, found some of his sketches and was impressed. She told George, "I'll bring you lots of paper and pencil tomorrow. Draw some Christmas cards for me and I will pay you." George was elated to receive $2.00 for doing two dozen cards. "That was the first money I earned from my art. When I went home I had ten dollars in my parka and I thought that was big money. But at home I had no paper so I ask mother for sealskin. Ever since I use skins for my paper, — reindeer, caribou, seal or moose." Preparing each skin took six to eight hours of scraping, stretching and 30 days of drying and bleaching. George worked very hard to develop his skill and was able to sell more of his work.

He married Kara Allockeok of Shishmaref. When their first child was born the Shishmaref pastor wrote in his newsletter, "George Ahgupuk stopped by to tell me, 'Today there is another little Lutheran in the village!'" Everyone belonged to that Lutheran Church for it was the only one in the village.

# NOTED ALASKAN ARTIST, GEORGE AHGUPUK

In Shishmaref, George continued to develop his talent. A few tourists came to their village and some were glad to purchase his art work. But he received very little for his work. "I often got one dollar for something I would get $100 for today." Then a lady in Nome, Mrs. Oliver Weaver, saw his work and offered to circulate and sell his art.

In 1936 Rockwell Kent, the New York artist, visited Alaska and was impressed when he saw his work. He purchased Ahgupuk's painting, *Reindeer Roundup* for one dollar. Back in New York Kent told his friends, "I have discovered the greatest of Eskimo artists." He showed two of George Ahgupuk's art pieces he had bought. Kent praised Ahgupuk for his "strong sense of both the pictorial and the dramatic." TIME Magazine and the New York TIMES quoted Kent when he praised Ahgupuk's work. The Associated American Artists elected Ahgupuk as a member and shipped him pens, ink, drawing paper and lithographic stones. They sold some of his drawings as Christmas cards and his works were exhibited in galleries. George Ahgupuk was becoming known back east, but still few people in Alaska knew about his talent.

In 1948 George and his family moved to Nome then in 1951 to Anchorage. where more people would see his work. Many tourists were visiting Alaska and they were glad to purchase his art. He was invited to exhibit his work in Seattle, San Jose, and Gallup, New Mexico.

George illustrated the 1951 Report of the Alaska Housing Authority Annual Report which won a national award. Then he illusrated a book for a Shishmaref teacher.

While Edward L. Keithahn had taught school at Shishmaref, George's sister, Bessie translated the legends told by the elders of the village. Keithan gathered these and hoped some day to publish them. Some years later Keithan asked Ahgupuk to illustrate the book "Igloo Tales" which was published in 1953 by the Bureau of Indian Affairs. Now well known, he was asked to illustrate five other books and his work appeared in many magazines and journals.

When asked why people like his art so well, he replied, "Well, I don't know. That's a thousand dollar question. I try to make it neat. Best as I can. I don't copy photographs. Mine is just freehand work." Preparing skins kept him busy for he needed 150 to 200 skins each year to fill the orders he received. He was one of the best known Alaskan artists.

Later George injured his knee cap and again had surgery. After that he needed crutches to get around. In his last years he made few sketches. When he learned that the Memoirs of Helen Frost would be published he gladly gave permission to use his art to illustrate the book for he knew income from the book would help support the Native Lutheran ministries in Alaska.

George Ahgupuk died on April 1, 2001 and his funeral was held in Central Lutheran Church in Anchorage. He will be missed not only by his family and his many Inupiat friends, but by thousands who appreciated his remarkable talent and ability to portray Inupiat life in Alaska.

# A TRIBUTE FROM THE PASTOR OF THE MISSION PLANE

*For nine years Pastor Norval Hegland was the "Flying" Superintendent of the Lutheran ministries on the Seward Peninsula. Norval and Helen had become good friends and he kept in touch her after he left Alaska. When he learned we were preparing her Memoirs, he sent this tribute to Helen.*

"Humanly speaking, Helen Frost is the reason why I went to Alaska. I was a mission pastor in South Dakota and flew a mission plane to get around my churches. She gave an Alaska presentation at a Circuit meetings at Pollock, South Dakota. She was so enthusiastic about her subject that she missed her bus for her next day's appointment. So I was asked to fly her to Brookings, S. Dak where her brother was a teacher. As we flew along she compared the terrain to Alaska's and later asked how I would like to go to Alaska. I told her I would be pleased to go. She told our Missions Director, Dr. Philip Dybvig about my interest and soon I had a call to be Superintendent of the Lutheran Eskimo Missions. We flew up in the new Mission plane and on September 13, 1951 landed at Teller, Alaska. Teller was our home for nine years. When we arrived in Alaska Helen was there to give me suggestions and guidance. I felt we were a good team. She was very wise, understood the Eskimo and was respected by them.

"When my wife was hospitalized in Seattle, I needed someone to care for our children when I was out on my flying missions, and Helen came to my assistance. I am highly indebted to her and owe her a debt of gratitude for all she did for me.

"Helen was Danish and she gave me the complete works of Hans Christian Andersen in Danish. Whenever I read them I think of Helen.

"I recall Helen as a happy person and she had 'chosen life.' She never allowed herself to sink into despair or discouragement. Her Danish persistence and good humor saw her through many an obstacle.

"Once when we were flying from Fairbanks she told me she was curious to learn about the historic village of Unalakleet. So we landed there and met the Mission Covenant Missionaries. They were kind and gave us a rare present — fresh vegetables!

"From Unalakleet we flew on to Nome where I landed at the old City Airfield. I told her while I tied down the airplane she should go to the rest rooms. She came back and said, "There ain't no such animal!"

"After Helen had moved to Carlsbad I kept in touch with her. I have some of her letters and her spirit and her faith were still strong. On May 28, 1986 I wrote to Helen, telling her: " I continue to thank God for you and all you have meant to me and my family. Those were great days, working with you in Alaska, and I cherish those memories. You are an unusual person, giving gentle guidance, but not being bossy. You were a great help to us "Cheechaukers." I always felt that with you there, things would work out O. K."

"I corresponded with her toward the last and respect her as one of our Saints to the Eskimo. Her last letter to me was dated Feb. 1, 1986. She was having much physical pain but was strong spiritually. She wrote: "So I am quiet in bed. Pray that I may get back on my feet. Isaiah 41:10 has been my daily help. 'Fear not, for I am with you, says the Lord. I will strengthen you, I will help you, I will uphold you with my victorious right hand.' I repeat it many times a day. Much love in Christ, Helen"

"My next letter to Helen was returned, marked "Deceased."

"As I reflect on Helen's life and work, I conclude that she was one of God's special angels (messengers) who had a profound influence on my life which has lasted to this very day! Blessed be her memory. I thank God for Helen Frost."

*.....Norval Hegland   August 4, 1999*

# HELEN'S GOOD FRIEND, ETHEL

"I knew Helen when she first came to the Lutheran Orphanage across the Bay. She was very busy with her work there so it was later at Igloo that I really got to know and love her.

"Mother and I were running the little Trading Post in the small village of Igloo where Helen was the missionary nurse. Each morning we would see Helen with her nurse's kit going to visit her people. One morning she would visit those on one side. The next day, those on the other side.

"She made much of holidays. A very accomplished seamstress, she made jackets and parkas for the girls and boys from used coats that had been sent in mission boxes from friends in the "States." They were good looking and very warm.

"One some occasions she made bag lunches for everyone. Baked loaves and loaves of bread. Many times it was pop corn balls, —tubs of them. Mother and I liked to help make those pop corn balls which everyone in Igloo enjoyed so much.

"We shared unique experiences. One spring she received a telegram that she was needed in Shishmaref to fill in for the missionaries who were leaving for the summer. The supply ship would be in Teller in a few days and she needed to be on it. She knew the only possible way she could get there would be by taking her boat and trying to get past the ice covered Lake by using the sloughs that ran parallel to it. There were many sloughs and the trick was to find the right ones to take. The teacher, Mr. Burkher drew us a map which helped a lot. We finally made it to the Agaipuk River where some native people from our village were camping on their way to their fishing camps. A crack had opened up on the lake and they were hurrying to use it before it closed. We had to portage across to them, dragging our boat and supplies. Just made it and were on our way again. Made it nicely the rest of the way across the lake and through the Tuksuk channel and a way down Grantly Harbour before we struck solid ice at Deece Creek. We camped on the shore until the wind changed and moved the ice out, then we continued our journey. Helen just made it in time for the ship that took her up to Shishmaref.

"We were both in Nome one summer when a disastrous fire broke out that took nearly all of the business district and the first two streets of Nome. I was staying with friends who had a jewelry store. We tried to save their most valuable things but they had a terrible loss. They started up again from scratch when it was over. Helen's hotel burned. The hospital was spared and the nurses asked Helen to stay with them.

"In later years when Helen was living in California, she often came back here. It was always a happy time when she came. In the last two years of her life, when she was not able to travel, I went to Carlsbad to see her. I spent a week with her early this spring. She was not at all well, —mostly had to be in bed. Still she was glad to have me there and, on her better days, we had many nice visits. Shortly after that she had to go to the hospital and in a short time passed away. I feel so grateful I had those days with her."

*....Ethel Marx Vogen,* December 1986

# "Helen Frost Visited our Church"

"I grew up in a parsonage. During my elementary school years, our family lived in a small town in central Wisconsin and we had many missionaries come to our church. They would talk to the Sunday School and always teach us a song and a Bible verse in their "other" language. Then they would deliver a sermon to the congregation. I enjoyed those special people from China, Madagascar, and Alaska. Of course, we were particularly fortunate because they stayed at the parsonage for there were no motels or good hotels in our small town.

"One of the missionaries who I remember was Helen Frost. She brought fur mukluks, toys of fur and she wore her own fur jacket! I was amazed at the lovely fur items and I wondered how cold it must get to wear such a warm jacket.

"Helen Frost was a tall lady and when I see her in my mind's eye, she appears brown hair and clothes. She was a fairly soft spoken person. When she told the stories of her life, at what seemed to me to be the end of the earth, she came alive. I could not imagine how she could be a nurse, doctor, teacher, post mistress, store keeper and much more! She seemed fearless. "As I thought about Helen Frost and her life so isolated and alone, I kept thinking how lonesome I would be for my parents, sisters, Grandpa and cousins.

"The logistics in having one or several missionaries as house guests was interesting. Of course we four girls would double up and even triple up so the missionary would have a good room. The bathroom was another story. One bathroom in a household was common— so when you have guests it is different. For example, we did not lock the bathroom door since we were four girls. On several occasions the missionary guest would open the bathroom door and there would be one of us. My favorite time — when my sister looked up and said, 'Hi!!'

"My Mother was Lutheran Daughters of the Reformation Advisor for years. The words 'Shishmaref' and "'Teller" still stir up memories in my mind. Helen was very important to the L.D.R. girls. I was privileged to see Helen again after she retired and was a resident at the Carlsbad home. She really had not changed much. She still had her camera— and told us she still look long walks on the beach. There will never be another person like Helen Frost."

............ Mary Tanner Egdahl, Lafayette, California; Nov. 5, 2000

---

## *Too Many Layettes!*

The Eskimo ministry had many friends who prayed, sent offerings and each summer sent many boxes of clothing, — gifts for the Christmas season. But one year they had a big problem. Their friends responded to one request with far too many gifts!

Letters had been sent asking for layettes for Eskimo babies. This special emergency appeal apparently touched so many that soon an unending stream of packages was on the way to Nome. Air pilots struggled with the extra weight of these bundles. Post office staff at Nome could not believe so many packages were being sent to the Lutheran Church! For days and weeks the boxes kept coming until the limited storage space at Our Savior's was filled with layettes. Many more than were needed for all the new Eskimo babies up and down the coast. What should they do? Then someone suggested, "Share this good fortune with others!" That is what they did! They shipped many layettes to missionaries in Asia. The mission workers there were pleased by the generosity of their friends in Alaska who solved a puzzling problem. Some say that, even today, one should not mention the word, *"layette",* in Nome.

# MEMORIES OF EARLY DAYS AT TELLER

Teller's rich history started years before Helen Frost arrived. When the Mission celebrated an Anniversary some of the elders shared their memories of the Brevigs who were the first missionaries. Some who spoke had been children cared for by the Brevigs in the Orphanage they started after the tragic epidemic.

Many of the spontaneous talks by the Eskimos were stories of their childhood years at the Mission. These outpourings of their hearts as they searched the past for childhood memories help us understand the early years at Teller, even before the Orphanage opened.

One of the men, Jerry Kaloke, spoke in a straight-forward way. "God called Brevig to come to us. He landed right at this spot where we are, 63 years ago these days." Jerry had come to Teller Mission at Christmas time 1918, after the loss of his parents in the epidemic, and he stayed until the following Spring. The mission house burned while he was here and was rebuilt on the same place.

Jerry had married Dora Kakiluviluk who was the lone survivor of her family. Her parents and five brothers and sisters had died in the epidemic and her childhood was spent in the orphanage. Dora told her story, " I remember that I was weak and cold and lying beside my parents but I did not know they were dead. Rev. Fosso and my brother came to take me but I refused to go. My brother coaxed me and tried to tell me that I would have a nice new home, but I refused to leave. When he promised me my little sled and puppy, I went with him. That is how I got into the children's home. I was well cared for and had enough to eat, though there were many of us. Dagny Brevig taught me my ABC's."

Robert's wife, Annie, dwelt with simplicity on her childhood at Serpentine River, where Rev. Brevig came to preach. "The natives would go from family to family to pray and then come a long way to the mission for baptism and communion. Rev. Brevig was wonderful in telling us about our Savior. So many people got saved."

Robert Otiktituk told his story: "I got acquainted with our first missionaries about the last three years of Mrs. Brevig's life. It was in April or May that my parents and I were baptized by Rev. Brevig. Fourteen other persons asked to be baptized. Some came with their families long distances from Okpik and Shishmaref to learn more about this "God of love." When they learned they wanted to be baptized and later to receive holy communion. People traveled by dogteam to Teller Reindeer Station from Okpik and Shishmaref for Bible study, baptism and later for holy communion. That was long ago."

Tom Rock told of being at the Mission as a child. "My parents died in the flu. Rev. Fosso found us two children near by them and he wrapped us in blankets, took us to the mission and saved us." Then he recalled hearing from older Eskimos of the time that Rev. Brevig's wife, Julia had died. They told Tom that Rev. Brevig stood at the graveside of his wife and said to the Eskimos, "She rests in the land of the people she loved and for whom she labored and died. Her most glorious monuments were in the mission which was her life."

The history is rich and tells of many faithful people who suffered great hardship. Today the history moves on in all the congregations as new chapters are being written each year.

# HELEN FROST

| | |
|---|---|
| 1896 | Born in Council Bluffs, Iowa where her father served a mission church |
| 1900 | Family moved to Sheyenne, ND; her Mother died when Helen was four |
| 1904 | Her father married again, later four more children, Esther, Reuben, Gerhart and Florence were born |
| 1907 | At age 11, Helen began playing organ for father's services |
| 1913-14 | Studied at Sioux Falls Normal School, receives Teacher's Certificate |
| 1916 | Major flu epidemic- Helen cares for family &considers becoming a nurse |
| 1918 | Reads about nursing training at Lutheran Deaconness Hospital in Chicago |
| 1919- 1921 | Studies at Deaconess Hospital, completes program |
| 1921- 1922 | Works at the Hospital, decides to take further study to earn R. N. Degree |
| 1923- 1924 | Completes her R. N. Degree program at Ancker Hospital in St. Paul |
| 1925 | Did private duty nursing |
| 1926 | Receives letter from Sister Anna Huseth in Teller, Alaska "We need you here. I think you are just the one for this place!" After prayer and a talk with her Pastor father, she accepted the Call. |
| 1926- 1929 | Teller Orphanage, then her first furlough back home in Minnesota |
| 1930- 1935 | Igloo, no furlough for five years |
| 1935- 1938 | Served at Indian Mission in Wisconsin, — but homesick for Alaska |
| 1938- 1949 | Back at Igloo, stays eleven years, — until the Igloo Mission is closed |
| 1950- 1951 | Teller Town |
| 1951- 1955 | Shishmaref — visited Nome and located lot for a new Church there |
| 1955- 1961 | Sitka Lutheran, working with native students at Mt. Edgecumbe School |
| 1962- 1986 | Retires: Later moved to Carlsbad-by-the-Sea, Carlsbad, California |
| 1986 | Died May 19, 1986. Funeral at the Carlsbad Chapel on May 21. |

Wrote her Memoirs. In 1969 King of Kings Lutheran Church, where she worshipped, mimeographed them,.but it was never printed.

Some of Helen's family were with her for several days before she died. Pictures of her family were on the bulletin board near her bed and her ever-present camera was hanging on the bed rail. She reached for it, handed it to Jean and asked her, "Take a picture of Jack and me!" Though she was weak, she was able to tell Jean and Bernie just what to do with her things. "Please give my camera to my friend Val who works at the desk." The lovely plant sent by two of her nieces was planted by the gardener near her apartment.

**CARLSBAD BY THE SEA**

# Celebration of the life of
# Helen Caroline Frost

August 28, 1896- May 19, 1986
Wednesday, May 21, 1986
Carlsbad- by-the-Sea Chapel

## From the Funeral Service Meditation by Pastor Stewart D. Millon

"I want to begin with a word from *Kept Moments,* a book by Helen's brother, Gerhard Frost, who is not able to be with us today.

## The Question

"Today as we talked,
Friend to friend,
she shared this memory with me.

"Keeping vigil at her sister's side
with death only moments away,
she longed to share thought and feeling,
but the dear one had moved beyond,
out of reach as she lay
in comatose stillness.

"Suddenly she stirred
and startled the waiting one
with a question, 'Yea' what, Ethel?'
Some seconds of panic
(What does she mean? What does
she want? I mustn't fail her now!)
and then as a gift, the answer came:
'Yea, though I walk through the valley
of the shadow of death, I will fear
no evil, for thou art with me.'

"The dying one smiled and said,
'I will fear no evil, for thou art
with me, ..with me. . .' and on this
she pillowed her head."

"Those could well have been Helen's words. I can imagine her saying
"Yea – what?" and smiling as she hears, 'I will fear no evil for thou art with me.'

"Helen lived an adventurous life; a style of life which few of us have known. She lived that life for 35 years because it was her call; because she walked with God all the way. She walked hand in hand with Him as she served Him in a very unique way. On the back of the bulletin today is a brief summary of her life, the places in Alaska where she served so well.

"Hers was a life of sacrifice of self in the service of God, by reaching out to others. She lived a Christ-like life and today we have come to celebrate her life. Helen was a friend; a Christian sister; and we miss her. So many here today have been touched by her. She served not only in Alaska, but also for the past twenty three years here at Carlsbad-by-the-Sea,. She continued to give of herself, here in the residence and in the Health Facility. She was truly gifted — gifted by God's Holy Spirit, with those gifts listed in Galatians, 'love, joy, peace, patience, kindness, goodness, faithfulness, gentleness, self-control.' "

Continued..... *the Service at Carlsbad- by-the-Sea*

Helen's brother, Reuben, spoke at the Service.

"I am here to represent Helen's family and first of all I want to express our appreciation. Our sincere thanks to the Lutheran Church which owns and operates Carlsbad-by-the-Sea, to all who have worked with Helen and for her, and the many fine friends she has made here.

"As a member of King of Kings Lutheran Church, Helen would want me to express her special appreciation to Pastor Millon and the members there and also her gratitude to Chaplain Wharton and Chaplain Brandt. The family is thankful for the over-whelming outpouring of concern and the expression of friendship by those who have lived, worked and visited with Helen. All of her family appreciates the professional help and care Helen received during her illness.

"When the news came of Helen's death, we were visiting our daughter, Nancy and her family in Texas. There was a lull then Nancy spoke and referred to Matthew 25, "When I think of Aunt Helen I am reminded of the Bible verse, 'Well done, thou good and faithful servant.' That verse always makes me think of Aunt Helen." Jean and I felt that the entire family would have agreed.

"My brother, Gerhard and I were brought up close together. I want to close with a short poem from his book, *Blessed are the Ordinary:*

> "The profoundest thing one can say of a river
> is that it is on its way to the sea.
> The deepest thought one can think of persons
> is that they are citizens of eternity.
> Moments and years, years and moments,
> pass like sea-bent streams.
> And I? I'm carried on the current of an all possessing love.
> I'm on my way, God's way for me,
> so let it be."

"Again, to all of you, thanks again for everything. "

-------

(Graveside services were held that afternoon at Eternal Hills Memorial Park.)

-------

Though Helen had lived in California for twenty three years, the bulletin that day revealed that her love for Alaska was still strong. Helen asked that any Memorials be sent to the Lutheran Native Outreach Ministries in Alaska. She still missed that Great Land and its people.

**"Alaska is my home; the Eskimos my people!"**

# APPRECIATION

**Editorial Advisory Committee:**
Rev. & Mrs. John Maakestad, Anchorage, Alaska
Mary Miller, Nome, Alaska
Helen Frost Thompson, Ft. Wayne, Indiana
Rev. Norval Hegland, Lakeside, Montana
Bishop Ronald Martinson , Anchorage, Alaska
Harvey Brandt, Sitka, Alaska

Many friends shared valuable materials.
Paul Daniels, Archivist, Luther Seminary
Bishop Clarence Solberg,
Rev. & Mrs.Otis Lee
Laura Samuelson, Director, Clara McLain Memorial Museum,  Nome, Alaska
Fr. Louis L. Renner, S. J., Catholic Diocese of Northern Alaska
Yvonne Mozee, Sitka, Alaska
The Pastors of the Alaska Native Lutheran Congregations:
    Teller, Brevig Mission, Shishmaref, Nome, Wales and Anchorage


**Sponsors**:

The Elders and Pastors of the Alaska Native Lutheran Congregations at
    Teller, Brevig Mission, Shishmaref, Nome, Wales and Anchorage
The Alaska Synod Bishops: Ron Martinson and Rev. Larry Jorgenson
Rev. and Mrs. John Maakestad
The Family of Helen Frost
Rev. Norval Hegland
Judith Simondson, Des Moines, Iowa
President Loren Anderson, Pacific Lutheran University
President Luther S. Luebke, California Lutheran University
President John Stamm, Trinity Lutheran College, Issaquah, WA
Rev. and Mrs. Mark Houglum
Lutheran Brotherhood Branch 8627, Contra Costa County, CA
Lutheran Brotherhood Branch 8279, Tacoma, WA
St. Matthew Lutheran Church, Walnut Creek, California
Good Shepherd Lutheran Church, Concord, California
Rev. Paul Daniels, Archivist, Luther Seminary
Prof. Patrick Keifert, Luther Seminary
Prof. James R. Nieman, Wartburg Seminary
Bishop H. George Anderson, ELCA, Chicago IL
Secretary Lowell Almen, ELCA, Chicago IL
Ms. Elisabeth Wittman, Archivist, ELCA, Chicago, IL
Rev. Richard Magnus, Division of Outreach, ELCA, Chicago IL
Dr. David Miller, Editor, The LUTHERAN, ELCA, Chicago IL
Rev. David Halaas, Augsburg /Fortress, Minneapolis MN
Sitka Lutheran Church,  History Committee
King of Kings Lutheran Church, Memorial Committee
Rev. Ludwig Siqueland, former Staff for Alaska Ministries
Richard Londgren, Editor, S.W. Washington Synod News
Harvey Brandt, Sitka, Alaska
The Officers and Friends of the Lutheran History Center of the West

# MANY FRIENDS HAVE HELPED

John and Louise Maakestad first encouraged us to publish Helen Frost's Memoirs. Two women have been especially helpful: Mary Miller, a native of Shishmaref, a staff member for LAMP on the Seward Peninsula and Helen Frost's niece, Helen Frost Thompson. She shared family papers and photographs. Harvey Brandt at Sitka Lutheran Church has given valuable counsel and provided information on Helen's Sitka years as she worked with native students at the high school and at Sitka Lutheran Church. Magdalena Spiegle shared her stories of Helen at Sitka. We were given permission to use material, art work and photographs from Alice Postell's excellent history, *Where did the Reindeer Come From?* Paul Daniels opened Helen Frost's fine collection in the Luther Seminary Archives. Michael Kurtz of the National Archives provided valuable documents. The Presbyterian Archives in Philadelphia shared photographs. Helpful material on the Nome fire came from Laura Samuelson, Director of the Carrie McLain Memorial Museum. US Congresswoman Lois Capps secured a copy of Dagny Dahle Nimmo's *Eskimo Phrase Book* from the Library of Congress. The excellent cover was designed by my nephew, Lance Hidy, noted graphic artist.

George Ahgupuk gave permission to use his outstanding native art depicting the history of the Inupiat on the Seward Peninsula. At first Helen Frost traveled by dog team and boat but later flew with Pastor Norval Hegland, pilot of the Lutheran Mission Plane. Norval shared photographs, new materials and some of Helen's letters. These told of her hope to encourage native youth to do graduate study to prepare to serve in Alaska.

Helen would be pleased that these native youth are at Trinity Lutheran College in Issaquah, Washington. Mrs Elaine Stamm taught their confirmation class at the Native Lutheran Congregation in Anchorage.

Left to right: Mrs. Elaine Stamm, Robert Gales, Deanza Hjalseth, Bobbie Kiyutelluk. Her husband, Dr. John Stamm, is President of Trinity Lutheran College, formerly Lutheran Bible Institute. Other Inupiat students have studied at Pacific Lutheran University in Tacoma. Some, like Mary Miller, have completed additional graduate studies.

## Emma Willoya - *one of the first orphans saved by the Brevigs*

Henriette Lund tells this story in her book *Of Eskimos and Missionaries.*

"A miner on a trail near Nome heard someone crying. In the snow he found a little girl who was almost dead. He picked her up, wrapped her in a fur blanket and quickly took her to Pastor Tollef Brevig and his wife, Julia. They welcomed her and cared for her for many years. Years later Henriette Lund met that child, now an adult.

"This is the nameless, almost forgotten lifeless little waif, nursed and tutored by Julia and Tollef Brevig, who was to become a treasured Christian worker and a distinguished citizen of the North. This is the story she told me:

"I do not know my real name or my birthday," Emma said in her soft voice. "I was born on a whaling ship in the Arctic and never knew my father. I don't remember my mother, a full-blood Eskimo, who had the measles sickness. A man who called himself my uncle found me beside my dead mother and took possession of me. He carried me around into drinking places to beg, and when I was no longer useful to him he threw me half naked into a snow bank. Someone heard me cry, picked me up from the snow, wrapped me in a fur blanket, and brought me to the Brevigs at the mission station. It took me almost three years to get warm, my eyes still foggy for my eye balls had been frozen."

"We worked hard at the mission," Emma remembers, "but it was good for us. We children helped bake tubs of bread, towed ice blocks for drinking water along three miles of beach, hauled driftwood seven or eight miles. Even after we grew up we came back to the mission for spring house cleaning. This was one way to show that we were grateful."

"To talk with Emma Willoya is to know that she is a precious person. Unbroken by pain and tribulation, never servile or ruffled, she is simple and unassuming as she goes about God's business among her fellowmen. Her faith is deep enough to rise above misery, which began the day of her birth.

At the age of "perhaps seventeen" Emma married the young reindeer herder, David Willoya, with 'Papa Brevig' officiating at the wedding. David had begun to work as a herder at the age of twelve and came back to the mission school one winter long enough to learn to write his name. The couple lived in a tent at a reindeer camp at Agiopuk for three years. They walked fifteen miles over frozen country each Sunday, carrying their babies on their back, to attend mission services and to have their children baptized. Their first child, born at the mission, was named Julia Kiahlie (Calm) in honor of her own mother and Mrs. Brevig, who had cared for Emma.

"Teller residents were surprised when Norwegian explorer Roald Amundsen landed his dirigible *Norge* at Teller after completing the first flight over the North Pole. The Brevigs and others gave him a royal welcome. Amundsen was amazed when Emma Willoya, in fluent Norwegian, sang their national anthem, 'Ja Vi Elsker dette Landet." That was Emma's first language, but she also fluent in Eskimo and English! Her linguistic skills kept her busy as a translator. She told Lund, "One morning I may interpret for a surgeon at the hospital, and in the afternoon for a judge in court."

# Emma Willoya - one of the first orphans saved by the Brevigs

Emma had a favorite sled reindeer, Whitey and at night she often curled up against his body to keep warm. Emma often said, "Whitey would never leave me. If Whitey is ever taken far away, —when he is turned loose, he will come back." Later Emma loaned Whitey to Mr. Shields, the reindeer superintendent, for a long sled trip way up to Point Barrow. Would she seeWhitey again? Three years later one morning Whitey stuck his head into Emma's tent! He had been turned loose about ten miles out of Point Barrow. Somehow, over trackless mountains and tundra, Whitey had found his way back to Emma's tent. Emma knew he would!

This brave young woman had a long and complex career, — as a reindeer herder, trapper, fisherman, fur sewer, advocate for native rights, and an ardent mission worker. Her education came from stark realities, not from her skimpy fifth-grade schooling. Her early experiences as she struggled to put them into words underscore her strength of character.

Her interest in the reindeer industry as a way of existence for the Eskimos never waned. She fought many battles for the protection of Eskimo reindeer rights. "When the white man entered the industry," she explains painstakingly, "it meant tragedy to the Eskimos. *My own family lost the herd for which they had given the best years of their lives.*"

In her role as an active member of the Nome Native Reindeer Company she wrote to the Government. "Something should be done to save the reindeer for us. The reindeer are useful, like your cows, and they are good for us Eskimos. They feed themselves on the moss, which grows only here where there are no trees. We use every bit of the animal. The meat is fine to eat, the sinews make strong thread, the hoofs can be cooked, the horns make tools, the hard skin on the forelegs is good for shoes, and the beautiful skin is for the warmest clothing and bedding ever made. The reindeer can lead and drive like a horse." She likes to add with a sparkle: **"Best of all, it was the reindeer that brought the Lutherans to us!"**

On September 1, 1937 the Congress passed the Reindeer Act. Now only the native herders could own reindeer. An appropriation of two million dollars was made to purchase the reindeer herds from other owners. However, it was several years before this was finalized. This Act was a great blow to the Lapp owners, the Saami, who had been brought from Norway to teach the natives how to herd the deer. Some had returned to Norway but others stayed, married, had families and also owned large herds. As a result of the Reindeer Act, the Lapps not only suffered great financial losses. They also were excluded from the occupation they loved. This tragic story is far too complex to report in this book.

The US Congress held hearings about a proposed law to forbid hunting of seals and other marine mammals. That would have made subsistence hunting illegal for the Eskimo. Many natives protested and Emma Willoya gave a strong testimony before the committee. "When the white man hunts it is for sport. The natives hunt so we can live. If this law is passed it will destroy our way of life." The law that was passed permitted subsistence hunting by the natives, but not for commercial purposes.

Emma, like other native women, was skilled in sewing skin garments. She helped organize the Eskimo women and for fifteen years Emma was the Director of the new Nome Skin Sewers Cooperative Association. She did this "so older ones can teach the

# Emma Willoya - one of the first orphans saved by the Brevigs

young." During the war the Nome women and those in other villages made thousands of mukluks, parkas and sleeping bags for servicemen in Alaska. President Truman sent a letter of thanks "for your selfless service in your country's time of need." Later the Nome Sewers also outfitted Admiral Byrd's South Pole Expedition. For that work Admiral Byrd, in his letter of thanks, included a bonus of $5,000! But handling the raw furs in the cold finally affected Emma's health. She was forced to withdraw as supervisor but she still supported this cooperative enterprise for gifted natives.

The Library of Congress in 1950 directed Emma, in her capacity as secretary of the Nome Eskimo Community, to assemble information about the history of the Eskimos. She gave this careful study. When asked about the effect of federal aid on the people, Emma replied, "Years ago, for a sick person unable to pay the medical bills, we had to wait for a wire from Juneau for permission to operate. When my own little boy, Joseph, became sick, I took him to the hospital. The doctor said it was appendicitis and sent a telegram to Juneau for permission to operate. My son died before the answer came from Juneau. Now better and quicker aid is given and we like it." Many hardships can be avoided by good housing and more jobs. With better schooling the young people will be more prepared to meet the difficulties than we who had so little."

She saw many changes after Alaska became the 49th State on January 3, 1959. Emma and other natives struggled until the Alaska Native Claims Settlement Act was passed in 1971. Through this act, the Eskimos, Aleuts, and Indians settled their claims to aboriginal lands with a cash settlement of $962.5 million and 40 million acres of land to be administered by village and regional corporations.

Emma had a large family, three daughters and nine sons — seven of whom were in war service. Her daughter Margaret, who had married a soldier and was living in New York, sent her a plane ticket to come to visit her new grandchildren. Without hesitation Emma undertook the long journey. On the crowded streets of New York City she had the courage to be herself and walked about simply dressed in clothes unfamiliar to her, with her braids of straight black hair. She smiled genially at passersby on the streets, greeting them, as she would have done on Main Street in Nome. Her main interest was purchasing gifts for her twenty-six grandchildren. But she couldn't tarry long. "It must be tomcod fishing time and the winter's cache of food must be put in." After her look at the world outside she was satisfied to go back to her Arctic home. "It was a nice place there, too lonesome, but I like going places and meeting people. We learn, — anyways, I do.'

Henriette Lund was impressed by this woman who had been saved by the Brevigs and helped by many others. "Emma is a product of the churches' effort. She is poor in worldly goods but rich in her understanding of what is important in life. Saving even one person such as Emma for useful Christian living seems to make worthwhile all the efforts and hardships of the workers of the Lord."

From *"Arctic Children of God"* by Henriette Lund (1974)

-------------------------------

When Emma's health began to fail she moved to a hospital in Anchorage. After a lifetime of service to her people, Emma died February 27, 1983. Several days later many gathered at Our Savior's Lutheran Church in Nome, for a "Celebration of Emma Willoya's Life." Emma was a devoted leader of this congregation for many years.

We include Emma Willoya's story for it tells how the Brevigs started the Teller Orphanage. Emma was a remarkable leader, but other Native people in Alaska have similar abilities, faith and dedication.

# The Seward Peninsula Congregations Today

The Lutheran congregations on the Seward Peninsula continue a ministry that is over 100 years old. People who live there must endure a harsh climate. In December the sun may shine only four hours each day. From October to April temperatures remain below freezing, often going down to 35 or 40 below zero. But in some summer days the sun never sets and the weather is much warmer. With all that sunshine the tundra is covered with flowers, later with berries. The natives catch and dry fish for their winter use.

**Pastor Tollef Brevig** arrived at **TELLER REINDEER STATION in 1894** and started the first congregation. When the tragic epidemic broke out, Tollef and his wife, Julia, opened their home to care for children who had lost their parents. Before the **TELLER ORPHANAGE** closed in 1933, it had cared for 85 children and youth. The Brevigs lost two children: Carl died on March 2 1896 and in 1898 his sister, Borghilde died of whooping cough. Then their Mother, Julia, with no physician near to care for her, died on March 10, 1898 at age 34. The whole community mourned her death. Many citizens in Nome sent gifts and a large stone marks her grave. To honor her memory and all that she had done, officials later changed the name of **TELLER STATION** to **BREVIG MISSION**. Today all 250 residents are active in the Lutheran Congregation there.

Another congregation, **TELLER,** is on the other side of Grantley Harbor. Pastor Brian Crockett serves both Brevig and Teller, commuting between them by boat in summer and snowmobile in winter. In Teller there is also a Catholic Church. Pastor Crockett says in these towns "everybody knows everybody and what people are doing. When somebody gets sick, everyone is affected. Also when someone does well — say, gets a walrus, a lot of fish, or a whale, everyone benefits." When a death occurs, church members come forward to dig graves and make crosses. People take care of those things no matter who died,"

In **WALES,** north of Brevig, **THORNTON MEMORIAL CHURCH** meets twice a week. Their services may last two hours with four or five choir numbers, songs, prayers and testimony. But Pastor Littau says, "People are in no hurry to end it," Wales was once the largest native village in Western Alaska but its population was decimated by the 1918 flu epidemic. Thornton Memorial is the only church in the village of 165 and the oldest building still in use. It needs repairs badly, for it suffers from dry rot, has warped floors and is not insulated. But building supplies are expensive —five sheets of plywood cost $217. At present two rooms are being converted for a health clinic which must move from their former location. From Wales, the westernmost part of the North American continent, you can see Siberia. They say it is the windiest spot on the Peninsula.

Farther north is **SHISHMAREF,** the northernmost congregation of the ELCA. For years residents traveled by dog sled down to Teller Orphanage to ask Pastor Brevig to tell them about the God of the Bible, this God of love. Some asked to be baptized. When he could, Brevig would travel north to visit them, teach a Bible class and lead worship. When he came, they always asked, "When can we have a minister here?"

**Sister Anna Huseth** had a special concern for Shishmaref. Her prayers and letters touched the Lutheran Daughters of the Reformation who adopted this Mission as their special project. They raised funds to call a pastor and build the church. Rev. Elmer Dahle, the first Pastor, directed the construction of the church which included housing for the Pastor and his family. Today it is a strong congregation. Music and education are the prime ministries of Shishmaref Lutheran Church. Senior, Young Adult and Teen Choirs practice weekly and sing songs in English and Inupiaq. All three choirs join in a monthly Singspiration of hymns and Gospel tunes. Members bring their tape recorders and record these hymns sings. Then they play the tapes in their homes, and everyone sings along once more. This is a singing Church!

**Pastor Tim Oslovich** reports, "Most children are involved in Sunday School and Vacation Bible School. During Advent every child in the village learns a Bible verse and participates in the Christmas Eve program. Last year more than 150 children took part. The Church is an important part of life in Shishmaref, and its ministry touches almost every member of the community.

OUR SAVIOR'S LUTHERAN CHURCH in Nome includes many families who have moved there from other villages. **Robert Iyatonguk,** now a respected elder, remembers his boyhood in Shishmaref. His father would whisper in his ear in Inupiaq the pastor's English sermon. While the pastors still preach in English, the opening prayer and Gospel are often read in Inupiaq. Favorite hymns, especially those that stress hope, comfort and assurance, are also sung in the native tongue.

Testimony is central in these congregations. In services at Nome, "members may stand and disclose pain over a loss, thank people for support during a difficult time, ask for forgiveness, or acknowledge God for blessings received."

At Nome weekly attendance at summer services drops by half for many members go fishing, seal hunting, crab fishing and berry picking. These subsistence activities allow people to live primarily or completely from the land. They do the same in all of the villages.

Youth gather at **SALMON LAKE BIBLE CAMP** which is located 35 miles outside Nome. They come from Anchorage and the Seward Peninsula villages for Bible study, outdoors activities, crafts and a good time. Youth from Anchorage, Wales, and Shishmaref must come by plane but those from Teller and Brevig travel by boat and truck. Pastor Frank Macht notes, "The Camp helps reunite urban kids with traditional culture and lets them bond with village kids they might not see otherwise."

Elders play an important role in all of the congregations. Revered for their knowledge of traditional language and culture— knowledge that is rapidly disappearing— elders occupy a special place in Inupiaq society. Like church council and Alaska Synod member Robert Iyatonguk, elders are strong leaders who are often consulted on community and church decisions. They are also a strong connection to the rich traditions of Inupiaq Eskimo culture.

Their faith in God offers healing and hope for the future to people marked by loss — loss of ancestral languages, cultures, and lands. Loss of life, first due to influenza epidemics that wiped out most of a generation, and left many children to be raised as orphans. More recently loss due to alcohol and suicide. Mary Miller conducts grief workshops in Inupiaq villages for LAMP, Lutheran Association of Pilots and Missionaries. "God promises that he will never leave us or forsake us, that through Christ he came to bind up the broken hearted and comfort those who mourn. We know that one day our tears will be wiped away by God himself, and our suffering and pain will end. Because of that, we can grieve with hope."

**Anchorage also has a Native Lutheran Church** which grew out of an outreach ministry aimed at serving urban Inupiaq who "were getting lost socially, economically, and spiritually as they moved from one world to another in the 1970's." They meet on Sunday evenings in the sanctuary of Central Lutheran Church. Twice a month everyone gathers early for a potluck featuring reindeer or moose stew, baked salmon, and "Eskimo ice cream" — berries mixed with seal oil or reindeer fat. Homeless people are often among the guests.

For over a century dedicated Lutheran lay leaders and pastors have been serving in these congregations. These ministries are directed by a Council of lay leaders and pastors who meet regularly to review the programs and make plans for the future. Serving as pastors today: at **Nome, Frank R. Macht;** at **Teller and Brevig Mission, Brian Crockett;** at **Wales, Matthew Littau;** at **Shishmaref, Timothy R. Oslovich**; and at **Anchorage, George and Karen Sonray.**

A closing devotion written by Mary Miller, a native of Shishmaref, now living in Nome

## "Encourage One Another"

*"Let us draw near with a sincere heart in full assurance of faith..Let us hold unswervingly the hope we profess....Let us not give up meeting together..but let us encourage one another."*
Hebrews 10:22-24     (New International Version)

"When I call on Inupiaq elders in their homes, I am often intrigued by their presence, particularly the times when their gentle courtesy and sincere caring for each other prevails over their time of visiting. Communication is from the heart, often with few or no words. I sense an openness, and acceptance, as they sit face to face. I struggle to comprehend the depth and magnitiude of what I am witnessing because it can be fully discerned only from a spiritual context.

"Then I recall Ghandi's insight: that God abides in the hearts of people, and if we hide our hearts from one another, in effect we hide God from one another. In the appropriate environment and expecially in each other's presence, elders come together in spirit, enfolded in God's love, their feet planted on higher ground. It is there that they care for one another, sharing their sorrows, burdens, struggles and disappointments. As their silent guest, I encounter their suffering. I see it in their faces and in their tears; I hear it in the tone of their voices.

"At times, there is joy and laughter from a generation of people who see the good in life, eager to celebrate, eager to remember their rich, vibrant past and history, drawing on the strength of spirit of their ancestors.

"Always there is the deep, enduring faith by which they encourage one another. At that place, where their faith abides, where God abides, they meet Christ, their Brother, their Friend. Broken and suffering, like them. Their Friend, who leads them to higher ground where hope abounds and where they are strengthened and sustained by an everlasting love. And where there is love, there is life. Once again, I marvel at how our Lord manifests Himself in our midst. And I thank Him, from a humble, grateful heart. "

**"Gracious, loving Father, thank you for the blessing of the saints among us who give us the example of living by faith, trust and abiding in your great love. In Jesus' precious name. Amen."**
.......Mary Miller, *Nome, Alaska*

**Mary Miller** is a staff member of **LAMP** who works with members of the Seward Peninsula congregations. The **L**utheran **A**ssociation of **M**issionaries and **P**ilots exists primarily "to help Christian fellowships develop, grow and and become self-sufficient within northern native cultures." They serve isolated villages in Canada and Alaska. Their Ship *Christian,* based in Wrangell, serves in southeast Alaska.

# BIBLIOGRAPHY

J. Walter Johnshoy *Apaurak In Alaska* Dorrance and Co. Philadelphia, 1944

Henriette Lund *Of Eskimos and Missionaries* 1974 American Lutheran Church

Henriette Lund *The Arctic Children of God* 1973 American Lutheran Church

*Eskimoland* and *Newsletters* from Shishmaref, Teller and Igloo - Luther Seminary Archives.

John L. Maakestad *The Lutheran Church in Alaska* 1978

Louise Maakestad *History of the Alaska Conf. of the Amer. Lutheran Church Women*- 1960-1987

Alice Postell *Where Did the Reindeer Come From?* 1990 Amaknak Press

Dagny Dahle Nimmo *Eskimo Phrase Book* Manuscript in the Library of Congress

*Eskimoland* and *Newsletters* from Shishmaref, Teller and Igloo - Luther Seminary Archives.

Alice Postell *Where Did the Reindeer Come From?* 1990 Amaknak Press

Ornulv Vorren *Saami, Reindeer, and God in Alaska* Waveland Press 1994

Rosemary Carlton *Sheldon Jackson, the Collector;* Alaska State Museums

Thomas R. Berger *Village Journey* Report of the Alaska Native Review Commission, 1985;
    New York, Hill and Wang

*Alaska in Maps A Thematic Atlas* Edited by Roger W. Pearson and Marjorie Hermans, University of
    Alaska, Fairbanks, Department of Education

Pirjo Varjola *The Etholen Collection* National Board of Antiquities of Finland, 1990

Hector Chivigny *Russian America* 1975 New York, Viking Press

*Russian America: The Forgotten Frontier* Edited by Barbara Sweetland and Redmond J. Barnett;
    Washington State Historical Society, Tacoma, WA

Melvin Ricks *Alaska Bibliography: An Introductory Guide to Alaskan Historical Literature* 1977
    Alaska Historical Commission

*Correspondence from Sitka* Lutheran Deaconess Archives, Gladwyn, Pennsylania:

*The Fire at Nome* Laura Samuelson, Director; Carrie McLain Memorial Museum, Nome

The Library at Sheldon Jackson College, Sitka, Alaska

Sitka Lutheran Church Archives; Oral Histories taken by Harvey Brandt

The Graduate Theological Library and Archives; Berkeley, California

The U. S. A. National Archives: Documents of the House of Representatives and the U. S. Senate
    Sheldon Jackson: 1886- Report on his study of the possibility of bringing reindeer from Siberia
        to Alaska for the establishment of a profitable industry and relief of a starving people.
    1891-1892 1892-93, 1893-94: *Report on Educational Affairs in Alaska*
        Sheldon Jackson *Report on the Introduction of Domestic Reindeer into Alaska*
        Miscellaneous US Senate Document No 22.
    *Cruise of the US Revenue Cutter Bear and the Overland Expedition to Rescue Whalers*

Personal Correspondence of Helen Frost, Norval Hegland, John and Louise Maakestad, Clarence
    Solberg, Sister Ruth Poetsch, Richard Solberg; Harvey Brandt, Helen Frost Thompson

Oral Histories: John and Louise Maakestad; Kiatcha Dahle Lief; Corinne Malmin Jones,
        Toivo Harjunpaa

Photographs: Helen Frost Family Collection; Luther Seminary Archives; John & Louise Maakestad;
    Norval Hegland; Carrie McLain Memorial Museum, Nome, Alaska; Sitka Lutheran Church, The
    US National Archives; Presbyterian Archives; "Where Did the Reindeer Come From? (Permission
    granted to use these photos.)

# A CLOSING WORD

Editing Helen Frost's Memoirs introduced me to the remarkable Christian nurse who spent years serving the people she loved. Helen was one of many devoted missionaries who came to serve in the harsh climate of northern Alaska. How did they survive in that Great Land? Because the Native People taught the missionaries their secrets.,— how to dress and live in this Arctic region. What a remarkable people they are and what a rich culture they have developed. Her story is really the story of the Inupiat who became so dear to Helen that she wrote, "Alaska is my home, the Eskimo my people."

Helen's Memoirs includes little biographies of some Native friends. We hope that more will be gathered and published. Here is the amazing story of Emma Willoya. And of George Ahgupuk who graciously gave permission to use his art in this tribute to his friend.

The Lutheran Church asked Henriette Lund to study their ministry and look to the future. Her observations on page 162 summarize her admiration for "*the gifted Inupiat who live in a world of ice and snow...*"

Alaska is a fascinating land and one who discovers its beauty and starts to read soon realizes there is much to learn. On the opposite page is a list of some of my personal library which has helped me understand more of the complex history of Alaska.

Each religious group had gifted pioneers, —courageous men and women who helped start various ministries in Alaska. Those pioneers faced many hardships, and some of them are buried in the cemeteries of Alaskan villages. Churches usually work together here. Ecumenical cooperation is expected, not the exception.

It has been a privilege to prepare Helen Frost's Memoirs. Income from the sale of this book will go to the Endowment Fund that helps support Alaska Native Lutheran Ministries.

Ross F. Hidy, Concord, California
Lutheran Pioneer Press

# THE ORPHANAGE AT TELLER

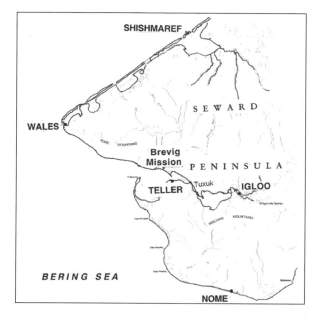

(Top left, counter clockwise) (1) Seward Peninsula Map showing missions. The Orphanage was at Teller Reindeer Station, later named **Brevig Mission** to honor the memory of Julia Brevig, after her death. (2) The mission building in summer. Tracks below used to haul up freight from barges to mission. 3) Mission in winter    (4) Digging out after a snow. (5)  Smiling boys making ice cream for children. They loved sweets, —cup cakes and Helen's pop-corn balls. (6) A reindeer from the mission herd.

# THE TELLER ORPHANAGE IN ARCTIC ALASKA

(Pictures, Top, Clockwise) Natives hunt polar bears on the frozen Arctic ocean in winter months. Temperatures often below zero (2) To visit Shishmaref and Igloo Helen Frost traveled by dog team 500 miles one winter with Pastor Elmer Dahle. (3) Boys use a sled to bring ice blocks to melt for water at the Orphanage. (4) Mrs. Julia Brevig helped start the Orphanage in 1894. The graves of Mrs. Brevig and her son, Carl are in the Mission cemetery. To honor her memory, Teller Station was renamed **Brevig Mission.** (5) Mission boys at a summer fish camp show Helen Frost fish drying for winter meals at the Orphanage (6) Two of the happy children (7) Helen Frost taught this Confirmation Class at Teller.

# LIFE AT IGLOO

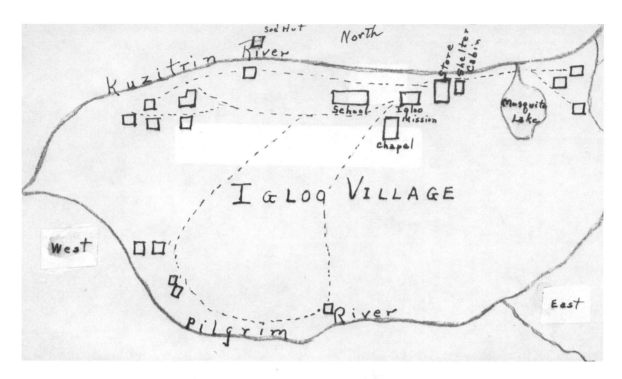

(Top, clockwise) Helen Frost's sketch of Igloo Village showing school, chapel, mission house and store. Igloo is between Kuzitrin and Pilgrim Rivers. (2) Natives enjoy Thanksgiving dinner at Igloo. Helen baked many loaves of bread and helped serve. (3) Picnic with the Mosquito family. (4) During the war Helen cared for the store during the war. Also radioed weather bulletins, sent telegrams and cared for the post office. Very busy days! (5) A Confirmation class at Igloo.

# Summer Fishing on the Tuxuk River

(top left, clockwise)  In spring the natives camped and fished on the Tuxuk River.
(2)  Helen Frost used her little boat, the Ark, with 4 hp motor, to visit the camps.
(3) Helen and Mary Oquillok at her tent   (4) Helen used her guitar to lead the singing for
services at various camps along the Tuxuk.   (5) fish drying in the sunshine.

# HELEN FROST AT SHISHMAREF

(Top, clockwise) The Shishmaref Beacon atop the Church is a welcome guide for travelers.Often the northern lights put on a dazzling display. (2) Warm native clothing keep Helen (right) and her friend warm in the coldest weather. (3) Helen was a talented sewer and she often surprised the children. These girls love their new aprons. (4) Over the years Helen made thousands of pop-corn balls for parties. Everyone loved them!

# HELEN FROST AT SHISHMAREF

(Top left, clockwise)  Shishmaref travel for years was by dog sled.  (2) Sled dogs were chained to poles and needed no shelter. (3) When Pastor/Pilot Norval Hegland came with the new Mission plane travel was different. Only 40 minutes from Shishmaref to Teller, —with a tail wind. (4) A greenhouse at Shishmaref produced flowers and a few vegetables. (5)  Noted artist, George Ahgupuk and his daughter, Stella.  (6) Air view of Shishmaref and Ocean.

# MISSION PLANE PILOT NORVAL HEGLAND

(Top left, , clockwise) Pastor Norval Hegland and wife, Margaret and children by plane. After plane was dedicated at Northfield, MN, Norval flew family along Alaskan Highway route to Teller. (2) Family in Alaska. Note their parkas and skiis on plane. (3) Plane motor would freeze in winter. Norval's solution: Heat from a small stove was piped up to heat covered motor. It worked! (4) Two Hegland girls with native friend in center (5) Ready for a flight: Mrs. Elmer Dahle, Henriette Lund, Pastor Elmer Dahle and Pastor Hegland (6) The Maakestads were at Nome before Our Savior's Church was dedicated. (7) Louise and John Maakestad with Laura, Walter, Gene and Ellen. They served at Fairbanks, Shishmaref, Nome and later in Anchorage. Beloved wherever they lived. John was born in Petersburg, Alaska where his father was Pastor.

# LIFE IN THE NATIVE CONGREGATIONS

(Top right, clockwise)   (1) Nativity Scene: Mary   (Roxanne Hjalseth)   holding Baby Jesus, (Douglas Weaver, Jr.)  at Alaska Native Church on Christmas Eve; (2) Nome Church in winter; (3) Sanctuary as people prepare for Spring Conference Service; (4) Pastor Brian Crockett and parishioner singing hymn in native language;  (5) In 1981, while making her study of the Ministry, 94 year old Henriette Lund visits Gramma Eeuck, age 104!, before Pastor Noeldner leads home Communion Service. (6) At spring conference everyone enjoys refreshments (6) At Shishmaref Beatrice Davis and Esau Weyiouanna on a clear day.

# LIFE TODAY ON THE PENINSULA

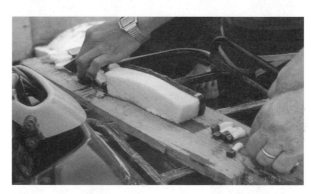

(Top left, clockwise) (1) When a barge brings heating oil for Shishmaref homes, it is pumped up to storage tank on shore though a long hose (2) Capt. Percy Nayokpuk and his crew have brought back a whale to share. (3) Whale blubber is cut into large slabs so every family may enjoy some of this delicacy. (4) For dinner at home pencil shape pieces are cut from larger slabs. The dark is the skin. (5) Today fewer families have sled dogs. Many now use snowmobiles to pull their sleds in winter. (6) At Nome there is lots of snow. Today industrial equipment makes snow removal much easier. (7) At Shishmaref winter storms for years have been eroding the shore. Will this house last through another winter? (8) Many come with shovels to fill sandbags to bank against the shoreline to slow the erosion. But it may be a losing battle.

# OLD AND YOUNG ENJOY WORSHIP AND PLAY

(Top right, clockwise)  (1)  Solo time for a little girl with her Mother (2) Everyone enjoys music.  An elder plays a hymn on his accordion (3) Children love to sing their favorite hymns  (4) Delegates to the 1999 Synod Assembly saw Youth from all of the villages do Native Dances (5) Boys wading in the Chuckchi Sea near Shishmaref. If you ask, "Is it cold?" They may say,  "Sure, but it's fun!" (6) Youth from all the villages enjoy the Salmon Lake Bible Camp north of Nome.   (7) Volleyball game at a church hot dog picnic on a summr day. (8) When Henriette Lund visited the Teller School in 1881, Teacher Dave Allen showed her some of the wood carvings done by the students. She was impressed!  (Dave, a National Champion wrestler at U of Iowa, later completed the Iditerod.)

# HELEN MOVES TO SITKA

Sea otter pelts brought the Russians to Alaska. These furs were so valuable that early traders sailed to the Aleutians in fragile ships to gather these pelts. The Russian American Company was chartered to direct this harvest and Kodiak was their headquarters. In 1798 Governor Baranov moved from Kodiak to Sitka, naming it New Archangel. This continued until 1867 when Russia sold its colony to the United States for $7,200,000. The Russian flag came down and the Stars and Stripes were raised at Sitka.

In 1841 when Arvid Etholen was appointed as the new Governor, his new bride was a devout Lutheran. So they brought with them to New Archangel the first Lutheran pastor, Uno Cygnaeus. Church services were in the Governor's residence until the Lutheran Church was dedicated in 1843.

After ministering to the Lutherans for five years Pastor Cygnaeus returned to Finland. Two other Lutheran pastors came to serve. After the American purchase, Chaplains often led services in the Church and civic services were often held there. But for many years the congregation had no resident pastor.

Uno Cygnaeus was an experienced educator. Finland hoped to start a common education program for their country, so they asked citizens to offer their proposals. The plan Uno Cygnaeus offered was chosen and Cygnaeus became the Founder of Finland's program of common education. Today his picture is in schools and the University he started as a training school for teachers.

In 1941 Pastor Hugh Dowler came to serve the Lutheran congregation and a new church building was erected. During the War, the church opened a Service Center. The men and women enjoyed the coffee and refreshments, a place to read, listen to music, and write letters home. Each spring as the fishing season began, Sitka's Pastor conducted a special service to bless the fishing fleet. Sitka Lutheran Church had entered a new vigorous chapter of ministry. After the war the Sitka Naval base became a High School for Native students from Alaska villages.

When Helen Frost came to Sitka to work with High School students, she also visited the adult patients in the Native Hospital. Knowing the students were homesick, she visited them, led a Bible study on Tuesday nights, and welcomed them to Sunday services at Sitka Lutheran Church where she was a member. After service, she had an Open House at her home just one block from the Church. The students loved to go there and often stopped by whenever they came over on the Ferry.

A new Sitka Community Hospital was being started and the administrator was a Lutheran Deaconess, Sister Ruth Ploetsch. Ruth was glad to have another Lutheran nurse nearby and she and Helen became good friends. They got together often and shared Christmas and other holidays.

Helen's Sitka years were very busy. She regularly visited the high school students and entertained them in her home. When many nurses became ill during a flu epidemic, the Hospital Head Nurse asked Helen to help on the night shift. She did, though night duty was very tiring. Helen soon became acquainted with the staff at other churches and at Sheldon Jackson College. Helen made so many new friends in Sitka that when she left, she was honored at a gracious farewell evening. Many leaders from the High School and churches came to thank her for her work at Sitka.

# HELEN ENJOYS SUNNY CARLSBAD

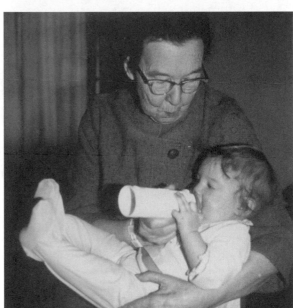

(Top right, clockwise) (1) A family photo. Standing, brothers Gaylerde and Reuben (Jack), (Herbert is not in picture.) Seated, her stepmother, Gina, Esther, Helen, her father, Hemming holding Florence. (2) Helen in her favorite chair (3) Happy 87th Birthday Cake (4) Helen worshipped at King of Kings Lutheran Church in nearby Oceanside (5) Helen cares for child of a lady who came to sing for residents.    (6) About 1978. The carved dog sled team under Helen's Christmas tree may be a farewell gift from a native family when she left Alaska.